ROMAN'S
PASADENA

2.—

Dr. and Mrs. Frank S. Schiff
1440 Circle Drive
San Marino, California 91108

THE GRAND CENTURY OF THE LADY

ABOUT THE BOOK

With the felicitous sense and sensibility of Jane Austen, Arthur Calder-Marshall brings to life the refined and dashing society of Georgian and Regency England. Surrounded by Nash, Adams architecture, Gainsboroughs, Reynolds, Romneys, Wedgewood, the most elegant and wealthy people on earth created a social life-style of ideal liberties especially for the complete lady, who is, astonishingly, the immediate ancestress of the modern woman.

ABOUT THE AUTHOR

Arthur Calder-Marshall was born in 1908 and educated at St Paul's School and at Oxford. He has two daughters and lives in London. His productive literary career includes nine novels (*Pie In the Sky*, *The Way To Santiago*, *The Scarlet Boy*), three volumes of short stories, children's books, travel books and biographies including his excellent biographies of Havelock Ellis and Robert Flaherty. He is a distinguished literary critic and widely known as a broadcaster.

THE GRAND CENTURY OF THE LADY

Arthur Calder-Marshall

GORDON & CREMONESI

Designed by Heather Gordon-Cremonesi
Set in 'Monotype' Caslon and printed in Great Britain
by W & J Mackay Limited, Chatham

ISBN 0-86033-011-7

Gordon Cremonesi Ltd
New River House
34 Seymour Road
London N8 0BE

Contents

Foreword   8

1 The Changing Scene   9

2 Breeding   14

3 Domestic Economy and Extravagance   20

4 Food and Drink   26

5 Fashion   36

6 Public Pleasures   49

7 Theatricals   60

8 Gambling Ladies   77

9 Ladies on Canvas   90

10 Women and Medicine   95

11 Old Maids   105

12 Marriages of Convenience   116

13 Mean Marriages   133

14 Notorious Ladies   142

15 Revolutionary Ladies   154

16 Revolutionary Daughters   164

Bibliographical Note   175

Index   177

List of Illustrations

Colour plates, following page 88

    I. Walking and morning dress, 1810 (*Witch Ball Print Shop, Brighton*)

   II. "You are clean, fair lady, but our ways and means are dirty" (*Witch Ball Print Shop, Brighton*)

  III. Walking and morning dress, 1813 (*Witch Ball Print Shop, Brighton*)

  IV. Sir John Halkett of Pitfirraine with his family (David Allan)

   V. Courtship: accepted, rejected, preferred (*Witch Ball Print Shop, Brighton*)

  VI. Some fashionable dresses of 1800 (*Witch Ball Print Shop, Brighton*)

 VII. Evening dress, 1818 (*Witch Ball Print Shop, Brighton*)

VIII. Morning dress, 1799 (*Witch Ball Print Shop, Brighton*)

  IX. Full dress, 1799 (*Witch Ball Print Shop, Brighton*)

   X. Promenade Dresses, 1802 (*Witch Ball Print Shop, Brighton*)

  XI. Promenade dress, 1818 (*Witch Ball Print Shop, Brighton*)

First section, following page 40

1. "Nine Months After" (Austin?) (*Witch Ball Print Shop, Brighton*)
2. "The Nursery" (J. Highmore's *Pamela*) (*Fitzwilliam Museum, Cambridge*)
3. "The Toast of the Kit-Kats" (*Radio Times Hulton Picture Library*)
4. *Marriage à la mode*, "After the Marriage" (painting by Hogarth) (*National Gallery*)
5. *Marriage à la mode*, "Toilette Scene" (engraving by Hogarth) (*Witch Ball Print Shop, Brighton*)
6. "The Lady's Maid" (*Witch Ball Print Shop, Brighton*)
7. "The Wig" (*Mansell Collection*)
8. "Her Majesty Queen Caroline & Ladies" (*Witch Ball Print Shop, Brighton*)
9. "The Ladies Disaster" (*Witch Ball Print Shop*, Brighton)
10. "Sensual Love—or A Sop in the Pan" (*Publisher's Collection*)
11–14. Cruikshank's *Definitions of Drawing*: "Covetiveness", "Size", "Secretiveness" and "Order" (*Witch Ball Print Shop, Brighton*)
15–18. Family Fashions, Walking, Morning and Full Dress: the Fatima Robe (*Witch Ball Print Shop, Brighton*)
19. Silhouette of Mr and Mrs Smith (F. Torond) (*Victoria and Albert Museum*)

Second section, following page 72

20. Promenade Dresses, 1810 (*Witch Ball Print Shop, Brighton*)
21. French and English Dresses, 1770 (*Witch Ball Print Shop, Brighton*)
22. "The genteelest Head-dresses of 1772" (*Witch Ball Print Shop, Brighton*)
23. The Fashionable English Dresses, 1774 (*Witch Ball Print Shop, Brighton*)
24. Ten fashionable headdresses of 1785 (*Witch Ball Print Shop, Brighton*)
25. London headdresses, 1800 (*Witch Ball Print Shop, Brighton*)
26. Walking Dresses and a Full Dress, 1805 (*Victoria and Albert Museum*)
27. "Lady Archer in Full Dress and Lady Waldegrave in Undress" (*Witch Ball Print Shop, Brighton*)
28. Two Ladies in the Dress of 1775 (*Witch Ball Print Shop, Brighton*)
29. Ladies in the Dresses of 1782 (*Witch Ball Print Shop, Brighton*)
30. Full Dresses for August 1798 (*Witch Ball Print Shop, Brighton*)
31. Walking Dress, 1810 (*Witch Ball Print Shop, Brighton*)
32. Promenade Dresses, 1803 (*Witch Ball Print Shop, Brighton*)
33. Evening Half-Dress, 1805 (*Witch Ball Print Shop, Brighton*)
34. Evening, Theatre or Opera Dress, 1814 (*Witch Ball Print Shop, Brighton*)
35. Evening Dress, 1810 (*Witch Ball Print Shop, Brighton*)
36. "Newest Fashions for July 1829, Morning Dress and Fashionable Head Dresses" (*Witch Ball Print Shop, Brighton*)
37. "In the Hunting Field" (Rowlandson 1807) (*Witch Ball Print Shop, Brighton*)
38. "Up & Down", the chariot of 1820 (*Witch Ball Print Shop, Brighton*)
39. "Packing Up After a Country Ball" (R. Dighton) (*Witch Ball Print Shop, Brighton*)
40. An Evening Walk (*Witch Ball Print Shop, Brighton*)
41. "Outside the Opera House" (I. R. & G. Cruikshank) (*Witch Ball Print Shop, Brighton*)
42. "Sarah Siddons as herself" (J. Downman) (*National Portrait Gallery*)
43. "Kitty Fisher as Cleopatra dissolving the Pearl" (Reynolds) (*The Iveagh Bequest, Kenwood House*)

Third section, following page 104

44. "The Harlot's Progress", plate 2 (Hogarth) (*Publishers' Collection*)
45. "The Coterie Quadrille Party" (*Witch Ball Print Shop, Brighton*)
46. "Mrs Thornton", the Lady Jockey (*North Yorkshire County Library*)
47. "Discipline à la Kenyon" (Gillray)
48. Georgiana, Duchess of Devonshire (Gainsborough)
49. Jane Austen (by her sister Cassandra) (*National Portrait Gallery*)
50. Lady Mary Wortley Montagu in Turkish Dress (*Radio Times Hulton Picture Library*)
51. Catherine, Third Duchess of Queensberry (after C. Jervas) (*National Portrait Gallery*)
52. Mrs Laetitia Pilkington (Nathaniel Hone) (*Radio Times Hulton Picture Library*)
53. Mr and Mrs Andrews (Gainsborough) (*National Gallery*)
54a. The Linley sisters, Mrs Sheridan and Mrs Tickell (Gainsborough) (*Dulwich College*)
54b. Mary Countess of Howe (Gainsborough) (*Greater London Council*)
55. Jane, Countess of Harrington (Reynolds) (*Henry E. Huntington Library*)
56. Mrs Lascelles, later Lady Harewood (Reynolds) (*Henry E. Huntington Library*)
57. Penelope, Viscountess Ligonier (Gainsborough) (*Henry E. Huntington Library*)
58. Fanny Burney, Madame d'Arblay (Edward Burney) (*National Portrait Gallery*)
59. Mrs Siddons as the Tragic Muse (Reynolds) (*Henry E. Huntington Library*)
60. *Marriage à la Mode*, "The Visit To the Quack Doctor" (Hogarth) (*National Gallery*)
61. "A Peep Into the Pump Room" (*Witch Ball Print Shop, Brighton*)
62. "The Old Maid's Petition" (*Witch Ball Print Shop, Brighton*)

Fourth section, following page 136

63. "The Spinstress" (Romney) (*Greater London Council*)
64. *Marriage à la Mode*, "The Marriage Contract" (Hogarth) (*National Gallery*)
65. *Marriage à la Mode*, "The Death of the Earl" (Hogarth) (*Publishers' Collection*)
66. Pamela and Mr B. in the Summer House (J. Highmore) (*Fitzwilliam Museum*)
67. Pamela Shows Mr Williams (J. Highmore) (*Fitzwilliam Museum*)
68. Fashions in Flirtation (*Witch Ball Print Shop, Brighton*)
69. "A Wit Outwitted" (*Witch Ball Print Shop, Brighton*)
70. "The Nine Living Muses of Great Britain" (Samuel 1779) (*National Gallery*)
71. Abigail Adams, wife of John Adams (*Radio Times Hulton Picture Library*)
72. Lady Caroline Lamb (miniature) (*Radio Times Hulton Picture Library*)
73. Charlotte Charke (after Gravelot) (*Radio Times Hulton Picture Library*)
74. Mrs Fitzherbert (*Witch Ball Print Shop, Brighton*)
75. Mary Wollstonecraft, Mrs William Godwin (J. Opie) (*National Portrait Gallery*)
76. Angelica Kauffman (self-portrait) (*National Portrait Gallery*)
77. Harriette Wilson (engraved by Cooper from a drawing by Birch) (*Radio Times Hulton Picture Library*)
78. Mary Wollstonecraft Shelley (R. Rothwell) (*National Portrait Gallery*)

Foreword

I have written this book for the pleasure of myself as "a general reader". Here and there may be some tit-bit to tickle the taste of a Georgian scholar. But most of these highways and byways are familiar.

There is no argument connecting chapter with chapter. For those unfamiliar with the period, the first chapter may be useful as a sort of time-map, like those plans for motorists which show only major roads. I advise well-versed readers to skip it. It is filled with infuriating generalisations and over-simplifications.

The next eight chapters might have been arranged equally well in any order, like the cards in a player's hand. Each chapter is roughly chronological: but all the chapters are, so to say, simultaneous. I have not attempted to lead a march down the decades. This is not even anything as purposeful as a journey. It is rather a perambulation, a leisurely ramble through Georgian landscapes. With the inconsequentiality Laurence Sterne indulged in *Tristram Shandy*, I wander up inviting culs-de-sacs, if there is something curious at the end. Why, the critic may ask, should I in a chapter on Ladies' Fashions digress to examine the Prince Regent's vast cellar of snuffs, which with great elegance he conveyed to his nose without partaking of them? The truth is that this quiddity amused me. If forced to justify myself, I would suggest that many Georgian ladies copied him, even though they abominated snuff, because of the opportunity it afforded of displaying elegant wrists and fingers.

The chapter on Women and Medicine acts as a sort of pivot, swinging from the general to the particular. Something can be gained by reading the remaining chapters in sequence. Though human nature may not change, human behaviour is susceptible to rapid changes. The American war of independence and the French Revolution, followed by the Napoleonic Wars (which future historians may classify as the *First* World War) had immense repercussions on the way people thought and behaved.

British sympathies were divided. There were many partisans of the American colonists in Britain; and many who admired what the French revolutionaries had done in France (while rejecting it as a recipe for their own country). It is for this reason that I have devoted my last two chapters to Revolutionary Ladies and their Revolutionary Daughters. The majority of Georgian ladies remained true to the establishment; and in so far as they reacted from the dissoluteness of the Regency, it was towards that ideal of middle class probity, failure to achieve which stamped the Victorian as the age of hypocrisy. The revolutionary ladies and their daughters were the pioneers, and victims, of tendencies which were to appear to triumph in the beginning of the twentieth century, and are now seen to be failing. These ladies were naive, immature and overoptimistic. But the future lay with them, rather than with those who accepted two codes, two moralities, two types of justice; one for the rich, the other for the poor.

CHAPTER ONE

The Changing Scene

The century 1720–1820 spans almost that period known as the Georgian era. Though there is no such creature as *the* Georgian Lady, of Georgian Ladies there are—what should be the collective noun?—bevies? bouquets? packs? assemblies? regiments?

When we think first about these ladies, it is not really of them, but of their clothes, their hats, their headdresses, their *maquillage*; and of these, not as they were, but as painters chose to portray them in full beauty. How many Georgian complexions were ravaged by the small-pox, and how few Georgian portraits!

If we study the caricaturists, we encounter an opposite falsity. Hogarth, Rowlandson, Gillray, Cruikshank and their fellows were connoisseurs of human imperfection. They collected comic noses as assiduously as Linnaeus collected plants, and invented bellies that outrivalled Lunardi's balloon. Between obesity and scrawniness there was little mean; but enough diversity to dispel any illusion that such a type existed as the Georgian Lady.

Though I use the phrase "the Georgian era" in the course of this book, it is intended merely to indicate the period of time between 1714 when George I ascended the throne of Britain and 1830 when his great-great grandson died. The only significance of the period 1714–1830 is that during that time the King's name happened to be George.

Politically "the Georgian era" partakes of two periods. The first began with the "Glorious Revolution" of 1688 and ended with the bloody suppression of the Jacobite Rebellion in 1745. The second did not end until the passing of the Reform Bill in 1831, the year after the death of George IV, though its origin also dated back to 1688. In fact the whole period 1688–1831 can be seen as a protracted argument over the significance of the Glorious Revolution.

It was viewed in two ways. From the point of view of William and Mary, Anne and the Hanoverians, the monarchy remained supreme, even though James II had been deposed and his legitimate successors were passed over, because of their Catholic beliefs. They ruled by right of legitimate Protestant succession.

From the point of view of the Whigs and their supporters, William and Mary had come to the throne at the invitation of Parliament (and some would add, the people). Under William and Mary, the Whigs enjoyed all the favours of court and parliamentary office. The Tories were ostracised and in some cases dispossessed, because of their Jacobite sympathies. Queen Anne, reacting against William and Mary, was more sympathetic to the Tories; and on her death, there was a strong movement to recognise the Stuart pretender, rather than George, Elector of Hanover, whose only claim to the British throne was that he was the nearest-related Protestant, being a great grandson of James I through the female line.

The fortunes of political families fluctuated throughout the Georgian era, according to what party was in power; the Tories in eclipse for the first part and the Whigs for the later. These fluctuations were felt as much by the ladies as by their gentlemen.

After 1745, the argument took a different turn. The Glorious Revolution was seen not as a conflict between Protestant Hanoverians and Catholic Jacobites but one between the King and the People, with Parliament as the battleground. The King used his money and power to buy his representatives in the Commons. Various Whig and Tory noblemen commanded a sufficient number of seats to offer assistance or resistance to the King's men. And finally there was a number of country MPs without fixed party affiliations. But none of these groupings was based upon the people as a whole. The system of Parliamentary elections was outmoded, corrupt and unrepresentative. As the century advanced, agitation for Parliamentary reform became more and more vocal and resistance more and more repressive. When finally the Reform Bill was passed in 1831, constituency boundaries were redrawn and the franchise extended, but only to include £10 householders, a minority of the male population. The *vulgus mobile*, in brief "the mob", was for the moment deprived of trained leadership. At the same time, the powers of the monarch were curtailed. From the battle between King and People, Parliament had emerged the victor.

During the whole period the exercise of power was in the hands of members of the Church of England, as by law established. Roman Catholics were (at first wisely) disfranchised as likely Jacobite traitors. By 1780, such fears were out of date. Catholics were as needed to serve in the Armed Forces as any other Britons. But the prospect of Catholic Emancipation let loose the Gordon Riots ("such a time of terror you have been fortunate in not seeing", Dr Johnson told Mrs Thrale). It was not until the Catholic Emancipation Act of 1829 that these penalties were relaxed.

The Church of England throughout the period lost ground, through its corruption, indolence, pluralism and identification with the secular establishment. Religious enthusiasm was whipped up by the Wesleys and Whitefield. In his essays on England, Voltaire devoted more space to the consideration of Methodism than to any other contemporary religious or philosophical manifestation. But there was a host of other philosophic-religious positions. Freemasonry, with its blend of rationalism and gnostic ritual, appealed to intellectuals, such as the

Encyclopaedists. Those who could not accept the Divinity of Christ embraced Unitarianism (regarded with indulgence by the Establishment). Gentlemen could hold what views they liked, in private. But Deism was regarded with sorrow and Atheism with horror. God was good for the poor. Piety made for peace, Christian resignation for civil obedience. Atheism among working folk went hand in hand with Revolution. Black Magic, which flourished in this so-called Age of Reason, was pursued by rakes so jaded by debauchery that they needed the stimulus of turning religion arse over tip. The women who participated in the orgies at Medmenham Abbey were mostly whores; the story that Lady Mary Wortley Montagu participated seems to me most unlikely. The only woman Freemason was Mlle D'Eon, that picturesque transvestite whose sex was the basis of wild bets during his lifetime, and whose masculinity was only established post-mortem. Georgian Ladies were often as non-conformist as their menfolk in their minds; but they were conformist in their Sunday observances, as a good example to the children and the servants.

They were even more a prey to literary fashion than their husbands. Reason gave way to sentiment, sentiment to sensibility, sensibility to romanticism. At first nature was classically ordered, then artifically disordered, then most admired when sublimely rugged. Such changes in taste wrought changes in feeling, and *vice versa*. It may, or may not, be true that human nature does not change. But human thoughts, feelings and emotions do change according to the vocabulary of their expression, and the sanctions of society.

So the ladies who flourished at the beginning of the reign of George I were different sorts of people from those who flourished at the end of the reign of George IV.

What does one mean by "flourished"? Sarah, Duchess of Marlborough, was born in 1660 and did not die until 1744, thirty years after the accession of George I. But I do not regard her as a *Georgian* lady, because the years of power in which she flourished were over before Queen Anne died. On the other hand, though Lady Mary Wortley Montagu eloped in the days of Queen Anne, she flourished as a Georgian lady. At the other end of the scale, though Mary Shelley and Claire Clairmont lived well on into the reign of Queen Victoria, they had ceased to flourish with the deaths of Shelley and Byron.

Between them these ladies saw more material changes in the 116 years of the four Georges than there had been in the previous half millennium. The first George came to a Britain of men and women whose lives depended on the work of their hands and domestic animals. The fourth George left a Britain powered by steam-driven machines, railroads, ships. Yeomen farmers had been ruined by the Enclosure Acts; but agriculture by these same Acts improved as never before. The cottage industries which had been dovetailed into peasant farming had been wrecked: but machines produced by the thousand what had been made in ones and twos laboriously by hand.

At the beginning of the period, the fastest mode of travel was cross-country on horseback. Roads were cart-tracks, dusty in summer, in winter muddy and waterlogged. Most heavy goods were transported by sea. Passengers from London to Edinburgh by swift sea-skiff might take three weeks on the voyage. Crossing the Channel sometimes meant a wait of weeks in bad weather. Inland, few people travelled by road, except on business. By coach from London to Oxford took two days.

With the building of bridges, the construction of turnpike roads, things started to change. People travelled for pleasure. The country opened up. Whole families moved around, discovering for themselves beauties, wonders, novelties and antiquities that they had only heard of by repute. Society moved from spa to spa, the old in search of health, others for love or money. The market for produce widened. The Great Wen, as John Byng and William Cobbett called London, grew yearly in size, drawing to it the adventurous in search of fortune, the vagrant in search of livelihood, the errant in search of anonymity. Rivers were buried. Farms became streets and squares. Villages were engulfed.

Great landlords discovered coal beneath their green pastures. To bring it to the ports, to rivers or industrial centres, they cut canals and built the greatest aqueducts since the Romans. Prices of transport plummeted.

Lovers of the past like John Byng lamented. Workers like the Luddites tried smashing the machines which increased production and unemployment. But a new class of men (and women) was arising; men who saw Britain not as this demi-paradise, this other Eden, but as the raw material from which, by means of industry and industriousness, fortunes could be made to put their owners on a level with the great Whig and Tory families who had gotten their places by past ruthlessness. They were not, of course, driven on merely by greed. The will o' the wisp, Progress, the pursuit of which we now fear may overwhelm the human race, was then enormously exciting. William Blake saw the threat of those "dark Satanic mills". But most eyes were turned towards the future rather than the past in search for a golden age.

Just as the face of Britain changed in the Georgian era, so did the concept of the inhabited globe. The American colonists revolted and achieved independence, but this was a temporary hitch in Britain's pursuit first of trade and then a colonial empire. Imperial greatness was less a matter of policy than the consequence of oversea commerce. Britain blundered her way to world dominance.

The side-effect of this vast haphazard expansion was that economists and political philosophers began to contemplate the possibility of planning society. Theorists like Voltaire, Diderot and Rousseau worked from first principles, without any knowledge of facts. Sir Frederick Morton Eden, who published *The State of the Poor* (1797) was a new type of thinker, compiling facts (however inadequate) as a basis for informed action.

The reason why 18th century political and social writers were so far from the realities of their time was because not only were there no facts, but also there was no machinery for collecting them. For example, no Census of Population was taken until 1801. The population was then found to be 8,873,000 for England and Wales, 16,300,000 for the British Isles.

In 1696, Gregory King had speculated about the growth of the population in *Observations on the State of England*. He estimated the population of England in his day at 5½ million. He reckoned that in the next six hundred years, the population would have doubled. "The next doubling after that will not be, in all probability, in less than twelve or three hundred years, or by the year of our Lord 3500 or 3600. . . . At which time the Kingdom will have 22 millions of souls . . . in case the world should last so long."

King was unusual in thinking that the population was growing. During most of the 18th century it was believed that the population was decreasing. Estimates were made either on taxation returns (containing enumeration of hearths or homes) or on parish registers of christenings, marriages and deaths. The Bills of Mortality for London (which were published monthly in *The Gentleman's Magazine*) showed consistently more deaths than christenings. In March 1731, for example, there were 1,954 christenings against 2,388 deaths, which included 907 children under the age of two. Causes of death numbered 239 from smallpox, 312 from fevers and 340 from consumption.

Estimates of population, based on Church of England parish registers of christenings, ignored large numbers of non-conformists. Taxation returns did not include houses not liable to hearth or window tax. They were as inaccurate as the figures on which the Rev. Malthus based his *Essay on Population* in 1798, prophesying imminent doom through over-population.

Georgian women, in fact, were breeding almost non-stop. Despite everything the population of England and Wales rose in the first half of the 18th century, probably from six millions to 6½ million. In the latter half (due to inoculation, improvements in sanitation, etc.) the population increased by nearly 2½ million; a rate of growth five times as great as that during the first half of the century

The reason why this increase was not plain for all to see was that during that half century there had been a greater movement of the population than at any time. Villages appeared depleted, but meanwhile other villages had grown into towns and towns into cities. And, of course, there was no representation in Parliament of these new centres of population and industry.

Where better, then, should we approach the Georgian lady, than in child-bed?

CHAPTER TWO

Breeding

"Language has always been changing," noted Lady Susan O'Brien in 1818, looking back to 1760. "It has been said, as morals grow worse language grows more refined. No one can say 'breeding' or 'with child' or 'lying in'. 'In the family way' and 'confinement' have taken their place."

However expressed, when they were not "breeding" or "in the family way" (which meant "entertaining without undue fuss or ceremony" until 1796 when Mrs E. Parsons gave it pregnant significance), most Georgian wives were "lying in" or being "confined" (as Mrs Delany first said in 1772, using a word hitherto synonymous with "imprisoned").

Whores and mistresses were for wantonness or pleasure, wives were for bearing children. And what fecund examples were set by the Hanoverian Court! The only exceptions were George I who had divorced his wife for adultery after she bore him an heir and George IV who as Prince of Wales refused to sleep with his odious Princess, Caroline of Brunswick, once he knew she was with child.

Generation seemed to outvie generation. Caroline of Anspach gave George II five daughters and four sons, of whom only one died in infancy. Their eldest son Frederick, Prince of Wales, predeceased George II, but not before begetting nine children on Princess Augusta of Saxe Gotha. The survival rate was lower, one of his five sons died at fifteen, and only two daughters reached maturity.

George III and Charlotte Sophia of Mecklenburg-Strelitz almost doubled the Hanoverian record. Seven of their nine sons reached maturity and five of their six daughters. The reproduction rate also increased. Queen Caroline took seventeen years to produce her brood of nine, the Princess of Wales fourteen. Queen Charlotte took only 21 years to produce enough for a rugby football team.

The fact that, after the death of Princess Charlotte, the Prince Regent's only child, there were no grandchildren of George III to succeed, was due not to infertility but to the Royal Marriage Act of 1772, whereby any marriage contracted without the King's consent was null and void, respecting the succession.

The Princes had their mistresses and morganatic marriages and to the future William IV was presented a quiverful of Fitz Clarences by the actress Dorothy Jordan.

Where Queens and Princesses led, peeresses and lady folk followed, believing despite the ever-crowded nurseries and the long entries in the Family Bible, that in some mysterious way the population of these islands was growing smaller and smaller. Breeding and lying in were a wife's highest duties. But there was many a woman who dreaded the conjugal onslaughts resumed so rapidly after each child-birth; who saw around them women friends and relatives brought to premature deaths by over-frequent pregnancies; who bitterly resented that while they were "in the family way" and "confined", their husbands were abroad, at their clubs, the theatre, opera or the pleasure gardens, flirting with what in Lady Susan's youth were called "women on the town" and "kept mistresses", but had by 1818 become "fair Cyprians" and "tender" or "interesting connexions".

Once she had given birth, there was a host of servants to assist the wealthy Georgian Lady. There was the Head Nurse and the Nursemaid, the Governess, the Tutors, the Teachers of music, dancing, drawing, languages, history and divinity. With families running into double figures, the progenitrix needed this retinue, if her husband could afford it. If not, the elder sisters played little mothers with the younger children, learning the early care of infants by washing the baby's "limbs morning and evening, and likewise its neck and ears; beginning with warm water, till, by degrees, it will not only bear, but like to be washed with cold". Elder brothers served as tutors to their juniors.

But even with such care many children died in infancy; and with such over-breeding many mothers died before their prime. It was not unusual for a Georgian gentleman to sire families by two or even three wives. Ladies married twice only when they had started by marrying an elderly fortune.

Why did Georgian women submit to this bondage? They had been ordering these matters better in France for two centuries. Henri Estienne in 1566 counselled noble ladies that there was no need for abortion or infanticide, when there were preventives to avoid pregnancy. "Disport yourself as you like, and give me pleasure," remarked one of the Abbé de Brantôme's gallant ladies, "but take care not to sprinkle me inside, not with a single drop, or it will be a matter of life or death." The use of a sponge, soaked in brandy, placed at the entrance to the womb and retractable by a thread may have begun with French prostitutes, but by the 18th Century this form of contraception was used by women of the aristocracy, the bourgeoisie and peasantry. French women of all classes seem to have recognised that intercourse between man and wife was healthy and delight-ful in itself and the production of children should be limited to what could be afforded for the good of all.

The reaction of Englishmen was hysterical. Daniel Defoe, who should have known better, published in 1727 an anonymous pamphlet called *Conjugal Lewd-ness: or, Matrimonial Whoredom*. It showed the confusion which was to bedevil discussions of contraception. 42 pages were spent deploring "of Marrying, and then publickly professing to desire they may have no children, and of using Means physical or diabolical to prevent Conception".

There must have been some amount of birth-control among married people to provoke this attack. But we know nothing of birth-control from the letters and journals of Georgian ladies, discussing the scandals of their day. We know that Casanova wore a *"redingote d'Angleterre"*, that Boswell engaged "in armour" or "safely sheathed". We know that there were various ladies running "Cundum Warehouses" in London; Mother Lewis in St Martin's Lane (not a step from Dr and Fanny Burney), one Mrs Phillips at the sign of the Golden Fan and Rising Sun in Orange Court off Leicester Fields and her rival another Mrs Phillips at the Green Canister "machine warehouse" in Bedford Street, just off the Strand, on a site which is now part of the Civil Service Stores.

But Casanova's English Ridingcoat (which the French were to christen the *capot d'anglais* and the English the French letter) was primarily a prophylactic against disease. Made laboriously from the intestines of animals, it was, even in its Superfine grades, tied at the base with the prettiest of ribbands, insensitive and unsatisfying. Agreeable young Alice Gibbs, when Boswell picked her up on May 17, 1763, and took her down a lane to a snug place "begged that I might not put it on, as the sport was much pleasanter without it, and as she was quite safe. I was so rash as to trust her, and had a very agreeable congress."

How many Georgian ladies soaked sponges in brandy or encouraged their husbands, or lovers, to engage in armour we have not the slightest idea. But the fact that the size of some families tended to decline towards the end of the 18th and during the early years of the 19th centuries makes one suspect that the upper and middle classes were beginning to exercise, not sexual, but reproductive restraint. Lady Melbourne (1752–1818) for example did not breed to capacity. At seventeen she married Sir Peniston Lamb, who had more money than sense. In giving him an heir, also christened Peniston, she felt that she had done her wifely duty. She had many lovers. Lord Coleraine is said to have sold her to Lord Egremont for £13,000, passing some of the purchase money over to her. Lord Egremont was almost certainly the father of her second son, as the Prince of Wales was of her fourth son, George. Who sired Frederick and her two daughters is anyone's guess; but few guess Sir Peniston, later Viscount Melbourne, an ineffectual man who was saddened when his true son died prematurely. Lady Melbourne was discreetly unfaithful, giving progeny to those whose influence might help her and her family. In this she was unlike Jane Elizabeth Harley, the Countess of Oxford, whose children by a variety of fathers were known as the Harleian Miscellany.

In an expanding economy, such as the British was compared to the French, breeding children was an investment for the nobility, the merchants, the bankers, the industrialists and the exploiters of colonies. Despite all these boasts of Norman blood, class in 18th century Britain was no more, and probably less, embattled than the Daughters of the American Revolution are today. Money had a persuasive tongue. Titles could be traded for marriage settlements. A rich banker, like Coutts, lent a fortune to Georgiana, Duchess of Devonshire, was treated like a tradesman by her husband, but succeeded in marrying his daughters off into the peerage or baronetage. Money, power, privilege and places spread around. Estates might be entailed, but the Georgian lady by breeding as fast as possible helped to extend the family tentacles. Husband and wife ran a family business, the wife being the production line and the husband the managing director, assisted by his wife in the complicated matter of matchmaking.

Children were assets as long as the jobs, or sinecures, increased proportionately to the population. But the pinch came when there was unemployment. For younger sons there were openings in the Colonies of North America and the West Indies or in the service of the East India Company. During the American War of Independence and the long struggle with Revolutionary and Napoleonic France, the army and navy needed men. It was the educated women who first felt the humiliation of being under-employed, under-used or under-rewarded by society.

Mrs Catharine Macaulay, in 1790, published her *Letters on Education* and, in 1792, Mary Wollstonecraft her *Vindication of the Rights of Woman*, which echoed the sentiments of Mrs Macaulay but was also a protest against Talleyrand's *Report on Public Instruction*. Talleyrand had proposed that girls and boys should be educated together at public schools, but after the age of eight, the girls should be sent home to learn the domestic crafts which would be their concern in later life.

Macaulay and Wollstonecraft argued that intellectually and spiritually women were as strong as men and that their weakness was due to bad education, unequal social position and economic dependence. They wanted women to be able to engage in business, practice as doctors, represent their sex in politics. Mrs Macaulay added "A Modest Plea for the Property of Copyright"; which if it had been successful would have enabled her contemporary Fanny Burney to enjoy part of the fortune which her publisher Thomas Lowndes made from the purchase of sole rights in *Evelina* for twenty guineas.

If, as I suspect, ladies of rank took to the sponge towards the end of the 18th century, it was not information that they spread about. Malthus may have given a moral justification for family limitation but the lady of quality would have considered enthusiasm for birth-control even worse taste than religious enthusiasm. It was men of the middle class who became the propagandists, pitying the condition of working class women driven to infanticide by poverty and desperation. Joseph Townsend (1739–1816) first qualified as a doctor at Edinburgh and later took holy orders. It was when travelling in France that he learned about the vaginal sponge. He passed on the information to his friend Jeremy Bentham (1748–1832). Bachelor Bentham was far too occupied in writing thousands of pages of learned studies, which he handed over to others to make of them what they could, to do more than hand on the information to Francis Place (1771–1854).

Place was a man of action, an early trade union organiser, member of the

London Corresponding Society, and radical reformer as well as becoming a wealthy fashionable hatter. He was a backstairs politician, using others to do the active work. Bentham's information was of little personal use to him. He had already begotten fifteen children, five of whom had died in infancy. The gospel must be passed on to others. He wrote a couple of leaflets explaining the sponge methods of contraception in terms easily intelligible to working class husbands and wives. But he left the hazardous task of distribution to others.

John Stuart Mill (1806–73) who vividly recalled seeing in childhood the murdered corpse of a newborn babe in a London park, sallied forth at the age of seventeen, with a group of friends, to distribute Place's leaflets among the wives and daughters of mechanics and tradesmen or to slaveys scrubbing area steps. It wasn't long before Mill and his friends were arrested, at the instancy of indignant citizens, and brought before the magistrate, who sentenced them to fourteen days, which was commuted to four days after Place had induced witnesses to come forward to explain that contraception was not the synonym of infanticide, but its opposite.

The incident might have been forgotten if Thomas Moore had not penned four lines about John Stuart and his father James Mill.

> There are two Mr M-lls, too, whom those that like reading
>   Through all that's unreadable, call very clever;
> And, whereas M-ll Senior makes war on *good* breeding,
>   M-ll Junior makes war on all *breeding* whatever.

Place's second attempt was equally cluck-handed. He despatched via Edward Taylor, founder of the *Manchester Guardian*, a parcel asking it to be forwarded to Mrs Mary Fildes, a lady celebrated since Peterloo for her interest in, and sufferings for, the working people. Mrs Fildes opened the parcel, which contained 26 copies of a leaflet "To the Married of Both Sexes" accompanied by a letter signed "A well-wisher to the working classes". Whether Mrs Fildes was scandalised by the pamphlet or not does not matter. A victim of Peterloo who knew the role *agents provocateurs* had taken in the Spa Field Riots and the Cato Street Conspiracy, she immediately smelt a rat and turned the leaflets over to the authorities.

She knew, as did the Georgian ladies who had no sympathy with her radical policies, that any control of breeding was something which you could not agitate about in that very agitated time. We only know her public behaviour. What she said to midwives or to over-laboured women of her acquaintance is another matter.

It was probably what French ladies had been telling British ladies, travelling abroad, maybe to have in secrecy a child by some lover, which after delivery would be adopted as a son or daughter of a continental friend or farmed out with a foster-mother and later married to a dependent squire or despatched to service in India. In the time of hoops and stays these European excursions with the family, in which mother made a brief detour during which she dropped her by-blow, were possible.

What Malthus urged, fashion commanded. The classic mode could not conceal great expectations. Among ladies of breeding, the simple formula of unconfinement was confided in the intimacy of the boudoir, "in a family way" as they used to say when Lady Susan O'Brien was a young girl. That young Mill should have scattered this information through the marketplace must have shocked them. There are ways of doing things; and to make public matters which are of their nature private offended their sense of delicacy as much as William Godwin's and Mary Wollstonecraft's open advocacy of Free Love, which robbed liaisons of clandestine charms.

CHAPTER THREE

Domestic Economy and Extravagance

There was in Georgian England such a discrepancy in the incomes of those who aspired to the title of Ladies and Gentlemen that even Samuel and Sarah Adams, the authors of *The Complete Servant*, found it necessary to discriminate. Published in 1806, *The Complete Servant* was "a practical guide to the Peculiar Duties and Business of all descriptions of Servants from the Housekeeper to the servant of all work and from the Land Steward to the Footboy, with useful receipts and tables". Samuel and Sarah had spent fifty years as "servants in different families"; and though they had read Dean Swift's sardonic *Directions to Servants*, their purpose was to instruct not only servants in the way they should behave, but also their Georgian employers.

"Next to the care and attention due to your husband and children", they quote another female author as writing, "your servant claims, as your nearest dependents; and to promote their good, both spiritual and temporal, is your indispensable duty. Let them join your family devotions, and endeavour to make them spend their Sabbath properly."

Mistresses were advised to be firm in their manner to servants without being severe, and kind, without being familiar. "Let them see that you will not pass over any neglect of orders. . . . Praise and reward them when you can. . . . Never keep servants, however excellent they may be in their stations, whom you know to be guilty of immorality . . . when servants are ill, their mistresses will, doubtless recollect that she [sic] is their *patroness* as well as their employer."

They quote William Cobbett on domestic economy. "Strange as it may appear to those in affluence, an income of £150 to £200 a year, will be enough to maintain a man and wife, with two or three children, and a servant girl."

In an age bereft of labour saving machines, retinue rose with income. A household based on a family income of £4,000 to £5,000 should consist, the Adams suggest, of eleven female and thirteen male servants. They quote "the present Household Establishment of a respectable Country Gentleman, with a young family, whose Net Income is from £16,000 to £18,000 a year, and whose expenses do not exceed £7,000". It consisted of fifteen female and twelve male staff. This appears extravagantly labour-intensive, by modern standards. But there is no modern family in any of the developed countries which does not draw on the part-time services of hundreds or thousands of other people to provide the materials and services which this country gentleman for the most part produced on his own estate.

In 18th century households of this size there was a system of delegated control. At the head could be the master of the house, the mistress or their man of business. Below came the housekeeper in charge of female staff and the welfare of male and female lieutenants, such as the Man-Cook, the Butler who controlled the Footmen, the Teacher and the Head Nurse. The mistress normally controlled within doors. But this was not always so. Mrs Thrale, for example, complained of her husband in her early married life: "Confidence was no word in our vocabulary; and I tormented myself to guess who possessed that of Mr Thrale; not his clerks, certainly, who scarce dared approach him—much less come near me; whose place, he said, was either in the drawing room or the bed-chamber. We kept, meantime, a famous pack of foxhounds at a hunting-box near Croydon; but it was masculine for ladies to ride. We kept the finest table possible at Streatham Park, but *his* wife was not to *think of the kitchen*. So I never knew what was for dinner till I saw it. Driven thus on to literature as my sole resource, no wonder if I loved my books and children. From a *gay* life my mother held me fast. Those pleasures Mr Thrale enjoyed alone; with *me*, indeed, they never would have suited, I was too often and too long confined."

If the mistress did lead a *gay* life, when she was not breeding or lying in, government of the household might pass to a relative, her mother, a sister-in-law, whoever might be more dominant with the master of the house. The master usually confined himself to without doors, the stables, the gardens, the game preserves, the farms and woodlands. But where the husband was indifferent, the wife could take over. Many of the great family empires were built by women. Bess of Hardwick founded the fortunes of the Cavendishes. Sarah, Duchess of Marlborough, acquired a landed empire for the Churchills and the Spencers by her business acumen. Mary, Countess of Berkeley, renovated her husband's estates even before she legally married him, leaving to him the honour of turning his hounds, for the first time, to the pursuit of the fox instead of the stag.

Though *The Complete Servant* was published after the French Revolution, the philosophy it embodies dates from mid-18th century. It perfectly illustrates the conventional attitude which it was the object of Rousseau, Tom Paine, Mary Wollstonecraft and the romantic revolutionaries to overthrow.

ADVICE
TO SERVANTS IN GENERAL

The supreme Lord of the universe has, in his wisdom, rendered the various conditions of mankind necessary to our individual happiness: some are rich, others poor—some are masters, and others servants. Subordination, indeed, attaches to your rank in life, but not *disgrace*. All men are servants in different degrees. The nobles and ministers of state are subservient to the king, and the king himself is the servant of the nation, and is wisely submissive to its laws. It manifests a divine superintendance that civil life should be thus composed of *subordinate* and superior classes. By this wise arrangement, all *may* enjoy an equal share of real happiness ... those are the most worthy characters who best perform the various duties incumbent upon them, *in that state of life unto which it has pleased God to call them*. Perhaps, there is not a more *useful*, a more numerous, nor a more indispensable necessary description of persons in society, than those who are denominated *Servants* ...

It is not surprising that Karl Marx writing in 19th century London, when this philosophy was still accepted by some servants as by almost all masters and mistresses, should have described religion as the opium of the masses.

The Lady's Maid, according to the Adamses, should be a paragon: higher than other servants, neater, cleaner, better educated, a girl of taste, fashion and re-sourceful anticipation. Up with the lark, she should see the housemaid make the fire, and prepare her lady's clothes. After a day spent dressing, undressing, re-dressing her lady, for morning, afternoon and evening, she should be alert to clean and press the clothes her mistress has spotted and crumpled at the opera, ball or masquerade before herself retiring to bed.

Her spare time should be engaged in mending, sewing, making special gifts for her mistress or improving her elocution so that she can "acquire a proper style and manner of reading, in all the varieties of poetry or prose, ode or epistle, comedy or sermon; avoiding alike the dull monotony of the school girl, and the formal affectation of the pedant". For this, her wages were from 18 to 25 guineas a year, "with tea and washing".

In addition to these routine duties, she was expected to prepare cosmetics, hair lotions, dyes, cleansing materials for different fabrics, grease-removers, infallible corn-plasters, toothache remedies and draughts for curing bad breath (with or without costiveness).

Whiteness of skin was necessary for beauty. For freckles of the skin, she applied overnight Roman Balsam, a paste made from an ounce of bitter almonds, an ounce of barley flour and "a sufficient quantity of honey". Next day a variety of chemical treatments was available ranging from the simple Freckle Wash, made of dilute hydrochloric acid to Grape Lotion or Dr Withering's Cosmetic Lotion. To concoct the last, the Lady's Maid took a tea-cupful of soured milk, cold, into which she scraped "a quantity of horseradish, let it stand for 6 to 12 hours" then strained and applied it to the affected parts twice or thrice daily.

From the late 17th century onwards beauty spots or patches were used to cover blemishes. But by the beginning of the 19th century, pimples had been classified and *The Art of Beauty* prescribed different treatments. Blackheads, or "the worm pimple with black points" were squeezed and rubbed with Roman Balsam. For "the small red pimple", Bateman's Sulphur Wash, Knighton's Lotion or Darwin's Ointment (made of mercury, flour of sulphur and hog's lard) were preferable to such nostrums as Gowland's Lotion or Kalydor. For "the livid buttony pimple" which "in its most severe form nearly covers the face, breast, shoulders and neck" Mr Plumbe "recommends the pimples to be pricked with a needle, or lancet, in order to irritate them, and spur them to suppuration." After squeezing the matter out, treat three or four times daily, with a solution of $2\frac{1}{2}$ grains of oxymuriate of mercury in four ounces of spirits of wine. The Bardolph pimple could in time be cured with plain diet and abstinence from high-seasoned pishes, pickles, cayenne, mustard and strong liquors.

With so much to do, and learn and make, it is small wonder that Ladies' Maids sometimes fell short of perfection. Compared with the wage of a village labourer (a shilling a day on which to keep himself and family) 25 guineas a year with tea, washing and mistress's cast-off clothes as perquisites, was a handsome salary. But compared with the Georgian lady's necessary expenditure, it appeared a pittance. Jonathan Swift had consolations to offer.

> If you are so happy as to wait on a young lady with a great fortune, you must be an ill manager if you cannot get five or six hundred pounds for disposing of her . . .
> If you serve a lady who is a little disposed to gallantries . . . three things are necessary. First, how to please your lady; secondly, how to prevent suspicion in the husband, or among the family; and lastly, but principally, how to make it most for your own advantage. . . . I need not warn you to employ your good offices chiefly in favour of those, whom you find most liberal; yet, if your lady should happen to cast an eye upon a handsome footman, you should be generous enough to bear with her humour, which is no singularity, but a very natural appetite: it is still the safest of all home intrigues, and was formerly the least suspected, until of late years it hath grown more common.

To be waited upon by domestics for services provided today by turning a tap, depressing a switch or inserting a plug imposed inhibitions upon Georgian ladies. To be able to converse in French gave privacy, except in those families where the Governess or Lady's Maid was French. In that case a third language, German or more likely Italian, was useful. "Pas devant les domestiques", were probably the first French words most Georgian children learnt.

It was an age of scandal, above and below stairs. Mistresses were not above receiving intelligence about their neighbours relayed through the domestic underground or below supplying by the same channels false information for the confusion of their best friends and enemies. Gossip, true or false, but all the better if malicious, was whispered from behind fans or confided in alcoves. Rooms planned for public receptions were designed with pillars, niches and corners convenient alike to spy from or avoid being spied on. The skilful knew the acoustics of passages; where one could speak without being overheard, where one could overhear without being seen.

Men when they were together talked bawdy and damn the servants if they overheard. Ladies were cautious in what they wrote and said. Letters could be steamed open or read through the transparent paper. A hint was more suggestive than a downright declaration. Men and women did not convey their feelings and sentiments in so many words when it was more diplomatic to imply them in so many more words.

Lovers addressed one another by aliases, preferably classical, Celia, Chloe, Sacharissa, Strephon. Each circle had its nicknames so that it was possible to gossip without being intelligible beyond the immediate clique. This was the more important, because society was small and inter-related enough for hundreds to be eagerly interested about trifles which in a larger community, with more fragmented groups, would have been totally ignored.

There was also nicety about language which anticipates the prudery of the Victorians. "I was reading the 'Spectator' to Sophy, while my maid papered my curls yester-morning," wrote Mrs Thrale to Dr Johnson. "It was Vol. iii, p. 217, where the man complains of an indelicate mistress, who said, on some occasion, that 'her stomach ached', and lamented how 'her teeth had got a seed stuck between them.' The woman that dressed me was so astonished at this grossness, though common enough in Addison's time one sees, that she cried out, 'Well, madam, surely that could never have been *a lady* who used expressions like those.'"

Clearly Dr Johnson would have known what Mrs Thrale thought was nice. But what would her maid have thought ladylike? A pain in the belly? Abdominal distress? Gastric discomfort?

Lady Susan O'Brien took a more aristocratic view, commenting on changes in language between 1760 and the early 19th century. "'Cholic' & 'bowels' are exploded words. 'Stomach' signifies everything. This is delicate, but to very many unintelligible, and in writing would be entirely so, very difficult for a foreigner to translate; or a medical man to understand that was not on the high *ton.*"

The high *ton* of one decade became the *comme il faut* of the bourgeoise matron the next and the vulgarism of below stairs thereafter. Great ladies talked broader than inferiors uncertain of their social status. But even great ladies were terrified of scandal.

Where fortunes hung upon legitimacy, the hint of bastardy might precipitate a lengthy lawsuit. As for the natural consequences of indiscretion, they were best accommodated across the Channel. As Laurence Sterne observed, "They order, said I, this matter better in France".

Perhaps the most terrifying illegitimate birth was that of Lady Hamilton in London. All London knew that Sir William was sterile, so that when she arrived in London pregnant by Nelson, the utmost secrecy had to be kept from the servants. Lady Hamilton "caught flu" so dangerously that Sir William and the servants were forbidden her chamber, until her mother, midwife as well as housekeeper, had delivered a daughter Horatia and spirited her out to wet-nurse.

"Not before the servants" was a precept which became geometrically progressively more terrifying the more servants there were. The country gentleman instanced by *The Complete Servant*, spending a mere £7,000 a year on 27 servants, was more liable to treachery than Cobbett's humble household of a man and wife with two or three children maintaining a servant girl on £150 to £200 a year.

There might have been a tyranny of servants over masters and mistresses in such a situation if the good laws of the land had not provided that the theft of a sum more than £1 was punishable by the sentence of death or later by transportation to the colonies, and if the magistrate had not been the parson, appointed by the Lord of the Manor.

CHAPTER FOUR

Food and Drink

"I dined at the Chaplain's Table . . . upon a roasted Tongue and Udder," James Woodforde noted in his diary on February 17 1763. "N.B. I shall not dine on a roasted Tongue and Udder again very soon."

He lived for another forty years, chronicling in his diary all the memorable events of his life as a country parson, of which his daily meals were the most frequent. His prophecy as a young man of 23 was correct. He ate dubbin of beef, forequarter of Harridan "very insipid", ham "spoiled by hoppers", pigs' ears, pheasant "eat up with maggots", calf's head, pigg's face, larks, leveret with stuffing in his belly, snipe, teal, whistling plovers, sparrow pudding, cygnet, green goose without the least seasoning, oxheart, tripe, brawn and Calf's Pluck, viz. Heart, Liver, and Lights. But never again did he dine on roasted Tongue and Udder.

Parson Woodforde was fortunate in his position. His Norfolk parish of Weston gave him fresh meat and vegetables and was not far from Colchester oyster beds and fresh fish from the sea. The cattle and the poultry that were driven to market had not come so far that their condition had been run down on the journey. London folk were worse off. There were market gardens all round the city, but foreigners complained of the salads, which they said were spoiled by the deposits from the sea coal which hung in clouds over the city. Cattle, sheep and even chickens, turkey and geese had to walk to market considerable distances. The fish offloaded at Billingsgate was seldom fresh and in hot weather frequently stinking by the time it got to market.

Ladies were wise to do their own marketing or if they left that business to the housekeeper (who frequently received a commission from shopkeepers for her patronage), she was well advised to inspect what was bought to see that it was fresh. The shopper needed to keep all her senses about her, to poke, to sniff, to taste, to observe the colour of flesh and fat, the eyes of fish, the feet of birds for their age, the tightness of their vents for freshness.

The Reverend Dr Trusler who was an authority on many subjects such as The Principles of Politeness, Blackstone's Commentaries, Roads, Farriers, Gardening and the Way to be Rich and Respectable, instructed the housewife in the Method of distinguishing good Provisions from Bad. He had this to say of *Mutton*:

> If mutton be young, the flesh will feel tender when pinched; if old, it will wrinkle up and remain so; if young, the fat will readily separate from the lean; if old, it will stick by strings and skins. The fat of ram-mutton feels spungy, the flesh close-grained and tough, not rising again when dented by the finger. If the sheep was rotten, the flesh will be pale; the fat, a faint white, inclining to yellow, and the flesh will be loose at the bone. If you squeeze it hard, some drops of water will stand on it like sweat; as to the freshness or staleness, you may know them by the same marks as in lamb, (which see). Fat mutton is by far the best. A wether five years old, if it can be got, is the most delicious; its natural gravy is brown. If after mutton is dressed, the flesh readily and cleanly parts from the bone, the sheep had the rot. Ewe-mutton is worth a penny a pound less than wether, the flesh paler, the grain closer, and the leg of a ewe may be known by the udder on its skirt; fat on the inside of the thigh.

It may appear niggling that Dr Trusler should cheapen prices by a penny a pound; but when it is realised that a workman's wage, on which he might raise a family, was only a shilling a day and the joints bought by the gentry were chines, forequarters, saddles or legs, the difference of a penny a pound amounted to a great deal over the year.

Dr Trusler wrote for honest folk dealing with dishonest butchers. But in Georgian times there were as many grand folk, whose gambling and other debts were so pressing that they might either forget to pay their butcher or even find themselves in the Marshalsea or the Fleet. It was for this reason that the butcher might add a leg or two of mutton to the monthly bill or palm off measly pork (that "may be known by little kernels like hail-shot in the fat") on some simple housewife, who did not realise that the sale of such meat was punishable.

One cannot help feeling some sympathy for the unfortunate butcher. The shopper was counselled to test the freshness of pork by putting a finger under the bone that came out of the leg or spring. "If it be tainted, you will find it by smelling your finger." But what of where the finger had been, before being put under the bone? In none of the eighteenth century books of cooking that I have seen is there any mention of washing hands before the dressing of food.

Rancid butter was very common. If purchasing tub-butter, the housewife was told to taste it on the outside of the tub, because the inside would be sweet, when the outside was "rank and stinking". How was the proof of the outside made? With a dirty fingernail, a spoon or knife not washed after it had been licked.

The Georgian housewife chose foods in their season. Some of the great land-owners could afford the luxury of an icehouse. Smaller houses had a cellar with slate or marble slabs to keep food from going bad. Eggs could be kept in wood-ash, turned every week. Vegetables and herbs were pickled, bottled or dried (though brass pans could be poisonous with "verdigrease").

Meats and fish were potted; and for them there was a great variety. Beef could be potted to eat like venison; ham with chickens; salmon (2 ways); all kinds of small birds; lampreys; lobster; hare; char; eels; marbled veal; moor game, etc.

In the winter, the Georgian larder was stuffed full with delicacies more toothsome, if less exotic, than those purchaseable today from the Piccadilly house of Fortnum & Mason.

Homemade wines, as opposed to those imported from Spain, Portugal or (if possible smuggled) from France, were necessary to every household not teetotal.

One of the most delicious home made wines I have ever tasted was made by Mr Adams of Bethersden, Kent, from the flowers of dandelions. It was at the same time potent and very smooth. None of the 18th century books I have seen deigns to mention the gentle dandelion as a key to alcoholic bliss. Mrs Raffald's receipt for "Lemon Wine to drink like Citron Water" reads more like cheating.

Pare five dozen of lemons very thin, put the Peels into five Quarts of French Brandy, and let them stand fourteen Days, then make the Juice into a Syrup, with three Pounds of single refined sugar, when the Peels are ready; boil fifteen Gallons of Water with forty pounds of single refined Sugar for half an Hour, then put it into a Tun when cool, add to it one Spoonful of Barm, let it work Two Days, then tun it and put in the Brandy, Peels and Syrup, stir them all together and close up your Cask, let it stand three Months, then bottle it, and it will be pale and as fine as any Citron Water, it's more like Cordial than Wine.

The idea of using five quarts of French Brandy seems to us fantastic. But the cognac used for Lemon Wine would probably have been smuggled. The imposition of custom duties on wines, spirits, tea, etc., led to an enormous contraband trade. Fleets operated across Channel into Chichester and Poole harbours, Rye, Dymchurch, the Romney Marshes on the south coast, up the Thames estuary and along the coast of East Anglia. The respectable Parson Woodforde recorded in his diary for February 6, 1777, that he had paid the smuggler Richard Andrews £1.15s for half an Anchor of Rum and £1.5s for half an Anchor of Geneva, brought about ten in the evening. There is no entry in the full *Oxford English Dictionary* indicating the fluid capacity of an Anchor. I assume that spirits were smuggled in hollow anchors which on the approach of a revenue cutter could be cast overboard, either in pretence of a genuine anchor or jettisoned attached to a buoy and recovered later. From the price the parson paid, it seems as if half an anchor was the same as a Tub. In 1782, Woodforde paid £1.5s for a Tub of Gin, bought by Clark Hewitt in a basket. A smuggler's tub contained four gallons, which worked out at thirteen and a half pence a pint. If we reckon Mrs Raffald's five Quarts of French Brandy at ten shillings, the cost of over twenty gallons of Lemon Wine cannot have been more than a few pence a bottle, for a homemade liqueur.

Apart from wines, most households brewed their beer and ale. Some also made various meads from honey; sack mead, cowslip mead, and walnut mead. They also made shrub (a gallon of milk, two quarts of red wine, six lemons, four

Seville oranges, two gallons of rum, one of brandy and two pounds of double refined sugar). They drank "mountain wine" from Malaga, Madeira, port red and white, Lisbon, Calcavella burgundy, claret and sack. For punch they used arrack, as well as gin and rum. Homemade English Usquebaugh bore no resemblance to Scotch or Irish whiskey, which was not frequently drunk in England and Wales.

It is impossible to be precise about Georgian meals. They varied according to time and place. Parson Woodforde, for example, was a gentleman of fairly settled habits. But for him there was no breakfast routine of egg and bacon. In the years 1782–87, we find him breakfasting off meat and beer once, four times off milk only, twice off oysters and tea, twice off pork and beer. One day it might be six o'clock, another at nine o'clock. But for those ladies and gentlemen who turned night into day in London, Bath or Brighthelmstone, breakfast might, if eaten at all, be at 4 or 5 p.m.

The aristocracy would have two different regimens, if not three. For London the morning would last until 3 or 4 p.m., when luncheon was served. The theatre or opera, ballet or harlequinade would start at 6 p.m. and go on until 9.30 or 10 p.m. Then there would be dinner, which would last until midnight, with a supper in the small hours in the morning.

The same people in the country might be up at 6 a.m. to chase the fox and be in bed by 10 or 11 p.m., having eaten and drunk as much but at different times of the day.

Life at the suburban retreat, Chiswick, Kew, Richmond, Roehampton, Wimbledon and so on could be of either pattern: somewhere one could retire to recuperate from the ardours of the metropolis; or a place, especially in summer, where because of proximity to London one could invite a few score or hundreds of friends to a conspicuous assembly.

It was an age of obesity. In fairs a common exhibit was the fat man or woman. The fattest Georgian was Daniel Lambert, a victim not of gross appetites but clearly of dropsy and some glandular disease. He was a great sportsman in his youth, ate moderately and drank nothing but water. He began to swell when he reached his majority; but it was not until the spring of 1806, when he was in his middle thirties, that he was persuaded, perhaps out of necessity, to exhibit his colossal person. After showing himself in London for five months he went on the road and on June 20, 1809 he arrived at the Wagon & Horses Inn, in St Martins, Stamford Baron, advertised to exhibit himself to the public next day and for the duration of the ensuing races. He had shown dropsical symptoms for some time, but no hint of the illness from which he died during the night. His last performance was posthumous, a progress to the graveyard. His coffin measured six feet four inches long, four feet four inches wide, two feet four inches deep, and contained 112 superficial feet of elm. It was built upon axletrees and four wheels, upon which his remains were drawn to their place of interment. His grave was dug with a gradual sloping of many yards, and upwards of twenty men were employed for nearly half an hour on getting his massy corpse into its last abode.

His gravestone recorded that he had in personal greatness no competitor. He measured 3 ft 1 in round the leg, 9 ft 4 in round the body and weighed 728 lbs.

Most of the fat men were colossal eaters, such as the baker in Pye Corner, who frequently devoured a five pound shoulder of lamb at a sitting. He weighed 476 lbs, but by dieting on brown bread and water gruel for a year, he reduced by 200 lbs.

The actresses Kitty Clive and Hannah Pritchard (of whom Dr Johnson observed that it was wonderful how little mind she had) developed such large bodies that they found it difficult to stoop on the stage. As Lady Easy and Edging in Colley Cibber's *Careless Husband* they put this to advantage. Mrs Pritchard, as Lady Easy, asked the Clive as Edging to pick up a letter she had dropped. Looking first at herself and then at the corpulent Pritchard, Mrs Clive said, "Not I, indeed; take it up yourself if you like it." This got a laugh which the author had never intended; and a servant was beckoned from the wings to end the dispute.

One can understand the Georgian tendency to obesity, when one studies the menus of the time.

On October 4, for example, Parson Woodforde gave dinner and supper for six persons. For dinner at 4 p.m. he served a dish of fine tench which he had caught out of his brother's pond, ham, and three fowls boiled, a plum pudding; and for second course, a couple of ducks roasted, a roasted neck of pork, a plum tart; pears, apples and nuts after dinner. With the meal they had white wine and red, beer and cider. After it, coffee and tea. Then at ten o'clock, they had hashed fowl, duck and eggs and potatoes.

Dinner was the main meal of the day; and one can assume that many families dispensed with luncheon altogether when a grand dinner was to be given (except for the servants who ate *their* dinner in the middle of the day, which usually consisted in the broken meats from the night before.)

The first course usually began with soup (one tureen being placed at the head; if two, one at either end.) These were then removed and replaced by main dishes which needed carving. The simplest dinner illustrated by Mrs Sarah Harrison's *Housekeeper's Pocket-Book* consisted of two courses, each of "one Dish with Furniture". One example of this is leg of pork boil'd, with pease pudding, greens and roots followed by a second course of fowls roasted or turkey, with tarts or cheesecakes and fruits. It was customary to have one dish roasted and the other boiled (if there was only a choice of two). This utilised the facilities of the kitchen.

It was not until the end of the 18th century that the iron range was invented. This was built into the wall and provided hot water on one side, an open fire in the middle and a separately fired baking oven on the other. Before this, frying pans, boiling pots and kettles were hung from chains over the open fire. The baking oven was either separately fired, or was a box-like contraption which was placed in front of the open fire on a trivet, in which the contents needed to be turned from time to time to secure even cooking. Meat was roasted before the fire on spits, sometimes turned by a dog in a treadmill.

The dinner party to which guests were invited might have according to size and munificence up to eleven dishes in each course. Mrs Ann Peckham gives a sample menu for a January dinner.

$$(1)$$
$$(2) \quad (3) \quad (4)$$
$$(5) \quad (6) \quad (7)$$
$$(8) \quad (9) \quad (10)$$
$$(11)$$

First course
- (1) A Pike
- (2) Stewed Oysters
- (3) A Boat
- (4) Scotch Collops
- (5) Bacon
- (6) Gravy soup
- (7) Boiled Chickens
- (8) Calf's Foot Pye
- (9) A Boat
- (10 Pork Griskins
- (11) A Chine of Mutton

Second course
- (1) A Fricasey of Rabbits
- (2) Oranges
- (3) Apricots
- (4) Cranberry Twist
- (5) Potted Hare
- (6) Lemon Possets
- (7) Lobster
- (8) Cheesecakes
- (9) Wine Sours
- (10) Quinces
- (11) Wild Ducks

In the diagram (1) represents the head of the table and (11) the foot. Main dishes were placed nearest the diners, the remainder in the centre. I do not know what A Boat is, unless it is a sauceboat. Scotch Collops were slices of veal fried in butter, yolk of egg, etc., served with mushrooms or forced meat-balls, garnished with sausages, lemon and slices of bacon. Pork Griskins were broiled steaks cut from loin of pork with gravy and apple sauce. Pike could be roasted, stuffed with oysters, suet, breadcrumbs, thyme, parsley, anchovies, mace, salt and eggs: but since the Chine of Mutton would be roasted, in this first course the pike would be boiled, probably with a sauce of butter, parsley and gooseberries. Wine Sours were plums preserved in sugar. Lemon Possets were made with a pint of cream, the rinds of two and the juice of one lemon, a jack of white wine, "blebbed" with a spoon and served either in glasses or a dish.

For a grand Table Mrs Raffald reproduced two copper plates, showing 27 dishes for the first course and 25 for the second. Even she, as late housekeeper to the Hon. Elizabeth Warburton, did not consider that it was essential to have all that number; but gave them as possibilities from which a hostess might make her choice in the month of January.

In *The Honours of the Table* Dr Trusler shows us how Georgian trenchermen and trencherwomen tackled these enormous dinners.

In all public companies precedence is attended to, and particularly at table. Women have here always taken place of men, and both men and women have sat above each other, according to the rank they bear in life. Where a company is equal in point of rank, married ladies take the place of single ones, and older ones of younger ones.

When dinner is announced, the mistress of the house requests the lady first in rank, in company, to shew the way to the rest, and walk first into the room where the table is served; she then asks the second in precedence to follow, and after all the ladies are passed, she brings up the rear herself. The master of the house does the same with the gentlemen. Among persons of real distinction, this marshalling of the company is unnecessary, every woman and every man present knows his rank and precedence, and takes the lead without any direction from the mistress or master.

When they enter the dining-room, each takes his place in the same order; the mistress of the table sits at the upper-end, those of superior rank next her, right and left, those next in rank following, then the gentlemen, and the master at the lower-end; and nothing is as a greater mark of ill-breeding, than for a person to interrupt this order, or seat himself higher than he ought. Custom, however, has lately introduced a new mode of seating. A gentleman and a lady sitting alternately round the table, and this, for the better convenience of a lady's being attended to, and served by the gentleman next her. But notwithstanding this promiscuous seating, the ladies, whether above or below, are to be served in order, according to their rank or age, and after them the gentlemen, in the same manner.

It was necessary for the host and hostess to know a great deal about their guests. The protocol of the higher echelons was comparatively simple, (i) King's Sons (ii) King's Brothers (iii) King's Uncles, etc. The Bishop of London preceded the Bishop of Durham who preceded the Bishop of Winchester, but thereafter the precedence of Bishops (and their wives) was according to the seniority of consecration. From here down, precedency was complicated. Daughters of Knights preceded wives of the Companions of the Order of the Bath, who preceded wives of the Esquires of (a) the Order of the Bath, (b) the King's Body, (c) the Knights of the Bath, (d) by creation, (e) by office, all of whom preceded wives of the younger sons of Baronets etc. Altogether Adams' *Complete Servant* lists 81 ranks of precedency among gentlemen and 67 among ladies.

Precedency could be relaxed at Royal behest. For example, when Betsy Sheridan went to Mrs Sturt's Masquerade at Hammersmith in 1789 (the year after Dr Trusler published his little book), there were three supper rooms, one for the Prince of Wales, one for the Duke and Duchess of Cumberland, and a third for the company at large. Precedency ruled in the general supper room; but not in the two royal rooms.

Royalty could do as they pleased. The Reverend Dr Trusler, who as a "clergyman not dignitary", ranked No. 74, above "Barristers at Law" but below "Gentlemen entitled to bear arms", could not take liberties with etiquette. Let us rejoin him in the dining room.

As eating a great deal is deemed indelicate in a lady (for her character should be divine rather than sensual), it will be ill-mannered to help her to a large slice of meat at once, or fill her plate too full. When you have served her with meat, she should be asked what kind of vegetables she likes, and the gentleman sitting next the dish that holds those vegetables should be requested to help her.

When there are several dishes at table, the mistress of the house carves that which is before her, and desires her husband, or the person at the bottom of the table, to carve the joint or bird, before *him*. Soup is generally the first thing served, and should be stirred from the bottom; fish, if there is any, the next.

The master or mistress of the table should continue eating, whilst any of the company are so employed, and to enable them to do this, they should help themselves accordingly.

When there are not two courses, but one course and a remove, that is, a dish to be brought up, when one is taken away; the mistress or person who presides, should acquaint her company with what is to come; or if the whole is put on the table at once, should tell her friends, that "they should see their dinner"; but, they should be told, what wine or other liquors is on the sideboard. . . . Sometimes a cold joint of meat, or a salad, is placed on the sideboard. In this case it should be announced to the company.

If any of the company seem backward in asking for wine, it is the part of the master to ask or invite them to drink, or he will be thought to grudge his liquor; as it is the part of the mistress or master to ask those friends who seem to have dined, whether they would please to have more. As it is unseemly for ladies to call for wine, the gentlemen present should ask them in turn, whether it is agreeable to drink a glass of wine. (Mrs . . . will you do me the honour to drink a glass of wine with me?"), and what kind of the wine present they prefer, and call for two glasses of such wine, accordingly. Each then waits until the other is served, when they bow to each other and drink.

Habit having made a pint of wine after dinner almost necessary to a man who eats freely, which is not the case with women, and as their sitting and drinking with the men, would be unseemly; it is customary, after the cloth and desert are removed and two or three glasses of wine are gone round, for the ladies to retire and leave the men to themselves, and for this, 'tis the part of the mistress of the house to make the motion for retiring, by privately consulting the ladies present, whether they please to withdraw. The ladies thus rising, then men should rise of course, and the gentleman next the door should open it, to let them pass.

Dr Trusler's instructions to servants are not very different from what we would expect today (supposing there were servants), except that "if each person's servant is present, that servant should stand behind his mistress's or master's chair." If there was a second course, crumbs were removed; if not the table was cleared of cutlery, the tablecloth rolled up to prevent crumbs falling on the floor, the table rubbed bright and clean and the wine put on the table from the sideboard.

Diners were counselled neither to eat quick or very slow. The former indicated that you had not had a good meal for some time, the latter, if abroad, that you disliked the food, if at home that you were rude enough to set before friends what you could not eat yourself.

> So again, eating your soup with your nose in the plate is vulgar, it has the appearance of being used to hard work, and having, of course, an unsteady hand. If it be necessary then to avoid this, it is so much more so that if smelling to the meat whilst on the fork, before you put it in your mouth. I have seen many an ill-bred fellow do this, and have been so angry, that I could have kicked him from the table. If you dislike what you have, leave it; but on no account, by smelling to, or examining it, charge your friend with putting unwholesome provisions before you.
>
> To be well received, you must always be circumspect at table, where it is exceedingly rude, to scratch any part of your body, to spit, or blow your nose, (if you can't avoid it, turn your head), to eat greedily, to lean your elbows upon the table, to sit too far from it, to pick your teeth before the dishes are removed, or leave the table before grace is said . . .
>
> If the necessities of nature oblige you at any time, (particularly at dinner), to withdraw from the company you are in, endeavour to steal away unperceived, or make some excuse for retiring, that may keep your motives for withdrawing a secret; and on your return, be careful not to announce that return, or suffer any adjusting of your dress, or re-placing of your watch, to say, from whence you came. To act otherwise, is indelicate and rude.

For the Georgians, palates were what peacocks' tongues were for the Romans. Connoisseurs of a cod's head and shoulders, eschewing the green jelly of the eye, made, some for the jelly about the jawbones, some for the palate and others for the tongue. Ox palates were stewed with veal gravy, Madeira wine, etc., and served with artichoke bottoms, forced meat balls and morels. They were fricassed with mace, nutmeg, cayenne, etc., and garnished with parsley and barberries or they were fricandoed with little bits of bacon, "fried in Hog's Lard a pretty Brown, laid round with stewed Spinach pressed and cut like sippets". That delight of Victorian England, the oxtail, was totally ignored.

The aristocracy employed French chefs as a matter of course. But the generality of housewives (or housekeepers) decried French cuisine with all its fancy sauces. De la Rochefoucauld, as a young man, found dinner "the most |wearisome of English experiences". This remark has always been taken as a comment on English cooking. It might as well be a reflection on his knowledge of English or his fellow guests' of French: or their sympathy. A long conversation is the better for good food and wine; but without good conversation the best banquet is a bore.

For every one who, like Mr Thrale, ate himself to death, there were thousands who starved. For every toper like Dr John Campbell who boasted of sinking thirteen bottles of port at a sitting, there were hundreds who drank themselves into oblivion in Gin Lane. But the contrasts we should make are not those between Georgian times and ours (which have their own terrors); but between

Britain at that time and the rest of Europe. Even bearing in mind the hunger in the Highlands of Scotland, the Irish famines, failures of harvests, the dispossessions, the bread riots, the burning of ricks and the wrecking of looms, Britons throughout the Georgian era fared and fed and drank comparatively better than the people of Europe.

Towards the end of the Georgian era new habits were forming. The world of Jane Austen was moderate. Food was enjoyed, but not guzzling. If too much drink was taken, it was not in front of the ladies. The Shelleys became vegetarians. Lord Byron needed careful handling if he was to be induced to take anything at all. Byron was careful about his figure. Without exercise, he ran to fat; and what fat poet could be romantic? He certainly went on a diet of dry biscuits and soda water. When he switched from soda water to brandy, it had results more frightening than his cosy lines:

> Claret, sandwich and an appetite
> Are things which make an English evening pass.

We associate sandwiches with picnics. Pique-niques were introduced from Sweden and Germany in the middle of the 18th century. They were bring-your-own food parties, food-equivalents to our modern bottle-parties. But by 1800, the English picnic had been adopted, as a cross-channel *fête champêtre*. In the summer a meal would be served out of doors, or an excursion taken to a beauty spot, like that fated one in Jane Austen's *Emma* to Box Hill, where an ambitious repast would be served from hampers, preferably "in shade from Phoebus' beams". But of course there would be nothing as simple as a sandwich, Britain's contribution to railway stations all over the globe.

The sandwich was the invention of John Montagu, the 4th Earl of Sandwich (1717–92), whose other claims to remembrance are slight. While celebrating a Black Mass at Medmenham Abbey imploring Satan to appear, he was pounced upon by a baboon that John Wilkes had clothed with horns, tail and talons; after which he became the most inefficient First Lord of the Admiralty in the history of a maritime nation. His main contribution to posterity was inspired by a twenty-four hour gambling session from which he could not tear himself away to eat. He sustained himself throughout with slices of cold beef "sandwiched" between slices of toast.

CHAPTER FIVE

Fashion

A winning wave, (deserving note,)
In the tempestuous petticoat,
A careless shoe-string, in whose tie
I see a wild civility,—
Do more bewitch me than when art
Is too precise in every part.

Robert Herrick, 1591–1674

The ladies of the Stuart Court knew how a sweet disorder in the dress kindles in clothes a wantonness. They appreciated as much as Herrick the liquefaction of their clothes. But with the glorious revolution of 1688, came a return to the stiff fashions of Elizabethan times. What the Elizabethans had called the fardingale was revived as the pannier or hoop; and this remained the ruling fashion throughout the continent of Europe and Britain until the French Revolution swept that and much else away. "Stiff with hoops, and arm'd with ribs of whale", Georgian ladies, like those of the court of Queen Anne, sailed their way through Palace and Pump-room in gigantic petticoats, their bodies hidden, like lights under bushels.

The spacious petticoat, in bright array,
Like a tall ship does all its pride display,
Swells with full gales and sweeps along the way.

The petticoat was an underskirt, worn over hoops made of osier, canes or whale-bone. It matched or contrasted with the gown or robe which opened below the waist to reveal the petticoat, and above the waist the bodice could be laced or allowed to open to reveal the glory of an elaborately decorated stomacher. Stays constricted the body into a wasp-waist. Sometimes they were underwear; at others, as in court dress, bodice and corset were combined, the *corps rigide*. That a fashion so undesirable should last for a century shows the feminine confusion between what hurts and what is smart. Since many women married at the age of seventeen and spent more than half their lives pregnant until death or the menopause brought relief from their labours, it must have been agony to be fashionable. Ugly, tight and uncomfortable, stays hastened the death of many tuberculous ladies. But according to Farington, Miss Laroche, daughter of the MP for Bodmin, owed her life to her stays. She was riding behind the aged and portly Dean of Clogher along the precipitous crest of Dovedale, when their horse stumbled. Both riders were hurtled down towards the rapid river Dove. "I felt every blow," she wrote her mother later. "In some places I fell perpendicular, in others I rolled and was dashed from rock to rock, there not being a bit of grass I defended myself with my hands, when within a few yards of the bottom a furze bush so entangled my hair that it stopped me and I hung by it." The portly Dean who had rolled not only down the scree but also over Miss Laroche once or twice, landed up half way down, stopped by a holly, the only tree growing on that side of the valley. Miss Laroche, who had fallen full four hundred feet, hung for three hours before she felt a dog licking her face and heard the voice of rescuing shepherds. When the doctor examined her, he found she was merely bruised. Thanks to her stays, no bones were broken.

Hoops kept ladies (who wore no underwear except petticoats and a chemise) cool in summer, but draughty in winter when icy winds got underneath the bell-hoops. "I have heard some great ladies lately complain of terrible colds they have caught through the too great concavity of their petticoats, which they seem to dread may end in rheumatism and scyatica's," wrote a correspondent to the *Spectator* in 1725.

Apart from that, hoops were confoundedly clumsy. In a theatre box a lady took up as much space as three men. Dining tables had to be lengthened or the number of guests curtailed. In eighteenth century houses, stairs were built grandly wide to enable ladies to pass, or walk side by side. Often trying to enter a hackney coach, the lady found—

> Yet found too late
> The petticoat too wide, the door too strait;
> Entrance by force she oft attempts to gain,
> Betty's assistance, too, she calls in vain,
> The stubborn whalebone beats her back again.
> Vex'd at the balk, on foot she trips her way,
> For woman's will admits of no delay;
> On either side a faithful slave attends
> And safe from harm the Petticoat defends.

Without the "faithful slaves", even walking the streets could be hazardous, especially in London on Mondays and Fridays when there were street markets. Displays of goods could be scattered and ruined by a clumsy petticoat.

The Female Spectator quotes the misfortune of a lady who "came tripping by with one of those mischief-making hoops, which spread itself from the steps of my door quite to the posts placed to keep off the coaches and carts; a large flock of sheep were that instant driving to the slaughterhouse, and an old ram who was the foremost, being put out of his way by some accident, ran full butt into the foot-way, where his horns were immediately entangled in the hoop of this fine lady, as she was holding it up on one side, as the genteel fashion is, and indeed the make of it requires. In her fright she let it fall down, which still the more encumbered him, as it fixed upon his neck; she attempted to run, he to disengage himself, which neither being able to do, she shrieked, he ba'aed, the rest of the sheep echoed the cry, and the dog who followed the flock barked, so that altogether made a most hideous sound. Down fell the lady, unable to sustain the forcible efforts the ram made to obtain his liberty. A crowd of mobs, who were gathered in an instant, shouted. At last the driver who was at a good distance behind, came up, and assisted in setting free his beast, and raising the lady; but never was finery so demolished. The late rains had made the place so excessively dirty that her gown and petticoat, which before were yellow, the colour so much revered in Hanover, and so much the mode in England at present, were now most barbarously painted with a filthy brown; her gauze cap half off her head in the scuffle; and her *tête de mouton* hanging down on one shoulder. The rude populace, instead of pitying, insulted her misfortune and continued their shouts till she got into a chair and was out of sight."

Enormous hoops and high head-dresses were at the same time so clumsy and so artificial that Mrs Delany prophesied in 1746: "I expect soon to see the other extreme of thread paper heads and no hoops, and from appearing like so many blown bladders, we shall look like so many *bodkins stalking* about." Mrs Delany lived for another forty years and though there was a memorable occasion in 1782 when Marie Antoinette appeared one April day in Versailles wearing a long white satin gown without a hoop and for a couple of seasons the *haut ton* in England followed suit, back came the hoops in 1784, big as ever, now embellished with artificial flowers or trimmings of feathers.

Why did the hoop survive for almost a century? It allowed many different forms. The bell grew as larger and fatter from Queen Anne to George I as did the reigning monarch. The size of the hoop depended upon the weight of the material. Damasks with gold and silver embroidery (costing £12 or more in those days, or by to-day's standards twenty times as much) were heavy. So were velvet petticoats, "wrought" petticoats, petticoats of cloth, heavy silk, chintz and holland, silk embroidered, even ermine petticoats, worn under fur trimmed velvet gowns.

The unfortunate whales were exterminated from the Bay of Biscay but others were discovered by the implacable Dutch off Greenland and their bones provided lighter, stronger hoops than those of cane or wood. At the same time from India came lighter fabrics such as calico and muslin to extend the fashion more outrageously in space for a longer time.

The human body had disappeared, like the frames of the puppets which, in default of fashion prints were sent around the capitals of Europe to illustrate new modes. As early as 1727 Lady Lansdowne in Paris was sending to her friend Mrs Howard, Lady of the Bedchamber to Queen Caroline, a doll dressed exactly in the

Paris fashion, with instructions to pass it on to Mrs Tempest, after her Majesty had "done with it". Mrs Tempest was a top London milliner, eager to be first with the new styles. Perhaps it was to avoid having her fashions stolen that Mlle Rose Bertin, Marie Antoinette's dressmaker, journeyed in her "berlin" coach round the courts of Europe with her own collection of model dolls and took orders and measurements.

After 1740 the round hoop (of which some complained that it projected so far that it made it impossible for a gentleman dancer to touch his partner's hand) gave way to the oval hoop, flattened front and back, or to pairs of panniers projecting at each side. These panniers were sometimes stitched to the petticoat itself, at others separate contrivances, covered with fabric and attached by tapes at each side of the waist.

Whatever the variation in stays and hoops, the female form was hidden (except when an upward gust of wind, to the infinite delight of passers-by, revealed all below.) Elegance consisted in texture, colour, contrast, ornament and ostentation. Petticoats came in velvets, cloth, silks of a dozen kinds. Brilliant colours were used, as if in defiance to the fog above and the mud below. A petticoat might be of one colour, the embroidery of a second, the gown of a third, stomachers or bodice of a fourth, the apron of a fifth, the cloak of a sixth and if a hat or hood was worn of a seventh. Vast were the opportunities for the exhibition of good taste, or bad.

"The single dress of a woman of quality is often the product of a hundred climates. The muff and the fan come together from the different ends of the earth. The scarf is sent from the torrid zone, and the tippet from beneath the pole. The brocade petticoat rises out of the mines of Peru, and the diamond necklace out of the bowels of Indostan." Thus Addison in *Benefits of Commerce*, when as throughout the century much agitation arose from the expensive import of fabrics, trimmings and accoutrements from abroad to the detriment of home industries. Holland linen was preferred to Scotch and Irish, Italian and French silks to those made by the Huguenot refugees in Spitalfields, Flemish lace to similar lace made in England by Flemish immigrants; Indian printed calicoes and cottons to those produced in Lancashire factories.

Import duties and total bans were placed on certain goods; only to stimulate the ingenuity of smugglers. Pitt imposed a tax on imported gloves, which he hoped, vainly, would bring in £50,000 a year. Importers smuggled their gloves in bundles consisting either of right or left hands. If one consignment got through, and the other was seized, the impounded bundle was sold at auction and bought for a song by the consignee who possessed the corresponding halves of the pairs. Coffins were used for the smuggling of lace shirts and ruffles. When Dr Atterbury died in Paris in 1731, the High Sheriff of Westminster discovered his corpse enshrouded in no less than six thousand pounds worth of French lace.

Conspicuous expenditure was an end in itself. For her marriage to George III, the 17 year-old Princess Charlotte of Mecklenberg-Strelitz wore a diamond tiara, necklace and stomacher valued at £60,000. Horace Walpole remarked that her dress, "an endless mantle of violet coloured velvet, lined with ermine, and attempted to be fastened on her shoulder by a large bunch of pearls, dragged itself and almost the rest of her clothes half-way down her waist" with the consequence that "the spectators knew as much of her upper half as the King himself."

As the century advanced, it was customary to wear a train or tail in the public promenades or gardens. "As a lady's quality or fashion was once determined here by the circumference of her hoop,' remarked the Chinese philosopher in Goldsmith's *Citizen of the World*, "both are now measured by the length of her tail. Women of moderate fortunes are contented with tails moderately long, but ladies of true taste and distinction set no bounds to their ambition in this particular. I am told the Lady Mayoress, on days of ceremony, carries one longer than a belwether of Bantam, whose tail, you know, is trundled along in a wheelbarrow." It was a fashion, both dirty and expensive. After sweeping the walks of St James's, of Ranelagh or Vauxhall Gardens a few times, a tail was no longer fit to be worn, however diligent the lady's maid, and more silk had to be bought to repair the damage.

The neck of the gown was cut low at front and back for full dress, but for ordinary wear it was often high at the back and square in front. No lady thought, in any time or weather, to cover the neck completely. A young lady in the *Spectator* writes to complain that her aunt allows her no protection except a scarf" about as thick as a spider's web, and pinned down to my mantua gown, which is no higher than the middle of my back." As behind, so in front; where cleavage was veiled, it was only by the flimsiest of neckerchieves.

Sleeves were elbow length, those of the gown ending high enough to show the lace sleeves of the chemise below. Aprons were worn not for use, but embellishment. In the language of the time "undress" was the alternative to "full dress" and a "night-gown" was worn in the evening, not in bed.

It was hard to distinguish where clothes ended and personal attributes began. Most confusing of all was the head. Just as the Middle Ages was a riot of "horns" and "steeples", so the eighteenth century was a proliferation of head-dresses of the most fantastic designs; towers, "commodes", "Fontanges" and so on. The origin of the Fontange was fortuitous. Mademoiselle Fontange when out hunting tied her unruly hair with a ribbon above her head and the "sweet disorder" was so charming that Louis XIV, her lover, begged her to wear it thus in future. The spontaneous arrangement became the rage among the court ladies. Disordered curls were artfully massed and puffed; to a single ribbon was added elaborate lace. The careless contrivance of a moment gave way to monstrous edifices, the Brussels or Mechlin lace for which cost from thirty to forty pounds (at a time when Dr Johnson reckoned a man could subsist on three pounds a year).

Though there was a revulsion against the Fontange brought about by Lady Sandwich, who delighted Louis XIV by appearing at the French Court with a low head-dress, heads started to rise again with the hoop, there being a need for height to counterbalance the width below. The preparation of these creations was

1. The first-born was greeted with rapture, muted if the sex was female. In this case, however, the cartoonist was speculating on an issue from the Prince of Wales' connection with Mrs Fitzherbert.

2–3. (*above*) Children were confined to the nursery, where a retinue of servants attended their needs; (*below*) the precocious emergence of Mary Pierrepoint, the future Lady Mary Wortley Montagu, as the toast of the Kit-Kat Club became legend.

4–5. Two scenes from Hogarth's *Marriage à la Mode*: (*above*) after a financially successful settlement and a hideous first night, boredom has set in; (*below*) but my lady finds consolations in the fashionable world which give her husband horns.

6–9. The toilet: (*top left*) the lady's maid prepares for the morrow after her mistress has retired to bed, ready perhaps for a late-night visit from the young master; (*top right*) by the early nineteenth century, the elaborate headdress had given way to the wig; (*bottom left*) but at Queen Caroline's court the old fashions still survived; (*bottom right*) the flaming headdress provided a dramatic incident in *The Sylph*, the novel published anonymously by Georgiana, Fifth Duchess of Devonshire.

10. Belowstairs the way to a man's heart was through his belly.

Order —

Secretiveness

Drawing —

Covetiveness —

Size

11–14. George Cruikshank shows the transition from the Regency to the Victorians: only secretiveness illustrates a joke at which Queen Victoria would not have been amused.

WALKING DRESS.

The Fatima Robe.

15–18. The Elegance of Fantasy.

MORNING DRESS.

19. The silhouette flourished in the eighteenth century; for German princelings, Meissen created tea and dinner sets in which each member of the family had his individual silhouetted plates, cups and saucers; here is a card of Mr and Mrs Smith of Hailsham and Aunt Everard by Francis Torond (c. 1777); we do not know for certain whether the dog is playing with Aunt Everard or Mrs Smith.

so intricate and time-consuming that they were often worn for days, if not for weeks. George Colman the Younger described one such edifice. "A towering toupée pulled up all but by the roots and strained over a cushion on the top of her head, formed the centre of the building; tiers of curls served for the wings; a hanging chignon behind defended her occiput, like a buttress; and the whole fabric was kept tight and water proof by a quantity of long single and double black pins." This was in 1770.

Later, the cushion, which was a pad stuffed with tow, horsehair or wool, was replaced by a wire frame over which the real hair was drawn and false hair added, before the structure was plastered with pomatum and covered with white powder. Being lighter, the wire frame caused fewer headaches: but either contraption was liable to become verminous. Little ivory claws on the end of long sticks, euphemistically described as "back-scratchers" were in fact implements to counter-irritate infested scalps. Of the hundreds who quote the homely wisdom of Robert Burns. "O wad some Pow'r the giftie gie us, To see oursels as others see us!" few know that the title of the poem is "To a louse" seen on the bonnet of a young lady in church.

On top of these headdresses were set fantastic collections of different objects, ribbons, jewels or flowers, real or artificial. Georgiana Duchess of Devonshire introduced vari-coloured ostrich feathers sometimes reaching a yard in height. It was impossible for a lady to travel in a hackney coach wearing a head-dress, unless she sat on the floor.

Topping these verminous and often malodorous concoctions, there had to be a hat, a cap, a chip-bonnet or a fly-cap, shaped like a butterfly and edged with garnets and brilliants.

At a very early age girls were taught the use of cosmetics, not merely for the face but for neck, arms, shoulders. In fact any part of the body which was not covered in clothes was covered with white, rouge, lip-salve, chosen to go with the dress. White paint was used as a cosmetic base. The cheaper type made from whitening, flour, ground rice and tallow soap, was comparatively harmless. The more expensive, a mixture of white lead, rice and flour, looked more elegant, but was as dangerous as the rouge, used for heightening the colour of the cheeks. This was made from red lead, mixed with vermilion or carmine.

Mr and Mrs Adams in the early 19th century *The Complete Servant* recommended white talc, applied by the finger, a piece of paper or preferably a hare's foot prepared for the purpose in ointment. Cosmetics extracted from minerals, they warned, were "more or less pernicious, but always corrosive. They affect the eyes, which swell and inflame, and are rendered painful and watery. They change the texture of the skin, on which they produce pimples, and cause rheums; attack the teeth, make them ache, destroy the enamel, and loosen them." Though this sounds alarming, the effects of lead- and mercury-based cosmetics were far worse. Mercury water and white lead (ceruse) was absorbed cutaneously and produced lead and mercury poisoning. Hair fell out; and after gastric disorders and tremblings, death might follow. This was recognised during the last half of the 18th century. Augustus Hervey casually remarked that the beautiful courtesan Kitty Fisher, a favourite model of Joshua Reynolds, died "a victim of cosmetics". Horace Walpole (1776) wrote of "that pretty young woman, Lady Fortrose . . . killed like Lady Coventry and others by white lead of which nothing could break her."

Rouge, prepared from red sandal-wood, root of orchanet, cochineal, Brazil wood or bastard saffron mixed with talc, though not lethal, could permanently damage the skin. Mrs Thrale used it so effectively in her early years that when she was 36, Charlotte Burney observed, "I fancy she is about thirty, though she hardly looks twenty eight." In her eighties she was forced to continue using it, because "it had introduced a dead yellow colour into her complexion, quite unlike that of her natural skin, and she wished to conceal the deformity."

Soaps were produced at Bristol and Windsor and imported from Spain, France, Italy and Turkey. But many ladies found the use of soap painful when applied to skin blanched with white lead or mercury water. They preferred cleansing creams and the deodorant properties of foreign scents or English lavender and rose water.

Cleanliness was not a universal practice, even among royalty. Writing to the Duc de Richelieu who was to bring to France a second bride for the Dauphin, his first having died in childbirth, Louis XV announced that the Dauphin had set his heart on the fifteen year-old Marie-Josephe of Saxony "and I gather that he would prefer her to be sweet-smelling; he had urged Madame de Brances" (the bride's maid of honour) "to see that she has a bath before he meets her, which confirms my suspicion that the poor late-lamented did not do this often enough."

Lady Mary Wortley Montagu wrote of court ladies, "All the women have literally rosy cheeks, snowy foreheads and bosoms, jet eye-brows and scarlet lips, to which they generally add coal black hair. These perfections never leave them till the hour of their deaths, and have a very fine effect by candlelight, but I could wish they were handsome with a little more variety."

Sometimes variety was introduced involuntarily; as when the lady playing cards at Tunbridge Wells drew her hand across her brow and shifted a false eyebrow into the middle of her forehead. As the other card players started to laugh, she joined in though she literally could not see the joke, even when at last her husband, noticing, went over and whispered to her.

Beauty patches were introduced in the sixteenth century. They were sometimes used to heighten a feature, at others to cover a spot or blemish. Addison refers to political patching among ladies at the opera, Whig ladies patching on one side of the forehead, Tories on the other. At the court of Louis XV, however, patching obeyed a different code. A patch in the corner of the eye was "impassioned", in mid-cheek "gallant" and on the lips "coquettish". In England patching among the elderly was noted with disapproval by the seventeenth century visitor Misson who wrote, "I have often counted fifteen patches or more, upon the wrinkled phiz of an old hag of three score and ten upwards." In France, patching was considered appropriate only for the young and beautiful.

The fan however was for every age. On her second birthday, Princess Charlotte was presented with a fan by her aunt, Princess Amelia, who herself had been painted at the age of three, wearing white gloves and carrying a fan. Fan play was learnt as behaviouristically as speech. It had its own language, codes, signals and cyphers. There was style as well as meaning in how it was opened or closed, fluttered, used to hide or reveal, peep through, over or aside. It was an advertisement, an article of dress, a political emblem, the signature of taste. Mrs Thrale recorded how after the success of *Le Mariage de Figaro*, Parisians carried "verses of this favourite piece upon their fans, pocket-handkerchiefs etc., as our own women once did those of the 'Beggar's Opera'."

There were fans of delicate gauze and painted silk, with jewelled mountings. At dances ladies tossed their fans on a table and the gentlemen drew them like tickets in a lottery and asked their owners to dance. A lady needed at least as many fans as she had sorts of occasions; fans for private balls and public masquerades, fans for the Haymarket in the summer and in the winter fans for Covent Garden or Drury Lane, fans for the Royal Birthday, fans for Matins in the Parish Church, fans for Handel's Messiah in Westminster Abbey, fans for mourning, for playing cards, drinking Spa waters or walking in the Pantiles, fans for the chaise bowling round the Park, fans for walking through Spring Gardens to the Mall.

There were other articles of adornment, of course; the muff of fur or feathers, satin or silk, enormously warm for winter, delicately elegant for summer; the reticule, the parasol, the scarf; gloves of fine lace or long gloves of doeskin for public display morning or evening; and at night for whitening the arms, cosmetic gloves of dog or chicken skin. But in this age of polite paraphrase and genteel euphemism, nothing was so expressive as the language of the fan which could invite without indelicacy and refuse without rudeness.

Snuff was a fashion as characteristic of the Georgian era as the fan; and since it was taken by both sexes, it was capable of even greater variety. As a habit among women, it was introduced by Queen Charlotte, who was a snuffer from the time of her marriage, in 1761, at the age of seventeen. She was not a beauty, though as she grew older, her Chamberlain considered that "the bloom of her ugliness" was "going off". It had been thought that her snuff-taking may have begun as an excuse for displaying her fine arm and delicate hand, as she applied her fingers to her nostrils (and momentarily hid her mouth, which was very large). It persisted into old age as an addiction. As an Etonian schoolboy, Captain von Gronow observed her walking on the terrace at Windsor with King George III. She applied finger and thumb to her gold box from which she "appeared to have fished a considerable quantity, for the royal nose was covered with snuff both within and without." As an old lady, she was amused when her granddaughter at a children's party, asked the musicians to play *What a beau my granny was* in her honour.

> What a beau she was!
> She took snuff and that's enough,
> And that's enough for me!

Queen Charlotte's favourite snuff was Violet Strasburg, made from Rappee and bitter almonds reduced to a fine powder to which were added ambergris and attargul.

As the first gentleman of Europe, the Prince Regent was perforce a connoisseur of snuff. His snuff cellar, worth thousands of pounds, was superintended by his Chief Page, assisted by periodic visits of inspection from Messrs Fribourg & Treyer. Rare and curious snuffs from all over the world were presented to him. He favoured different varieties according to the time of day: for the morning, Queen Charlotte's mixture; for afternoon Etrenne, Bureau, Martinique, Cologne, Old Paris, Havre, Rouen, Bordeaux. His favourite blend was The King's Carotte, expressly prepared by Fribourg & Treyer; but after dinner there would be a choice of a dozen different snuffs in boxes magnificent as works of art.

The taking of snuff was as much a matter of style as the play of a fan. The Prince Regent would hold his snuff box in his left hand, and, opening it with his right thumb and forefinger, in the words of Captain von Gronow, "introduce them into this costly reservoir of snuff, and with a consequential air convey the same to the nose; but never suffered any to enter: indeed those who were well acquainted with his Majesty, frequently told me he took snuff for effect, but never liked it, and allowed all of it to escape from his finger and thumb before it reached the nose."

Beau Brummell, who led his contemporaries in cleanliness and in taste, did not consider snuff-taking a messy habit. His admiring biographer, Captain Jesse, claimed that "he opened his box with peculiar grace, and with one hand only, the left".

For a gentleman to offer a pinch of snuff was politeness, to request one a discourtesy. Brummell's lifelong quarrel with the Prince Regent began with a snuff-tiff. Dining at Brighton Pavilion, the Bishop of Winchester took a pinch from Brummell's snuff box which lay open on the table beside him, without being asked. Brummell turned to his servant, who stood behind his chair. "Throw the rest on the fire or floor," he said. The Prince Regent was furious at the insult to the bishop and next morning gave Brummell "a good wigging".

Snuff boxes were for both sexes what canes were for men and fans for women; objects of art, occasions for elegance, expressions of taste or sentiment. The gift of a snuff box could convey a variety of messages. Women had boxes containing miniatures of their children and their lovers. A scene of amorous shepherds and shepherdesses, Cupid and Psyche, Venus and Adonis, Leda and the Swan could mean only what it showed or more. The lid of box might display a beauty in high fashion and, within, the same beauty unadorned: *Maya vestida* and *Maya desnuda*, a box appropriate for a masquerade. Proffered to a lady, it could discover whether she would like to take a pinch or something more. Ladies and gentlemen of the *ton* had snuff-boxes for all occasions.

It is significant that British fashionables thought of themselves in French, the *ton* or the *haut ton*. As a nation, most women dressed soberly, apart from those who moved as easily at Versailles as at Carlton House. The Quakers were as conspicuously simple in their dress as in their speech. Their puritanism and that of the evangelicals whether following Wesley or Whitfield was more typical of the Georgian era than the hedonism of the *ton*. In 1770 a Bill was introduced into Parliament, containing the clause: "That all women of whatever age, rank, profession, or degree, whether virgins, maids or widows, that shall, from and after such Act, impose upon, seduce and betray into matrimony, any of His Majesty's subjects, by the scents, paints, cosmetic washes, artificial teeth, false hair, Spanish wool, iron stays, hoops, high heeled shoes, bolstered hips, shall incur the penalty of the law in force against witchcraft, and like misdemeanours and that the marriage, upon conviction, shall stand null and void." No sumptuary penalties seem to have been inflicted against such practice of bitch-craft. But it expressed the Janus-headed nature of Georgian England. This was one face, the other was the delight that even the *vulgus mobile*, the "mob", took in the lavish splendours of the aristocracy, especially in society beauties, who provided the glamour furnished today by the "stars" of entertainment.

Marie Antoinette was not only Queen of France, but also Queen of Fashion. Her *robe à la chemise* anticipated the simplicity which was to become the keynote of the Revolutionary Age. But it was the storming of the Bastille and the ensuing terror which made that change inevitable. The hoop could not survive the tumbril, nor the head-dress the guillotine.

After the arrest of Marie Antoinette, Mlle Rose Bertin and her staff fled to London, the asylum of nobility. In Paris at first the fashion was to be simply inconspicuous in order to avoid the suspicion of high birth. But soon Republican France evolved entirely new modes, based upon those of the pre-Christian republics of Greece and Rome. Women wore high-waisted dresses, flowing straight to the ground, flat sandals fixed with a thong or ring. The breasts were partially or sometimes completely exposed. The contours of the body were revealed either through transparent muslin or by silks.

During the five years of the Terror, English ladies adhered, like the aristocratic *emigrées* whom they befriended, to hoops and stays. But with the rise of the *haute bourgeoisie* in the Directory, Parisian styles became again respectable across the Channel. Georgian ladies turned eagerly to the simplicity of the new classic style. They did not go to the extremes of *les merveilleuses*, two of whom appeared in Paris totally nude. But they welcomed the bodily freedom which these comparatively simple dresses gave them.

The artificially high waist remained the vogue for thirty years, even though when it was introduced in 1794, an occasional versifier complained:

> Shepherds I have lost my waist
> Have you seen my body?
>
> For fashion I that part forsook
> Where sages place the belly.
>
> Never shall I see it more,
> Till common sense returning,

My body to my legs restore,
  Then I shall cease from mourning.

Folly and fashion do prevail
  To such extremes among the fair,
A woman's only top and tail,
  The body's banished God knows where.

When Napoleon Bonaparte, aged 30, became First Consul of France, his beautiful Creole wife, Josephine, six years his senior, became the model of elegance, excelling in extravagance the late Queen, above whom she was to be exalted as Empress of France. Napoleon disapproved of scanty clothing. At a Luxembourg reception, he gave orders to stoke all fires to stifling heat, because the weather was cold and the ladies "practically naked". He liked to see new clothes. "Madame la Maréchale, your cloak is superb," he is said to have remarked. "I have seen it a good many times." White was his favourite colour. Obediently Josephine wore white and ordered so many clothes that even Napoleon was appalled at her extravagance.

Where Paris led, London followed. "White, and white only", was the message relayed from London to Bath, Brighton, Bristol, Cheltenham, Edinburgh, Dublin and wherever there were young ladies anxious to follow fashion.

The traveller and philanthropist Jonas Hanway (1712–86) had carried an umbrella in the streets, provoking the taunts of chairmen and hackney coachmen who felt he was trying to cheat them of their rain trade. The practice appeared absurd even to Samuel Johnson, who said Hanway "acquired some reputation by travelling abroad, but lost it by travelling at home." Ladies wearing hoops and stays had no use for the light umbrella. Going to and from their coaches, they would be sheltered by servants carrying the sort of umbrellas we use as sunshades for garden tables. But when the slender classical dress came into fashion, they began to carry light umbrellas for protection. There was still little regard for the different seasons; summer, winter, spring or autumn the same sort of dress would serve its daily occasion. The changes were made according to times of day, morning, afternoon, evening or night: or according to purpose, walking, riding, the garden or the seaside, the ball, the dinner, the opera or theatre.

For the first two decades of the 19th century, there were in effect two rival courts. For Queen Charlotte the hoops and stays that had gone out in the 1790's had still to be worn. The ageing princesses and the maids in waiting dressed as if time had stopped with the storming of the Bastille. But at Carlton House or the Pavilion fashion was freer. The Prince Regent still considered himself the First Gentleman in Europe, even though Beau Brummell's, "Who's your fat friend?" was evoked at the sight of his encorsetted obesity. Prinny and his mistresses were already past their prime. Young people did not find in Carlton House or the Brighton Pavilion the fashion to mirror. It was rather Madame Recamier or the Empress Josephine to whom young ladies like Lady Caroline Lamb looked.

After Waterloo, there was a brief possibility that Princess Charlotte and her husband Prince Leopold might establish a young court, which would have counterbalanced that of the Queen, her grandmother, and her father the Regent. The Princess's first duty, however, was to provide an heir to the throne. After one or two miscarriages, she had a foreboding that a third would be fatal to herself. She was correct. After fifty hours of labour she was delivered of a still-born boy. Five and a half hours later at 2.30 a.m. November 6, 1817, she herself died and with her died any hope of a young court successive to the Regent's.

In *La Belle Assemblée* and the fashion plates which were published in Ackerman's *Repository of Arts* from January 1809 to December 1828 one can see certain similarities running through the changing modes. Whatever the type of dress, Morning, Garden, Promenade, Carriage, Dinner, Evening, Full Evening, Opera, Theatre, Court, Sea-side, Mourning, each was planned within a small range of colours, shapes and fabrics. Shoes, head-dresses and parasols were usually of matching colours; but the head-dress was also linked to the dress, by colour, similarity of material or design. Instead of the wide colour range which had been combined in the hoop, bodice, chemise and head-dress in the 18th century, early 19th century designs were simple; lyrics compared to odes. Perhaps because each outfit was a simple arrangement, there was far greater variety between one design and another. The hem of the skirt was frequently ornamented so that it echoed the line of neck and sleeves an octave lower. Sometimes the connection was emphasised by a design running down the front or back of the dress.

This was customary in the high-waisted classical dresses when the hem line was above ground and it became axiomatic with the return of the waistline to its anatomical position in 1824 and thereafter. Neck line and skirt billowed and flounced while the waist was encorsetted. Corsets were used even for girls, mothers being counselled to place the child face down upon the floor, in order to get a tight grip on the laces.

Hats grew larger as the twenties advanced. While suitable for carriage costume on a windless day, they were public nuisances at the theatre for those sitting behind. They were also worn at the dinner table and tall men sitting between short women complained of the impossibility of seeing their food.

It was a great decade for sleeves; which could be short and puffed, long and double-puffed or treble-puffed. There was for the lady with beautiful arms, the attractive combination of the short opaque leg of mutton sleeve and the mid-arm billowy sleeve which by itself looked like elephantiasis of the elbow, but was attractive in conjunction with a billowing riding skirt.

Hair was arranged usually with curls over the forehead and a chignon at the back. Gone were the towering edifices of tow, pomatum and powder. In the evening, artificial hair was sometimes added, in what was called "the Apollo knot", fixed on top of the head and variously ornamented with feathers, flowers, bows or tortoiseshell combs. Necklaces, bracelets, tiaras, cameo brooches, crosses, jewelled or wrought gold clasps were popular, but there were few dress rings.

At the end of 1828, the *Lady's Magazine* issued an announcement and warning. For the winter it would be fashionable to wear dresses made of cloth. "They are very comfortable as a high dress in morning walks requiring only a pelerine in addition; but there is much to be said against them: never ought they to be retained as a fireside costume; for perhaps the next evening is devoted to a dress party or a ball, when the thinness of the texture and the nakedness of the neck and arms are sure to be the causes of violent colds, often ending in pulmonary complaints."

It was curious logic that ladies would be more likely to catch cold and develop pleurisy or pneumonia through wearing warm clothes indoors than through wearing muslin dresses in the winter streets. The warning went unheeded. By the time that George IV, holding his physician's hand "more strongly than usual" exclaimed, "My dear boy! This is death!" it had become accepted that cloth would be suitable for indoor wear during the winter of 1830/31.

CHAPTER SIX

Public Pleasures

Imagine to yourself, my dear Letty, a spacious garden laid out in delightful walks, bounded with high hedges and trees, and paved with gravel; part exhibiting a wonderful assemblage of the most picturesque and striking objects, pavilions, lodges, groves, grottoes, lawns, temples and cascades; porticoes, colonnades, and rotundoes; adorned with pillars, statues, and paintings; the whole illuminated with an infinite number of lamps, disposed in different figures of suns, stars, and constellations: the place crowded with the gayest company, ranging through blissful shades, or supping in different lodges on cold collations, enlivened with mirth, freedom and good humour, and animated with an excellent band of music.

Tobias Smollett: *Adventures of Humphrey Clinker*

The 18th century became the great age of pleasure gardens. There had of course been all sorts of minor pleasure gardens; as well as tea gardens; wells whose brackish waters were calculated to move the bowels, help pass the stone or relieve the gout; taverns with rooms set aside for gambling and gardens laid out as bowling greens. But it was Jonathan Tyers who started the fashion for sophisticated Pleasure Gardens in 1732, when he opened Vauxhall, which threw Lydia Melford into the ecstasies quoted above.

In Pepys's day there had been two of the old style gardens at Foxhall; the old Spring Gardens and the new Spring Gardens. Not far away, where the southern approach to Waterloo Bridge now is, there was Cuper's or Cupid's Gardens. But Tyers took over the lease of the new Spring Gardens for thirty years and produced something totally different, which he called a *ridotto al fresco*. If he had called it an "open air resort", Londoners would perhaps have argued that that was exactly what its predecessors had been. The new Spring Gardens had fallen into disrepute, the haunt of rakes, thieves, harlots and drunkards. The *ridotto al fresco* was to be very different. The opening night, June 7, 1732, was patronised by Frederick, Prince of Wales, the father of George III. The assembly was limited to four hundred guests, the price of admission one guinea (equivalent at that time to three weeks wages of a farm labourer). The first ladies and gentlemen began to arrive at 9 p.m. and the last left at 4 a.m. To ensure the safety of the Royal Party and the good behaviour of all a battalion of soldiers with fixed bayonets was stationed in the gardens. The guests wore lawyer's gowns or dominoes and everything passed off magnificently except that one of the waiters got tight and reeled around in a domino and a pickpocket stole fifty guineas, "but the rogue was taken in the fact".

So was inaugurated Vauxhall, the greatest, most popular and longest lived of London pleasure gardens. Tyers was able to buy the freehold of the 12 acres of grounds and attraction after new attraction was added by the Tyers family and their successors who carried on the Gardens until 1859.

Once Tyers had proved the feasibility of Vauxhall Gardens as a pleasure resort for family parties of all ages and classes, a host of rivals sprang up. W. and A. E. Wroth list 64 in their *London Pleasure Gardens of the Eighteenth Century*. The only two which presented a serious challenge to Vauxhall, were Marybone and Ranelagh. Marybone Gardens belonged to the Rose of Normandy Tavern in Marylebone High Street. At the height of its success, the gardens stretched as far east as what is now Harley Street and south as far as Weymouth Street (then called Bowling Green Lane). When Pepys visited it in 1668, he called it Marrowbone: and until converted to a pleasure garden on the Vauxhall model in the summer of 1738, it was patronised by the nobility either for bowling in the garden or gambling in the tavern. It never achieved the popular success of Vauxhall or the fashionable glitter of Ranelagh. Though it closed in 1776, Fanny Burney laid a scene there in *Evelina*, which was not published till two years later.

Ranelagh originated in the house built by the Paymaster-General of the Forces, Richard, Viscount (later Earl of) Ranelagh, in grounds on the east side of Chelsea Hospital. In 1733, the house and grounds were bought by Lacy, patentee of the Drury Lane Theatre. He retained Ranelagh House "very fine within, all the rooms being wainscotted with Norway oak" and in the grounds erected a Rotunda, which made the Vauxhall Gardens Rotunda look puny. Five hundred and fifty feet in circumference, one hundred and fifty feet in diameter, it was like the Reading Room of the British Museum, except that the surrounding walls were lined not with books but with two tiers resembling stage boxes in which visitors could sit, eat, drink and, most important of all, scrutinise the assembly, some of whom were seated at tables in the arena, while others promenaded around the pillared chimney of the gigantic central fireplace, listening to or ignoring the orchestra banked on tiers before the giant organ.

Ranelagh Rotunda and Gardens were opened on April 5, 1742. On April 12, Horace Walpole, inquisitive pleasure seeker, wrote to Mann. "I have been breakfasting this morning at Ranelagh Garden: they have built an immense amphitheatre, with balconies full of little ale-houses: it is in rivalry to Vauxhall and costs about twelve thousand pounds."

Back next month, he referred to "the vast amphitheatre, finely gilt, painted and illuminated; into which everybody that loves eating, drinking, staring or crowding, is admitted for twelvepence."

In June 1744, Walpole went "every night constantly" to Ranelagh, "which has totally beat Vauxhall." "Nobody goes anywhere else; everybody goes there. My Lord Chesterfield is so fond of it, that he has ordered all his letters to be directed thither." "You can't set your foot without treading on a Prince or a Duke of Cumberland." In 1748, "Ranelagh is so crowded that going there t'other night in a string of coaches, we had a stop of six and thirty minutes."

For all that we find him in 1750 visiting Vauxhall by water "with a boat of French horns attending". His party took one of the best boxes, near the orchestra. There was "the little Ashe, or the Pollard Ashe as they call her" and Lady Caroline Petersham, "with the vizor of her hat erect, and looking gloriously jolly and handsome". "She had fetched my brother Orford from the next box, where he was enjoying himself with his *petite partie*, to help us to mince chickens. We minced seven chickens into a china dish, which Lady Caroline stewed over a lamp, with three pats of butter and a flagon of water, stirring and rattling and laughing, and we every minute expected the dish to fly about our ears. She had brought Betty, the fruit girl with hampers of strawberries and cherries from Rogers's, and made her wait upon us, and then made her sup by us at a little table. . . . In short the whole air of our party was sufficient, as you will easily imagine, to take up the whole attention of the Gardens; so much so, that from eleven o'clock till half after one we had the whole concourse round our booth: at last, they came into the little gardens of each booth on the side of ours, till Harry Vane took up a bumper and drank their healths, and was proceeding to treat them with still greater freedom. It was three o'clock before we got home."

Seven chickens seem a large number to mince into a china dish. But Tyers was notorious for the minginess of his portions. His chickens, which cost half a crown, were no bigger than sparrows and his shilling slices of ham and beef were so thin that it was said you could read a newspaper through them. A current joke was that his carver was given the job because he said he could carve a ham so fine it would carpet the Vauxhall Gardens.

Far better for food was Marybone Gardens when it was taken over by John Trusler, a professional cook, whose daughter became famous for her cakes.

Snobbery, which does not exist in any society where class or caste barriers are firmly fixed, was rampant in 18th century Britain. In 1760, a fashionable lady complained that Ranelagh had too many tradesmen's wives (hoping to tread on a Prince or a Duke of Cumberland?) But in *High Life Below Stairs* (circa 1759) Lady Charlotte's Maid, on declaring, "Well, I say it again, I love Vauxhall." is snubbed by Lady Bab's Maid, "Oh, my stars! Why, there is nobody there but filthy citizens—*Runelow* for *my* money." In his *Reminiscences* Henry Angelo voiced the opinion that in their later days Marybone Gardens were "adapted to the gentry rather than the *haut ton*". But Angelo was writing in 1830 about scenes of his early youth. None of Fanny Burney's readers that we know of considered it an error for her to have placed Lord Orville there, when Evelina was taken by the vulgar Branghtons to see the fireworks.

The truth is that as in the theatres and in streets like St James's and Pall Mall high and low mingled, and were pleased to mingle. It was natural that visitors from the country and from abroad should take in both Ranelagh and Vauxhall. In *Humphrey Clinker* (1771) Miss Lydia Melford, with her brother, uncle and aunt, visited Ranelagh and Vauxhall Gardens on the same, to her rapturous, day.

Ranelagh looks like the enchanted palace of a genie, adorned with the most exquisite performances of painting, carving and gilding; enlightened with a thousand golden lamps, that emulate the noon day sun; crowded with the great, the rich, the gay, the happy, and the fair; glittering with cloth of gold and silver, lace, embroidery and precious stones.

So Miss Lydia, but to her uncle Ranelagh and Vauxhall appeared very differently.

"What are the amusements at Ranelagh? One half of the company are following one another's tails, in an eternal circle, like so many blind asses in an olive-mill; where they can neither discourse, distinguish, nor be distinguished: while the other half are drinking hot water, under the denomination of tea, till 9 or 10 o'clock at night, to keep them awake for the rest of the evening. As for the orchestra, the vocal music especially, it is well for the performers that they cannot be heard distinctly. Vauxhall is a composition of baubles, over-charged with paltry ornaments, ill conceived, and poorly executed, without any unity of design or propriety of disposition! . . . The walks, which nature seems to have intended for solitude, shade, and silence, are filled with crowds of noisy people, sucking up the nocturnal rheums of an aguish climate; and through these gay scenes a few lamps glimmer like so many farthing candles. In all probability, the proprietors of this, and other public gardens of inferior note, in the skirts of the metropolis, are, in some shape, connected with the faculty of physic and the company of undertakers; for, considering that eagerness in the pursuit of what is called pleasure . . . I am persuaded that more gouts, rheumatisms, catarrhs, and consumptions, are caught in these nocturnal pastimes, than from all the risks and accidents to which a life of toil and danger is exposed."

Smollett was a doctor. The testiness is in the character of gouty Squire Bramble but the views of the unsuitability of ladies' fashions for the night air were those of Dr Smollett. Lydia saw things with different eyes. While Squire Bramble, fearful of catching cold upon the water, went from Ranelagh to Vauxhall in the coach, Lydia went across in a wherry "so light and slender, that we looked like so many fairies sailing in a nutshell."

Humphrey Clinker is a comedy of different viewpoints. Lydia, closely chaperoned, met with nothing worse than a headache and a sprinkling of rain before they could take shelter in the rotundo, a building which Jonathan Tyers had constructed as soon as he realised that a *ridotto al fresco* was at the mercy of the weather, even in the best of seasons.

But Vauxhall was designed for every sort of pleasure, of which some were not so innocent; as Evelina Belmont discovered when the Branghtons took her there. The Branghton girls, who knew how to handle a slap and tickle in the dark walks, assumed that Evelina, from her country vicarage, was equally knowledgable or should be made so.

> I followed them down a long alley, in which there was hardly any light. By the time we came to the end, a large party of gentlemen, apparently very riotous, and who were hallowing, leaning on one another, and laughing immoderately, seemed to rush suddenly from behind some trees, and, meeting us face to face, put their arms at their sides, and formed a kind of circle, which first stopped our proceeding, and then our retreating, for we were presently entirely enclosed. The Miss Branghtons screamed aloud, and I was frightened exceedingly; our screams were answered with bursts of laughter, and, for some minutes, we were kept prisoners, till, at last, one of them, rudely, seizing hold of me, said I was a pretty little creature.

Evelina is fascinating as the sentimental education of an 18th century young lady, uncertain of her social status because of the mystery of her birth, uncertain of her behaviour in the sophisticated metropolis because of her upbringing in a country vicarage, uncertain of the romantic impulse of her heart and certain only of her taste, intelligence and moral integrity. When she describes the crowd of tipsy youths as a large party of "gentlemen", one can trust that they were indeed "gentlemen" and this was how they would normally behave with girls like the Branghtons adventuring, screaming, into the dark alleys. Young beaux knew the rules. If they took a social inferior, that was her look-out.

A further shock awaited Evelina in Vauxhall, when she escaped from the unknown into the arms of another group, of which one, Sir Clement Willoughby, had met her before at the Pantheon with Lord Orville. Sir Clement rescued her from his fellow rakes. "Gentlemen," cried he, disengaging them all from me in an instant, "Pray leave this lady to me." Evelina imagined that the gentleman whom she had met in polite company would be her *chevalier*. But Sir Clement, having found that she was the sort of girl who strolled in the dark walks of Vauxhall, jumped to the conclusion that she wanted to lose, if she had not already lost, her virtue. Having delivered her from his friends, he tried to take her for himself.

A later episode, in Marybone Gardens, completes our education of the unchaperoned girl. It is the nadir of the country ingenue in London. Evelina was bored until the pyrotechnics began.

> The firework was really beautiful, and told, with wonderful ingenuity, the story of Orpheus and Eurydice; but, at the moment of the fatal look, which separated them forever, there was such an explosion of fire, and so horrible a noise, that we all, as of one accord, jumpt hastily from the form, and ran away some paces, fearing we were in danger of mischief, from the innumerable sparks of fire which glittered in the air.
>
> For a moment or two, I neither knew nor considered whither I had run; but

my recollection was soon awakened by a stranger addressing me with "Come along with me, my dear, and I'll take care of you."

Accosted on all sides by amorous men, Evelina sought asylum with two "ladies" who turned out to be a pair of harlots, highly amused at her innocence. At that very moment, who should stroll by but Lord Orville, that peer of inestimable wealth and moral probity? When all girls dressed alike, how should he know that Evelina was not herself a harlot?

In *The History of Amelia*, Fielding described how even a young married woman, accompanied by her children and three men, one of whom was a clergyman, could be plagued by dissolute rakes and drunken noblemen. Lady Mary Wortley Montagu disapproved of the moral effect of her cousin Henry Fielding's novels. But she recognised that in Amelia and her husband Mr Booth, Fielding had painted a true portrait of his first wife and himself "some compliments to his own figure excepted".

The "Vauxhall affray" of 1773, similar in its provocation to that described in *Amelia*, was different in its outcome. The Reverend Henry Bate (1745–1824), alias "the Fighting Parson" was at that time the rector of North Fambridge in Essex, the editor of the recently founded *Morning Post* and a conspicuous man of pleasure. Mr Parson Bate, in Henry Angelo's words, "as magnificent a piece of humanity, perhaps, as ever walked arm-in-arm with a fashionable beauty, in the illuminated groves of Vauxhall, was promenading and chatting with the celebrated Mrs Hartley (a beautiful actress); her Woodstock glove gently rubbing against his sable sleeve; when Mr Fitzgerald (who was afterwards hanged in Ireland for some mal-practices), in company with Lord Littleton and Captain O'Bourne, most ungallantly gave offence to the lady and to her protector, by severally turning short round upon her, and, with the most marked rudeness, staring in her face." Unlike Amelia's male protectors, who preferred to hush the matter up, Mr Bate set on the three offensive gentlemen and trounced the lot. Not content with that, he held them up to ridicule and contempt in the *Morning Post*, while they replied in newspaper kind.

After some weeks a meeting was fixed at a tavern, ostensibly to effect a reconciliation. In fact Fitzgerald, Littleton and O'Bourne brought along a well-known prizefighter, whom they introduced as an Army Captain and who immediately provoked a fight. The Fighting Parson took the prizefighter on and so thrashed him that he was taken off, almost senseless, in a hackney coach.

It is typical of the 18th century that following this tavern brawl Lord Littleton asked Henry Bate to become his Chaplain and the fighting parson accepted the post.

Henry Angelo, who visited Vauxhall Gardens with Thomas Rowlandson, recalled that in 1776, the price of admission being then one shilling, Vauxhall was more like a bear garden than a pleasure resort, especially on Sunday mornings (which at that time lasted until 6 p.m.) A quarrel would be started in one part of the garden, in order to attract a crowd whose pockets could be picked; and then to distract pursuit another fracas would be staged some way away. Things were very different at Vauxhall when Angelo wrote his *Reminiscences* in 1830— at least in his elderly opinion. In his youth "the dashers of the day, instead of returning home in the morning from Vauxhall, used to go to the Star and Garter, at Richmond." He even recalled one morning "with a party going over Westminster Bridge, when, seeing a boat, one of them proposed taking it to go to the Tower, and to go by the Margate hoy."

But things weren't so very different if we are to believe Pierce Egan's account in *Life in London* (1821), when Jerry Hawthorn, Corinthian Tom and Bob Logic, the Oxonian, visited the Gardens. The ham, Logic bet Jerry, was not cut with a knife, but shaved with a plane. After burnt wine, sherry and arrack punch, Logic announced he was "now able to *reel* with any lady or gentleman in the gardens". "Yes," replied Tom, "but not to *dance*."

The elegant appearance and address of the Corinthian soon procured him lots of dashing partners; Jerry was not behind his Coz. in that respect; and the agility both our heroes displayed on the "light fantastic toe" attracted numerous gazers.

Logic, who was for "pushing along, keep moving", as he termed it, was interrupted in his pursuit by a *jack-o'-dandy* hero . . . Some sharp words passed, in reply, from Logic, when the *dandy*, who was rather *snuffy* as well as impudent, put himself in to a posture of defence, crying out, "Come on, my fine *fellow*, I'll soon spoil your day-lights." The *Oxonian* immediately gave the *dandy* so severe a blow on the head that he measured his length on the ground like a log of wood; and, on Logic's perceiving the fallen *dandy*, quite terrified, he assumed to be in a most violent rage, and addressed two of the sisterhood near him, with, "My dears, if you do not hold my arms, I am so tremendous a fellow, I shall certainly do him a mischief."

Vauxhall Gardens, it would seem, had not changed its character in the previous half of a century as much as the style of those writing about it, the vivacity of Fanny Burney, the humour of Smollett and the vigour of Fielding degenerating into the facetious clichés of Pierce Egan.

The summer pleasure gardens gave citizenry, gentry and nobility an opportunity of meeting friends and making acquaintance without the expense of those infrequent private assemblies, immense gatherings, as Mme de Staël complained, where London people "elbow one another as in the pit. Women are the majority there, but usually the crowd is so large, that even their beauty has not enough space to be seen, let alone any pleasure of the mind."

In 1760, Mrs Theresa Cornelys inaugurated an indoor alternative to the pleasure gardens, at Carlisle House, Soho Square, which she rented from the Howard family. "Cornelys," remarks Casanova, "was the name assumed by Theresa, daughter of the actor Imer, later wife of Pompeati, the dancer who had killed himself in Vienna, cutting his belly open with a razor and the mistress of the Margrave of Bayreuth." For a time she had directed all the theatres in the

Austrian Netherlands. She had sung at the Haymarket in Gluck's opera *La Caduta de Giganti* under the name of Mme Pompeati and later at Amsterdam under the name of Mme Trenti. In Amsterdam she became mistress of Cornelius Rigerboos, whom she ruined, but in memory of whom she assumed the name of Mrs Cornelys when she took residence again in London, with her daughter Sophie. Casanova claimed to be Sophie's father, but Mrs Cornelys preferred as the father the Marquis de Montperny. Either might have been right. But Sophie ended up as a "Miss Williams".

Mrs Cornelys hit on the idea of organising subscription balls, banquets and later morning concerts whereat the nobility and gentry could meet, without the cost of time and money in organising their own entertainments.

Lydia Melford thought that Carlisle House "for the rooms, the company, the dresses and decorations surpassed all description, but, as I have not great turn for card-playing, I have not yet entered thoroughly into the spirit of the place." Mrs Cornelys, in fact, catered for more tastes than card-playing.

Two years after Mrs Cornelys set up Carlisle House, Casanova brought over her son, Giuseppe Pompeati (known in Paris as Count d'Aranda, but renamed in London Mr or Sir Joseph Cornelys) to act as her business manager. Casanova gives the most intimate account of Mrs Cornelys, though like everything he wrote it is full of inaccuracies.

Mrs Cornelys refused to let Casanova (or the Chevalier de Seingault as he called himself in London) have a ticket to her assembly but was not displeased when he purchased one from Lady Harrington, a great patron of Carlisle House. The ball had not begun when Casanova and Lady Harrington arrived. Everyone remarked on the physical resemblance of Sophie to the Chevalier, and asked Lady Harrington if he was Mrs Cornelys's husband. To distract the gossip he danced a minuet with his nine year-old daughter. All the nobility and all the Royal Family were there, except the King, Queen and Princess of Wales. The ball lasted till dawn without a break, people going away to eat in side rooms in groups at all hours. There were fourteen rooms on the second floor, according to Casanova. The takings for the evening were more than twelve hundred guineas; but the expenditure and incidental thefts were enormous.

Mrs Cornelys had flair. She was always thinking up new types of entertainment. But her son was incapable of taking over the managerial duties she had planned for him. She became involved in law-suits. She was frequently attacked under the Alien Act: and where she had led, others were quick to follow.

On December 16, 1764, Walpole wrote George Montagu. "Almack's room, which is to be ninety feet long, proposes to swallow up both hers, (Mrs Cornelys') as easily as Moses's rod gobbled down those of the magicians." Almack's opened in February 1765, but Mrs Cornelys wasn't daunted. Bach and Abel directed her concerts in 1766 and a new door had to be built in Soho Square to accommodate the "society night" throng. Not only members of the British royal family but the King of Denmark and the Prince of Monaco attended assemblies in 1768 and in the following year she opened a new range of rooms and a gallery for the dancing of "cotillons" and "allemandes". For the King's Birthday on June 6, there was a grand assembly with illuminations and a grand concert under the direction of Guadagni. On February 27, 1770, the Duke of Gloucester and half the peerage attended a masked ball, organised by the gentlemen of the "Tuesday Night's Club", at which Miss Monckton appeared as an Indian sultana, wearing jewels worth £30,000. Carlisle House had reached its zenith.

For the following February, Mrs Cornelys planned the first of a series of "harmonic meetings". Opposition was threatened by the proprietors of the Italian Opera House, who considered she was poaching on their preserves. To appease her rivals, she donated a portion of the profits to the poor of the parish, but she and the other organisers were fined at Bow Street and an indictment was brought before the grand jury on February 24, 1771, for keeping "a common disorderly house". Though never common, Carlisle House in recent years had become raffish if not disorderly. Some members of the Society of Carlisle House started a schismatic institution "The Coterie" and in 1772, the Pantheon was opened at 173 Oxford Street. Walpole called it "a winter Ranelagh". For Mrs Cornelys, it was the last straw. The list of bankrupts of the *London Gazette*, November 1772, contained the name of Theresa Cornelys, dealer, and next month the contents of Carlisle House were up for auction.

The Pantheon was the 22 year-old James Wyatt's first major edifice and it made his reputation immediately. Walpole enthused:

> The ceilings, of the passages, are the most beautiful stuccos in the best taste of the grotesque. The ceilings of the ballrooms, and the panels painted like Raphael's loggia in the Vatican. A dome like the Pantheon glazed. It is to cost fifty thousand pounds.

Boswell recorded his visit to the Pantheon with Dr Johnson in the year the Pantheon was opened.

> The first view of it did not strike us so much as Ranelagh, of which he (Dr Johnson) said, the "*coup d'oeil* was the finest thing he had seen." The truth is, Ranelagh is of a more beautiful form; more of it, or rather indeed the whole *rotunda*, appears at once and it is better lighted. However, as Johnson observed, we saw the Pantheon in time of mourning, when there was a dull uniformity; whereas we had seen Ranelagh, when the view was enlivened for us with a gay profusion of colours. . . . I said there was not half a guinea's worth of pleasure in seeing this place. JOHNSON. "But, Sir, there is half a guinea's inferiority to other people in not having seen it." BOSWELL. "I doubt, Sir, whether there are many happy people here." JOHNSON. "Yes, Sir, there are many happy people here. There are many people here who are watching hundreds, and who think hundreds are watching them."

Sheridan's Mrs Hardcastle and thousands of country-bound ladies who had never been to London, pined for the Pantheon and other resorts of grandeur, real or imaginary. "Who can have a manner that has never seen the Pantheon, the

Grotto Gardens, the Borough, and such places where the nobility chiefly resort?"

Old Angelo, or to give him his full name Dominico Angelo Malevolti Tre-mamondo, who had taken over Carlisle House from Mrs Cornelys, as a school of fencing and equitation, would sometimes walk down Oxford Road, as it was then called, to act as Master of Ceremonies at the Pantheon, welcoming such distinguished pupils as the Prince of Wales and the Duke of Devonshire or his friends Garrick, Reynolds, Gainsborough and Wilkes. From the supper room of the Pantheon the Duke of York dismissed the Duchess of Gordon for rudeness to his mistress Lady Tyrconnel. In the dome of the Pantheon was suspended the balloon in which Lunardi made the first ascent from British soil. In the Pantheon gallery Lunardi himself, accompanied by his fellow aeronauts (a dog and cat), welcomed the crowds who paid a shilling each to witness this wonder. To the Pantheon migrated the musicians of the Haymarket after it had been burnt down in 1789.

Fire in those days of guttering candles, oil lamps and sooty chimneys was a perpetual hazard. In 1792, in the early morning of one of the worse frosts in history, a young friend of the architect Wyatt, living in Great Marlborough Street, two doors from the back of the Pantheon, was awakened at 2 a.m. by the sound of women shrieking and watchmen's rattles. He threw open the window and heard the cry of Fire. The watchmen and patrol were thundering on doors. Mr and Mrs Siddons who lived opposite had, *en chemise*, thrown up the sashes on their bedroom window and shouted that the Pantheon was in flames. Wyatt's friend dressed in an instant, ran down and climbed the garden wall, shouting, "Fire!" He knew some people slept back stage and he threw some stones, till he broke the window of a room where a man and his wife were sleeping. When they came to the window, he called "The Pantheon is on fire!"

Their room was too high for a leap, so he bawled, "Through the stage; the fire is at the Oxford Street end, fly for your lives." They escaped to the next door house.

The firemen were prompt . . . they were soon beyond the scene room, and upon the stage, being admitted through our premises. I was with them, where I stood looking into the body of the theatre, and beheld a sight . . . which can never be effaced from my recollection. . . .

In consequence of the cold temperature, the rush of air into the theatre was furious. The very large and magnificent chandeliers, that were suspended from the roof of the building, were whirled round; and the vast damask curtains, with which the upper parts of the house were enriched, majestically waved, like the spacious flags of a first-rate ship of war. Now the leathern hose from several engines in Marlborough Street, were brought through the passages of the houses, and the firemen directed the stream from the branch pipes to the boxes nearest the spreading flames, which were yet behind the theatre, in the upper and lower vestibules of this spacious structure towards Oxford-street. But, vain were the efforts of these powerful machines. The fire proceeded from north to south, and, bursting through the boxes and gallery, I distinctly saw this finest of modern temples, with its scaglioli columns and gorgeous embellishments, enveloped in flame, which, whirling to the centre of the roof, bursting a passage, exposed the interior of the lofty dome. This vast column of fire now finding vent, raged with such irresistible violence, that the firemen thought it prudent to retire.

At this time the Pantheon's architect, returning from the west country by post chaise, was on the heights of Salisbury Plain some 80 miles away. Seeing the sky glowing in the east, Wyatt said to his clerk, "That vast light is in the direction of London; surely, Dixon, the whole city is on fire," little realising that the first fruit of his genius could make of itself so great a blaze.

As far away as St Giles's Circus, Tyburn and Leicester Fields, roosting pigeons, startled by the explosions of that unnatural dawn, rose in flocks with clattering wings and circled bedazzled in the sky, until, drawn like moths to candlelight, feathers seared, they plummeted or burst in flight roasted on the wing.

In Blenheim Street, hard by, an anatomist named Mr Brookes kept a private zoo to which the public was allowed admission. His birds and beasts were not encaged but tethered by chains to rocks. Heat from the burning Pantheon was so intense that paint on the doors and windows of his house was blistered. His panicked creatures, an eagle, hawks, racoons, foxes and other animals tugged at their chains, screeching, squawking, yelping, trying to flee or fly from the fire, while a mob hammered at his gates, some furious that the animals might be roasted alive, others wanting to enjoy from his vantage point a better view of the blaze.

Next day, thousands who from as far away as the heights of Highgate and Hampstead, Harrow and Richmond, the Surrey and the Kentish hills had watched the pillar of fire which recalled that holocaust which had gutted London over a century before, went on foot or elsehow to see the embers of "the most beautiful building in England". They were astonished to see its ruin embellished even more grotesquely than its architect's fancy had designed. From the north front parapet and even from the windows depended clustered icicles twelve and fifteen feet in length, in girth as big as the branches of trees; glacial fossils of the firemen's failure.

Among those thousands who came, gawped, gasped and went away was one J. M. Turner, the 17 year-old son of a barber in Maiden Lane, who stayed, sketched and then painted The Pantheon the Morning After the Fire, the first picture to show the originality of the genius who in the next sixty years proved himself peer of past masters and the father of future.

CHAPTER SEVEN

Theatricals

In the eighteenth century, theatre-going was a blend of the formal and the informal.

Only persons of rank, quality or fortune sat in boxes: with the exception of two or three boxes on each side of the house which were reserved for ladies of the town, who used the theatre as a shop-window. They received communications from prospective clients by quizzing stares and notes passed across by the orange-sellers (who themselves were mostly for hire.)

The pit was occupied by men of letters or wit, law students, barristers and others who considered themselves arbiters of dramatic taste. Between acts they exchanged views: and after the show in coffee houses such as the Bedford, Covent Garden passed judgements, which could make or break a play.

On nights when capacity audiences were expected, an ampitheatre was erected back-stage, where spectators sat row upon row on seats which touched the theatrical clouds. In front of them, ill-dressed youths would sit or kneel, while in the wings young gentlemen of fashion lolled, watching the performance, exchanging remarks with one another across the stage or pointing out people in the auditorium who attracted their attention or wit. These interruptions were often resented by the apprentices and others sitting in the gallery, who would shy halfsucked oranges or apple cores to the hazard of those below.

The Georgian theatre was distinguished less by its plays than its players. Stage repertory was enriched only by six pieces, John Gay's two comic operas, Goldsmith's *She Stoops to Conquer* and Sheridan's three original comedies. For the rest, 18th century theatres drew either on Shakespeare or the Restoration dramatists, suitably emended to meet the nicer taste of Georgian society, or on contemporary tragedies in pedantic verse like *Mithridates King of Pontus*, or class comedies like Townley's *High Life Below Stairs*.

For a dramatist ever to succeed demands the happy concatenation of circumstances; but never more so than in the 18th century when patronage was powerful, political passion invaded the theatre and claques could break a good play, even if they could not make a bad one. The struggles of Gay are good examples.

John Gay was aged 42, when in 1727 he wrote *The Beggar's Opera*. Catherine Hyde, proud, beautiful and eccentric, had been his patroness since her marriage to the Duke of Queensbury in 1720. Alone or with coadjutors such as Pope and Arbuthnot, he had already made several assaults upon the theatre in a mixture of styles. *What d'ye Call it* was described as a "tragi-comi-pastoral farce" which puzzled more than it pleased. A tragedy called *The Captives* ran for seven days at Drury Lane, which in those days of short runs was a considerable success.

Swift gave Gay the germ for *The Beggar's Opera* as early as 1716 when he wrote to Pope "I believe that the pastoral ridicule is not exhausted, and that a porter, footman, or chairman's pastoral might do well. Or what do you think of a Newgate pastoral?" Gay modelled Peachum on Jonathan Wild, the notorious thief-taker, who had been hanged at Tyburn in 1725. But instead of a "Newgate pastoral" he chose to write a lyrical drama. "When first he mentioned it to Swift," wrote Pope, "the doctor did not like the project. As he carried it on, he showed what he wrote to both of us, and we, now and then, gave a correction, or a word or two of advice, but it was wholly of his own writing. When it was done, neither of us thought it would succeed. We showed it to Congreve, who, after reading it over, said, 'It would either take greatly, or be damned confoundedly."

When the management of Drury Lane rejected *The Beggar's Opera*, the enthusiastic Duchess of Queensbury undertook to recompense John Rich for any loss he might sustain, if he put it on at the Lincoln's Inn Fields Theatre.

While the play was in rehearsal, Rich suggested that the play would be improved by songs. The wits, sitting in as dramatic critics, disagreed. But the Duchess, coming to hear of it, was strongly in favour and songs were specially written by Swift, Lord Chesterfield and Sir Charles Hanbury Williams, in time for the opening night.

Pope was among those who attended the first night of *The Beggar's Opera*. "We were all in great uncertainty of the event," he wrote, "till . . . hearing the Duke of Argyle, who sat in the next box to us, say, 'It will do—it must do—I see it in the eyes of them.' " This was during the first act, which was received with strict attention but without applause. During the first interval, the gentleman critics seem to have made up their minds. When Lavinia Fenton, playing Polly, sang

> For on the rope that hangs my dear
>   Depends poor Polly's life

the applause was thunderous and by the final curtain, it was plain that here was no ordinary success, but something entirely new to the theatre.

The Beggar's Opera was performed at Lincoln's Inn Fields that season for the record number of 62 nights. It "made Rich gay and Gay rich." Box office takings were £11,199.14s and the author's profits from benefits, card-tickets etc., amounted to over £1,450. Its takings during the next year's London season were equally great. A note to Pope's *Dunciad* adds: "It spread into all the great towns of England, was play'd in many places to the 30th and 40th time, at Bath and

Bristol 50 etc. It made its progress into Wales, Scotland, and Ireland, where it was performed twenty four days together. It was lastly acted in Minorca. The fame of it was not confined to the Author only; the Ladies carry'd about with 'em their favourite songs of it in Fans; and houses were furnished with it in Screens. The person who acted Polly, till then obscure, became all at once the favourite of the town; her pictures were engraved and sold in great numbers; her Life written; books of Letters and Verses to her publish'd; and pamphlets made even of her Sayings and Jests."

The public loved *The Beggar's Opera*; but Sir Robert Walpole and his fellow ministers hated it, because everyone recognised it as an attack, equating statesmen with rogues and highwaymen. The story is told that when one evening Sir Robert Walpole was seen sitting in a stage box, the audience demanded an encore of the song "When you censure the age . . .", turning their attention towards the Prime Minister. When the encore was finished, Sir Robert joined in the applause and demanded another encore. This earned him a huzza from the crowd.

Flushed with success, Gay immediately sat down to write a sequel, *Polly*. The Prime Minister used his influence with the Lord Chamberlain to forbid its stage production. But they could not ban its being printed. The Duchess of Queensberry canvassed all her friends, including those at Court, for subscriptions (which brought Gay over £1,000); and in retaliation for this George II forbade her the Royal Presence. Her reply is famous.

> The Duchess of Queensberry is surprised and well pleased that the King and Queen has (sic) given her so agreeable a command as forbidding her the Court, where she never came for diversion, but to bestow a very great civility on the King and Queen. She hopes that by so unprecedented an order as this the King will see as few as he wishes at Court, particularly such as dare to think or speak the truth . . .

The Duke took the same opportunity to resign his appointments and attach himself to the Court of the Prince of Wales. He did not hold government office until the accession of George III.

The original Polly, Lavinia Fenton, retired from the stage to become the mistress of the Duke of Bolton, "£400 during pleasure" and £200 for life. She gave the Duke three sons and so much pleasure that when they travelled abroad, they took with them a chaplain to join them as man and wife as soon as the death of the first duchess was known. "Crammed with virtues and good qualities . . . despised by her husband, and laughed at by the public", as her friend Lady Mary Wortley Montagu put it, the first duchess survived till September 20, 1751, whereupon Miss Fenton "bred in an alehouse and produced on the stage" wedded her lord within a month.

Two other Polly Peachums married into the peerage. Miss Bolton married the Lord Chancellor Lord Thurlow, who, said Fox, "*looked* wiser than any man ever *was*": and Catherine Stephens, the star of opera house and concert hall from 1813 to 1835, at the age of 44 married the octogenarian Earl of Essex, whom she survived by 43 years. Quite apart from the marital prospects it offered, Polly was a peach of a part, over which actresses fought one another with all the guile and malice of their profession.

Between the first performance of *The Beggar's Opera* and the Licensing Act of 1737, controversy raged over London theatres. Only two were established by patent, the Theatre Royal, Drury Lane and Covent Garden. The theatres at Lincoln's Inn Fields, the Haymarket and Goodman's Field, as well as the theatrical booths at fairs, existed without licence. The Ministry's objections to all theatres were political. Plays were more capable of inflaming popular feeling than books. On the other hand, magistrates and the growing number of evangelicals were morally outraged. Actors and actresses were considered, if not vagrants, examples of immoral living: and in the neighbourhood of every theatre there were taverns, gaming houses, brothels as well as parades for prostitutes and their pimps. Most actors and actresses lived within the square comprising Covent Garden and Drury Lane to be handy for sudden calls.

According to the Licensing Act (which remained in force for the rest of the Georgian period), a performance of any drama of the stage, without authority, by virtue of letters patent, or without licence from the Lord Chamberlain, should be subject to penalties; and if without a legal settlement, the actors should be deemed rogues, etc., according to the Act of Anne. The authority of the Chamberlain in licensing plays and prohibiting those objectionable was affirmed. Representation under patent or licence was confined to the city of Westminster and places where the sovereign resided.

Under the Act, the Goodman's Field theatre and the Haymarket were closed down; and two plays were immediately prohibited, each of which in consequence gained their authors substantial sums by subscription.

The Act did nothing to suppress prostitution. The whores moved to other venues. Actors and actresses thrown out of work were more likely to lead immoral lives in order to keep body and soul together. Some, like Colley Cibber's errant daughter, Charlotte Charke, took to puppet shows, which could be performed without licence.

In London the patentees of Covent Garden and Drury Lane were in sharp rivalry for the patronage of the public; but sometimes, when there was a revolt among the cast of one company, the patentees would combine to suppress demands for better wages or working conditions. The Dublin theatres were second only to those of London. Ireland produced most of the best players and writers for the English stage. Among actors were Delane, Quin, Barry, Mossop, Thomas Sheridan, Charles Macklin and Master Betty, the infant Roscius: among actresses, Jenny Johnson, Kitty Clive, Peg Woffington, George Anne Bellamy: among playrights Steele, Farquhar, Goldsmith, R. B. Sheridan and Sheridan Knowles.

The Licensing Act, by limiting the number of London theatres, encouraged the building of provincial theatres and the enterprise of strolling players. The

Haymarket Theatre was half-reprieved. It offered shows of different kinds, operas, conjuring tricks, dancing dogs and monologue entertainments, until in 1766 Samuel Foote, through the interest of the Duke of York, secured a patent to present plays during the summer, when the two other theatres were closed.

The conventions of acting in the early eighteenth century were strange. No attempt was made at period costume. Julius Caesar or Othello would appear wearing full bottom wigs and the dress of the day. Speeches were declaimed, arms sawing the air to make rhetorical emphases. The convention was that terror made one's hair stand on end and this was achieved by jerking off the hat. The story is told of an actor called Hammond, playing Hamlet for his benefit in a house packed, stalls and pit thrown together, the amphitheatre full and beaux standing blocking the wings. The Ghost elbowed his way on, apologising for the inconvenience he was causing to spectators. When Prince Hamlet saw him, his hat dutifully flew off, expressing fright. Then as he said the air bit shrewdly and was very cold, a kind old lady in a red cloak got down from her amphitheatre seat and coming behind him picked up his hat and placed it on Hamlet's head. The Prince started in real terror. The house burst into peals of laughter. The Ghost took to his heels and fled and Hamlet, after a agony of indecision, followed suit.

Shylock was accepted as a low comedy part. Even Doggett played the Jew as broad farce. What was to be the preface to the revolution in acting came when Charles Macklin asked Fleetwood if he could play the Jew as a serious character. The rest of the company were appalled at this break with tradition. They petitioned Fleetwood to stop the experiment. But Macklin swore if he played Shylock straight just once, he'd pledge his life on its success. No one knew till the night what he intended. At rehearsals he mumbled his lines, without acting.

Came the night when Macklin staked his reputation, with Kitty Clive as Portia and Peg Woffington as Nerissa. Macklin tells the story. He came into the green room not as a clown. He wore a piqued beard, a loose black gown with coloured sash and a red hat. (He told Pope later that he had read that Jews in Italy, especially Venice, wore hats of that colour. The idea that an actor should study history for a part, instead of histrionics, was then unthinkable.) The company feared the worst.

Delane, who was playing the Merchant, came to Macklin and said the house was packed. Rumour had passed round that this Shylock was to be a Jew like no others and the critics had come for an autopsy. Looking through a slit in the curtain, Macklin said, "I shall be tried to-night by a special jury."

He felt a hand on his arm. It was Peg Woffington, his fellow countrywoman, by birth the daughter of a widow laundress, but one of the great ladies of the Georgian stage. "Courage, Mac, courage," she whispered. "Show them you can act."

"Commending my cause to Providence," he wrote, "I went boldly on the stage." He sensed surprise, though there was some applause; for him? his courage? his approach?

The critics were in the front rows of the pit. He could hear them almost as well as they could hear him. He caught the words, "Very well—very well indeed. This man seems to know what he is about." He took heart, reserving himself for the third act. He kept his strength to contrast his joy and triumph at the merchant's losses with his sorrow and despair at Jessica's elopement. Bewailing her loss, he rushed hatless on stage, face distorted by rage, eyes bewildered, hands clenched, every movement abrupt, convulsive. Never had audience or cast seen such a Shylock; but his passion lifted them like a whirlwind dust. The applause was thunderous. Even the company was impressed. Kitty Clive, who had always delivered her Portia trial scene as a parody of Lord Mansfield, was forced to play straight against a Shylock, pitiless, corroded by hatred and revenge, whetting the glittering knife to cut his pound of flesh so realistically that the audience shuddered with fear.

When it was over, the green room was crowded with lords, ladies and critics, who had come to quiz and stayed to praise. Among them was Fielding, who said to Kitty Clive, "And may I ask why you did not give us your imitation of the great man tonight?".

"In faith," said she, "when I looked at Shylock, I was afraid."

And the Woffington, broadening her brogue added. "It takes an Irishman to teach them what a Jew is like."

Pope's comment on Macklin went the rounds. "This is the Jew that Shakespeare drew." Macklin had won the first skirmish in the war for natural acting which David Garrick was to lead to victory.

Garrick had a genius for acting which he hesitated to indulge. The third of ten children born to an ill-paid English army officer and his Irish wife, David came to London to open a branch of his uncle's wine business, of which his brother Peter managed the head English office in Lichfield. David's shop was in Durham Yard, close to Covent Garden Theatre and the Bedford Coffee House, at which all the actors of the day congregated. There he met among others Macklin of Drury Lane, and Giffard who had reopened the Goodman's Field playhouse, by means of an ingenious evasion of the Licensing Act. Ostensibly the entertainment consisted of Vocal and Instrumental Music, for which the prices of admission were three shillings, two shillings and one shilling. But between the first and second parts of the concert there was a play for which no charge was made.

At the Bedford Garrick would hold forth about acting. (He had at the age of ten formed his own children's company and played Farquhar's *The Recruiting Officer*.) Garrick's views chimed with Macklin's. He abominated the burlesque of comedy, the artificiality of romance, the woodenness of declamation. His heart was obviously in acting, not in the wine business. But when Macklin and Giffard urged him to turn actor, Garrick held back for fear of displeasing his genteel family. The prejudice against the stage as a profession was perhaps even more deeply seated in the merchant class than in the nobility.

At length, however, encouraged by Peg Woffington with whom he had fallen in love, Garrick went privily to Ipswich, where Giffard presented him as Aboan, a negro in the tragedy of *Oroonoko*, under the stage name of Lyddal. In this and other pieces he scored such success among the people of Ipswich and around, that he agreed to try out the name part of *Richard III* at Goodman's Fields as "a Gentleman (Who never appear'd on any stage.)"

The version of *Richard III* was not as written by Shakespeare but as doctored by Colley Cibber, who had himself played the king, drawling and declaiming his lines in a shrill, feeble voice, strutting about the stage, in a way that audiences had found very satisfying. Garrick's Richard III was as startling as Macklin's Shylock. Like all the greatest actors and actresses, Garrick acted from his centre. He did not use his voice to stir the passions of his audience. The passions of the character he was portraying used him.

Few of the gentlemen critics attended that first night in Goodman's Field. They were too concerned with the rivalry of the two great theatres, each of which was presenting *As you Like It*, Peg Woffington and Milward playing Rosalind and Orlando at Drury Lane, Mrs Pritchard and Hale the same at Covent Garden.

But early next morning, Tuesday, October 20, 1741, the *London Daily Post* which seldom noticed even the most distinguished performance, ran a paragraph.

Last night was perform'd Gratis the Tragedy of Richard III, at the late Theatre in Goodman's Field, when the character of Richard was perform'd by a Gentleman who never appear'd before, whose reception was the most extraordinary and great that ever was known upon such an occasion; and we hear he obliges the Town this Evening with the same Performance.

The news spread like wild fire. Everybody who cared for the play, the nobility, wits, writers, blue stockings, fashionables, flocked to the city. The coaches coming from Westminster were blocked solid from Temple Bar to Goodman's Field; and everyone agreed that little David Garrick was a great genius, with the solitary exception of Horace Walpole, who considered that the verdict of any overwhelming majority must be wrong. He thought "the wine-merchant turned player" was an excellent mimic, but could see nothing in his acting "though it is heresy to say so". His neighbour at Twickenham, Alexander Pope, a critic more captious but without the need to appear clever, observed to Lord Orrery, seated beside him, "That young man never had his equal as an actor, and he never will have a rival."

That Garrick was an excellent mimic, he proved a few months later, when he played Mr Bayes, the stage manager in *The Rehearsal*. It gave him the chance of parodying the styles of all the actors of the old school, to which his natural acting was opposed.

That Garrick would never have a rival was incorrect. Spranger Barry, son of a Dublin silversmith, made his debut as Othello in Dublin two years after Garrick began in London. Spranger was tall, handsome, with a beautiful voice. When he came to London, Charles Macklin took him in train and had him engaged at Drury Lane, where, by then, Garrick was part-manager. In scenes of love and tenderness, Barry was unsurpassed. His height gave a dignity to Othello which the short Garrick could not encompass. As Quin said, Garrick "could not appear as the Moor; he must rather have looked like Desdemona's little black boy that attends her tea kettle."

Between the two stars, there arose a rivalry which one theatre could not contain. Barry went over to Covent Garden in the autumn of 1750 and the two great actors appeared before the town as if in mortal combat. Spranger chose to play Romeo with Susanna Cibber as his Juliet. Garrick who had trained them both knew their strength in combination. For his Juliet he chose George Anne Bellamy, as beautiful a young actress if not yet as experienced as Susanna. Rich at Covent Garden promised "An additional scene representing The FUNERAL PROCESSION of JULIET" accompanied with "a solemn Dirge never performed before and set to music by Mr Arne". Garrick merely advertised, "It is hop'd no Gentleman will take it ill that they cannot be admitted this Night upon the Stage, or in the Orchestra, on Account of the Scenery and Music that are made Use of in the Play."

Opening the same night, they ran together for twelve consecutive performances, until Mrs Cibber declared she could not endure the strain of a part so taxing. Garrick and the Bellamy won the test of endurance by playing for a thirteenth night. Enthusiasts would exchange seats hurrying from the Garden to the Lane between acts to compare performances. At coffee house and dinner table arguments ranged over who was better. One lady of quality vowed that if she had played Juliet to Garrick's Romeo, he was so impassioned she should have expected he would have climbed the balcony to her; but Barry was so seductive she would certainly have jumped down to him. Another said she had seen Romeo and Juliet at Drury Lane but at Covent Garden Juliet and Romeo. Garrick was "a modern lover", Barry "an Arcadian".

Barry played Romeo twenty five times during that season and often afterwards, while Garrick gave the part a miss. But Garrick had the discipline, the staying power and organisational ability. Barry's head was turned by the flattery of society. He spent wildly, put private pleasure before public performance, while Garrick stuck to his last.

Garrick was a great actor-manager, but a meanish man. He set up house with Peg Woffington, with the agreement that they should pay the bills alternate months. Here they entertained Samuel Foote, the wit and mimic, Mrs Porter the star of Queen Anne's day, Johnson, Fielding, Macklin, Colley Cibber. When Johnson was taking tea with them one day, Garrick complained that the tea was too strong, "as red as blood". It was his month to pay the bills.

For two years they lived together on the understanding that they would get married sooner or later. Garrick went as far as trying on a ring. But when the Woffington demanded marriage, Garrick pleaded, "the knowledge of the fact that we were chained together would make us miserable."

After a blazing row, she walked out, leaving him every present he had given her and asking him to return what she had given him. The only souvenir he retained was a valuable pair of diamond shoe-buckles. She waited a month before asking for them and when he replied that, "as they were the only little memorials he had of the many happy hours which passed between them, he hoped she would permit him to keep them for her sake," she did not answer and he continued to wear them after he had married Violette the dancer.

Peg Woffington went to live in Teddington and though she had sworn that she would never talk to Garrick again except on business, there was rather a touching performance which they gave there in a barn, fitted out as a theatre. It was a tryout for Peg Woffington's young sister Polly and her school-friend George Anne Bellamy, who wanted to go on the stage. The two girls played Hermione and Andromache to Garrick's Orestes, while Peg Woffington and Mrs Bellamy played the parts of attendants. The audience was drawn from the quality of neighbouring Hampton Court, Strawberry Hill, Marble Hill, Richmond, Twickenham and Cambridge Park.

Few girls have ever been privileged to have so public an audition. George Anne Bellamy showed such talent that Garrick took her into his company, Polly Woffington such charms that Captain Cholmondeley gave her his heart and his hand. He was a younger son of Earl Cholmondeley, whose pride was greater than his poverty. Hearing of the intended match, the earl, whose goods had been distrained for debt, posted off to Peg Woffington to call off the match.

"They love each other, my lord," she said, "and I see for both a fair prospect of success."

"The fellow has not a penny save his pay," he said, "this marriage will be their ruin."

Peg answered that Polly might be but the sister of a player, but her name was spotless, her education a gentlewoman's and she would not be dowerless. The last word and Peg's charm won the noble pauper over. As he left he begged her pardon for having been previously offended with his son's conduct.

"It is I who have cause for offence, my lord," she said. "I had but one beggar to support, and now I shall have two."

The daughter of a Dublin washerwoman, Mrs Polly Cholmondeley, married in 1746, became a "bright and airy matron", friend of Johnson, Reynolds and Goldsmith, and mother of four children, of whom two married into the noble houses of Townshend and Bellingham.

Being the sister of a well paid actress was less hazardous than being an actress married or unmarried. The Georgian gentleman considered that he need only behave as a gentleman to Georgian gentlefolk of either sex. Below that rank, it was his privilege to be impertinent to men or impudent to women. Evelina was assailed in Vauxhall Gardens under the impression that she was a pretty actress. Theatre managers, like the randy Irishman Daly, importuned their leading ladies and sacked them if they repulsed their advances. The horizontal elevation to stardom is no new thing. Most of the actresses of the eighteenth century were of humble birth. But though their education was meagre and their spelling and grammar primitive, they were in fact better trained than many of their social superiors in the speaking of English and the understanding of character. No Aspasias, they were gayer company than many dull daughters of nobility, better dressed, and warmer partakers "of the genial bed".

Like the Woffington and the Bellamies, Kitty Clive hailed from Ireland. Miss Catherine Raftor, as she was called before marriage, came of grandparents who had been impoverished by adherence to the Stuart cause and parents ruined by improvidence. With her friend Jenny Johnson, she "tagged after" the actor Robert Wilks from the age of twelve. Both girls secured engagements at the Drury Lane when in their 'teens. Jenny married Theo Cibber, rascally son of Colley, one of the Drury Lane managers; and Kitty, who from her first appearance made a name for herself in a "breeches" part, secured as husband George Clive. Jenny Cibber died young, having given birth to two daughters, and Theo soon after married the talented Susanna Arne, sister to the musician. Kitty lived long, but soon separated from her husband, who did not live up to the merits of his brother, Sir Edward Clive, a Baron of the Exchequer, or his second cousin, Lord Clive of India.

Susanna Cibber and Kitty Clive soon came into conflict. When *The Beggar's Opera* was revived at Drury Lane in 1736, Kitty considered that Polly was her part of right, though she would have been a perfect Lucy. Susanna Cibber thought, with justification, she was better suited. Both appealed to the public in *The Town*. "No two women of high rank ever hated one another more unreservedly than those great Dames of the theatre. But though the passions of each were as lofty as those of the first Duchess, yet they wanted the courtly art of concealing them." The quarrel was so public that the actor Woodward brought out a piece *The Beggar's Pantomine; or the Contending Columbines*, dedicated to the two actresses, "who had a violent contention for Polly". The silly feud lasted for twenty years and in 1756 Mrs Cibber succeeded in securing in *Rule a Wife* the comic part of Estifania for which Kitty Clive was far better qualified.

Kitty was a hoyden, a romp, a tomboy, a singing chambermaid, more suited for the plays of the first half of the 18th century than the second. Garrick used her, respected her talent. But the older she grew, the more prickly. She wrote obstreperous, illiterate letters, protesting for example about the date chosen for her Benefit.

> Sir.—I am sorry to give you this trouble but I really cannot comprehend what you mean by saying you expected I should thanke the managers for their tenderness to me. . . . If you still look over the number of times I have play'd this season—you must think I have deserved the monney you give me. You say you give me the best day in the week. . . . St. Patrick's Day is the very worst to me that can be. Mrs Yates' might be the strongest Benefit, as her interest and mine clash in the Box's. As to my *quaiviling* you are under a very great mistake. There is nothing I dread so much, I have not spirits for that, tho' have for acting . . ."

Garrick treated her with affectionate diplomacy. Dr Johnson enjoyed her company in private. "Clive is a grand thing to sit by," he said, "she always understands what you say." As for her acting, "Mrs Porter in her vehemence of rage, and Mrs Clive in her sprightliness of humour, I have never seen equalled. What Clive did best, she did better than Garrick; but she could not do half so many things well; she was a better romp than I ever saw in nature."

She retired to Twickenham in her late fifties, living at "little Strawberry Hill", a small house Horace Walpole had given her around 1753. She had her brother Jeremy Raftor, a less successful actor, to live with her. Lord Radnor, who lived close by, left her a legacy of £50. "You never saw anything so droll," wrote Walpole, "as Mrs Clive's countenance, between the heat of the summer, the pride in her legacy, and her efforts to appear concerned." In old age the Clive's face had become so flaming red that Lady Townshend remarked that Strawberry Hill "would be a very pleasant place, if Mrs Clive's face did not rise upon it and make it so hot."

When she died on December 6, 1785, Walpole, who in old age had lost his sting, but not his wit, set up an urn in his gardens with this epitaph.

> Ye smiles and jests still hover round;
> This is mirth's consecrated ground.
> Here lived the laughter loving dame,
> A matchless actress, Clive her name.
> The comic muse with her retired,
> And shed a tear when she expired.

Her rival Susanna Cibber had a shorter life and a worse husband. Theo Cibber ranks high among stage shits. "Should men say I used my first dear, and well-beloved wife, of ever blessed memory . . . with ill usage?" he asked. "Should they affirm, that when her all pale and breathless corpse was laid in the coffin, and I, with many sobs and tears and interjected sighs, had moaned to many a witness, my too unhappy fate, yet that same night had a brace of Drurian doxies vile in the same house?" Men did, and in view of the way he treated Susanna, whom he married within a twelvemonth, they were probably right.

Susanna Arne had started her career as a singer. Her voice, though not strong, was so sweet that Handel arranged one of the arias in his Messiah to suit her. But after marrying Theo, she was trained by her father-in-law, Colley, to act (with all the declamatory mannerisms of the old school), and was engaged at Covent Garden. Theo himself was a successful actor, but on Drurian doxies he squandered more than his wife's earnings and his own. A whore-master, he decided to turn pandar. He took as a lodger a wealthy young man named William Sloper, whom he introduced as "Mr Benefit . . . a romp and a good natured boy". He proved Sloper's good nature by borrowing from him £400, before being called on urgent business to France. On his return, he lodged at an inn nearby their lodgings in Kensington, spending the day with his wife and her lover and leaving them each evening on the understanding that Sloper footed all the bills.

Susanna fell in love perhaps with Sloper, certainly in hate with Theo. They eloped, leaving Theo without his source of income. He followed, determined to play the injured husband, and when Susanna's brother intervened, he brought a suit against Sloper for alienation of his wife's affections, claiming £5,000 damages. Theo's counsel admitted that "players were considered as not upon the same footing with the rest of the subjects", but urged that Theo was also a gentleman, son of a father renowned in the theatrical profession and grandson of the best statuary of his time, and on his mother's side related to William of Wykeham. The jury assessed Theo's damages at £10.

Mrs Cibber lived with Sloper until the end of her life. She never entirely lost the bad acting habits she had learnt from her father-in-law. But in her day she became as great a tragic actress as Kitty Clive was comic. When she died in 1766, aged 52, Garrick said "Then tragedy is dead on one side." Of course Tragedy no more died with the Cibber than Comedy with the Clive.

Eleven years before, in 1775, at the Shoulder of Mutton Inn, Brecon, Sarah Kemble, wife of Roger Kemble, a strolling player, and daughter of an actor manager was brought to bed of a daughter, also named Sarah. Roger Kemble was a Roman Catholic in which religion his four sons were brought up. As his wife was a Protestant, their eight daughters were baptised into the Church of England. Four of the girls died young, but all the eight other children made appearances on the stage; though only Sarah and her brothers John Philip and Charles were to make the grade in London.

Compared with Clive, Woffington and Bellamy, Sarah was a slow developer. She made her debut as "an infant phenomenon", reciting the fable of The Boy and the Frogs. She attended schools in Worcester, Wolverhampton or wherever the company was playing. At the age of twelve, the year before Mrs Cibber died, she performed with other members of her family in the great room in the King's Head in Worcester, the price of admission being the purchase of a packet of toothpaste. She played Rosetta in *Love in a Village*, Meadows being taken by William Siddons, her future husband. Siddons was a handsome young man who had joined the company from Birmingham and was said to be able to play any part from Hamlet to Harlequin. When it was plain that he and Sarah were in love, he was dismissed the company. At his farewell benefit, he recited some verse bewailing his misfortunes as a discarded lover, which so angered Mrs Kemble that she boxed his ears. To get over her infatuation, Sarah was sent as lady's maid to a Mrs Greathead, where she beguiled the company below and sometimes above stairs with recitations from Milton, Shakespeare and Rowe. Remaining true to Siddons for a couple of years she obtained her parent's consent to her marriage in November 1773, when she became eighteen.

The young couple acted in various country towns, pitifully poor but with a gathering reputation. At Cheltenham in 1774 her Belvidera won the praise of an aristocratic party which had come to scoff. Lord Dungarvan's daughter replenished Sarah's scanty wardrobe from her cast-off clothes. Lord Bruce thought so highly of her that he recommended her to Garrick, who sent Fighting Parson Bate to report on her performances: and on his recommendation she was engaged at £5 a week for Garrick's last season, the winter of 1775/76. Her first performance on the London stage was as Portia on December 29, 1775 when she was billed merely as a "young lady, her first appearance". Tom King made a poor Shylock and Sarah's Portia was written off as not considerable enough for a London theatre. Perhaps she was not accustomed to an auditorium of such size. She was cast for comedy, in which she had no talent; and it was not till the close of the season that she was billed under her own name. The season benefited her nothing, except for the experience of seeing David Garrick act.

Back they went to the provinces, where her genius was appreciated. Birmingham, Manchester, Liverpool, Bath: success after success in an ever expanding repertory. It was not until October 12, 1782, that she returned to London, the scene of her failure. She was 27, an old stager compared with previous actresses who had risen to fame. Her merit, said Davies, swallowed up all remembrance of present and past performers. "The person of Mrs Siddons is greatly in her favour; just rising above the middle stature, she looks, walks, and moves like a woman of superior rank. Her countenance is expressive, her eye so full of information, that the passion is told from her look before she speaks. Her voice, though not so harmonious as Mrs Cibber's, is strong and pleasing; nor is a word lost for want of due articulation. . . . She excels all persons in paying attention to the business of the scene; her eye never wanders from the person she speaks to, or should look at when she is silent. Her modulation of grief, in her plaintive pronunciation of the interjection 'Oh!' is sweetly moving and reaches to the heart. Her madness in Belvidera is terribly afflicting. The many accidents of spectators falling into fainting fits in the time of her acting bear testimony to the effects of her exertions." (*Dramatic Miscellanies*, iii, 248–9.)

Charles Dickens had the same ability of toppling his audience over. In Clifton, his reading of *The Murder of Nancy* produced "a contagion of fainting . . . a dozen to twenty ladies borne out, stiff and rigid, at various times. It became quite ridiculous." But then Dickens cheated. He fixed his eyes on likely candidates for vertigo and did not turn away until they collapsed. Mrs Siddons, like the greatest players, seemed unaware that there was an audience watching her or a dozen fiddlers waiting for her exit.

Her finest parts were Lady Macbeth, Isabella in Garrick's version of Southerne's *Fatal Marriage*, Zara in *Mourning Bride*, Elvira, Belvidera, Constance, Queen Katharine and Lady Randolph. Though her delivery was declamatory, her movement and gestures, the use of face and hands, were as of nature. She was not an actress whom audiences took to their heart. Christopher North described her effect as "divine, inspiring awe." "Not less than a goddess," Hazlitt found her, "or than a prophetess inspired by the gods. Power was seated on her brow, passion emanated from her breast as from a shrine." "If you ask me 'What is a queen?' " said Tate Wilkinson," I should say, Mrs Siddons." When Sir Joshua Reynolds painted her as The Tragic Muse, in the posture which, at his request, she chose upon the throne, Dr Johnson wrote his name upon the hem of her garment, remarking to that "prodigious fine woman", "I would not lose the opportunity offered to me for my name going down to posterity."

The respectability which David Garrick gave to actors, Sarah Siddons gave to

PROMENADE DRESSES.

21–22. Head Dresses 1805.

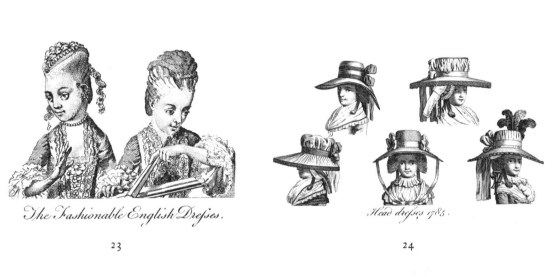

The Fashionable English Dresses.

23

Head dresses 1785.

24

LONDON HEAD DRESSES, JANY 1800.

25

26

Lady Archer.

Lady Waldegrave.

27

Two Ladies in the Dress of 1775.

LADIES in the Dresses of 1782.

28

29

30. Full Dresses, 1798.

31. Walking Dress, 1810.

32. Promenade Dress, 1803.

35. Evening Dress, 1810.

33. Evening Half-Dress, 1805.

34. Evening Theatre or Opera
Dress, 1814.

Newest Fashions for July. 1829.

W Alais 36

36

37–38. In Mrs Thrale's day it was un-ladylike to hunt. Though there was little traffic, the number of accidents was large; at first because of bad roads, later because of light carriages. Lord Peterborough built a travelling coach to seat six and sleep four, "a moving house having in and about it every convenience appertaining to a man-sion". It was so heavy that no horses could draw it over Contnential roads.

Up & down or the endeavour to DISCOVER which way your Horse is inclined to come down backwards or forwards.

PACKING UP AFTER A COUNTRY BALL.

39–40. Country balls were patronized by all and sundry, especially at election times, when the nobility and gentry condescended to the burghers and their folk; in the Mall was an equal mingling of sexes and classes.

Printed for & Sold by BOWLES & CARVER,   An EVENING WALK.   Nº 69 in St Paul's Church Yard, LONDON

41. At theatre or opera, the ton waited in the foyer until their conveyances were called.

42. The First Lady of the Stage, Mrs Siddons.

43. The beautiful Kitty Fisher, who died of lead-poisoning from cosmetics.

actresses. But like him, she did not escape the accusation of miserliness. When she played in Edinburgh in the summer of 1784, people came from as far away as Newcastle to see her play. For one performance of Belvidera at the Royalty Theatre, seating 630 people, 2,575 applications for tickets were made. Strangers trying to pass in the street were swept in by the crowd. Receipts for nine performances, including presents and £200 guaranteed to the manager by Edinburgh gentlemen (deftly annexed by Mr Siddons who had turned Sarah's business manager) amounted to over £967. Compared to the £10,000 a year which Edmund Kean later was reputed to have earned for eighteen years, Sarah's total earnings may have been comparatively small. But they were splendid in comparison with her predecessors'. If she was thrifty this is not surprising, considering early years of poverty and demands made upon her by dependents. She was believed to have charged a large fee for appearing in Dublin for the benefit of West Digges and also for Brereton. She denied the accusation. And when she resigned from the 1789/90 Drury Lane season, Sheridan could not deny her claim that he had left salaries unpaid and misappropriated the receipts from Benefit nights.

She retired from the stage in 1812 after a final performance of Lady Macbeth. Thereafter, she gave private readings to royalty at Windsor Castle and to friends in her house looking over Regent's Park in Upper Baker Street. She appeared only occasionally for the benefits of members of her family or for the Theatrical Fund. She did not bear the nineteen years of her retirement without a pang. "Oh, dear!" Samuel Rogers relates her saying, "at this time I used to be thinking of going to the theatre." But she knew that there is a time when even the greatest stage player should exit, in order to preserve the image of greatness.

Sarah Siddons, conscious that she stood upon the pinnacle of the theatrical pyramid, resented the possibility of anyone who might threaten her pre-eminence, even her brother John Philip Kemble, the manager of Drury Lane, whom she felt received perhaps more adulation than was his due. In fact she, her brother and the whole profession were for a brief period plunged into obscurity by an "adolescent phenomenon", "the young Roscius", the 13 year old William Henry West Betty, who chased Kemble from his stage, and reduced actresses to lunatic insignificance.

On Betty's first appearance at Covent Garden on December 1, 1804, Bow Street and the Piazzas were so crowded, not only by those who wanted to storm the theatre but also by those who wanted to watch those who wanted to storm the theatre and those who wanted to watch the watchers, that a strong detachment of the Guards was stationed outside, and a numerous body of peace officers within the theatre to preserve not just order but lives. James Boaden, who attended the first night wrote, "When the passages were all choked up, the house filled, and thousands still pressing towards the avenues, the shrieks of those, who had vainly attempted to go forward, and now as vainly tried to go back, that while they had breath to call out, they summoned the soldiers to save them; and only soldiers could have done it. They soon divided the ins from the outs, by forming in front, and then allowed of exits, but no more entrances; by which measure, the almost exhausted at length secured a retreat; and the light fingered gentry, now heavily laden, made their exit along with them, complaining dreadfully of the pressure."

Master Betty had a genius for imitation. His tutor was his prompter William Hough; his evil genius his grasping father. In 56 nights he drew £34,000 at the box office and saved the Drury Lane from bankruptcy. For his first three nights, he was paid £50 a night, thereafter £100. From his two benefits he netted £2,500. But Master Betty-mania did not last. When he tried Richard III, he was hissed. When his father, knowing that theatres were closed during passion week in London, tried Master Betty out in Coventry, the bishop banned him. When Master Betty was asked to give a benefit for the Theatrical Fund for elderly actors and their families, he refused. And finally, he cast his teacher William Hough off without a penny. The infant Roscius had kicked the ladder away from himself and collapsed, to the relief of the Kembles, the Siddonses and the profession as a whole.

Though Sarah Siddons acknowledged that she had had three possible rivals during her career, she did not mention Dorothy Jordan, who was originally brought to London from Leeds as her understudy. Perhaps the reason was that Dorothy Jordan could never be a threat to a tragic actress. She was like Kitty Clive and Peg Woffington a romp, a tomboy, a comedian. She was also the living example of the truism, "the woman always pays".

She was, as the result of birth and upbringing, the most adaptable of women. Her maternal grandfather was a Welsh cleric named Phillips, whose three daughters, since the Holy Ministry was denied to their sex, chose the stage. Her mother, Grace, had Dorothy, a son and another daughter, by a gentleman named Bland, who was afraid to marry her, because his family had so disapproved of his elder brother when *he* had turned actor. Mr Bland, in due course, married a lady of whom his family approved, and who probably had enough money for him to support, in a modest way, his ex-mistress and three bye-blows.

Dorothy came out at the Smock Alley Theatre, Dublin, under the manager Daly. Daly liked to put young ladies under contract and give them parts on the stage according to the way they acceded to his pleasures. When Dorothy refused him, he kidnapped and raped her. Pregnant by him she and the family fled to England. At Leeds, Dorothy was auditioned by Tate Wilkinson, the "Wandering Patentee" who asked what she could do. She answered "All"; and, greatly hesitating, he allowed her to sing *The Greenwood Laddie* at the end of playing a tragic part. The audience took her to their hearts.

Her equivocal positions in life were shown in her variation of surnames. Her true name was Phillips. But she was known as Miss Francis, Miss Bland, Mrs Jordan, Mrs Ford and then Mrs Jordan once more. Her life was always abnormal, but never perverse. Under Wilkinson, she had Daly's child, a daughter called Fanny. When she went to London, she had two more children by one Richard Ford who considered himself far too much a gentleman to marry her. This did not prevent his feeling outraged when the young Duke of Clarence proposed to set her up with £1,000 a year and a pension. In a public letter, Mrs Jordan announced that she was settling on her children by Daly and Ford all her savings and half her future earnings. Dorothy was 31 and the Duke of Clarence 27. She had previously lived in the centre of London. Now she went to live with the Duke of Clarence at Petersham and rented for the children a house on nearby Ham Common.

Her reputation as an actress had hung in the balance while she made the transition from Richard Ford to her royal master. When the balance came down in her favour, it went against both her lovers; against Ford for not having married her, against the Duke for not properly supporting her. The promised £1,000 a year was often in arrear and many household bills at Petersham and later at Bushey were paid out of her theatrical earnings.

The Duke and Mrs Jordan lived together for twenty years, during which time she bore him ten FitzClarences and between childbirths played to audiences (including King George III and Queen Caroline), who applauded her as "the child of nature, to hear whose laugh was to drink nectar". When Clarence paid her off she was a matron of fifty, a tomboy running to fat. He was a bachelor of 46, thinking of settling down with an heiress who could keep him more in the manner to which he felt himself born.

Dorothy was playing at Cheltenham when she received the Duke's message that he wished her to meet him at Maidenhead to discuss their separation. She went back for the last act in which she was meant to burst into that laughter which had enchanted audiences for decades. But at the critical moment, she dissolved into tears. The actor playing opposite her "dried" for a moment. Then he brilliantly improvised, "Why, Nell, the conjuror has not only made thee drunk; he has made thee *crying* drunk."

The terms of the promised settlement were not ungenerous. Dorothy was to have care of their four youngest daughters, with £1,500 a year and £600 for their house and carriage. But *if Dorothy returned to the stage*, the girls and the money should be forfeited to their father. Dorothy herself was to receive £1,500 a year and £800 to share between her first four daughters.

All would have gone well perhaps if Fanny, the child she had by Daly, had not involved her in the debts incurred by Fanny and her husband. Mrs Jordan returned to the stage, losing control of her four youngest children. Never a wife, she was always a good mother; as one after another of her children got into scrapes, she struggled to get them out. She herself sank deeper and deeper into debt, hounded by John Barton, Prince William's man of business, without the Prince's knowledge. Fearful of arrest, she fled to France and died at St Cloud, July 3, 1816.

In 1818, the father of her ten FitzClarences married Amelia Adelaide Louise Theresa Caroline, Princess of Saxe-Coburg Meiningen in the hope of providing a legitimate heir or heiress to the throne. He was 52 and Adelaide 25. A well-known portrait shows her as a delicate beauty; but Lady Brownlow, her lady-in-waiting, describes her as rather small, with pale blonde hair and eyebrows, weak eyes and a gingerbread complexion. In beauty she was no match for Dorothy Jordan, nor was she for "breeding". She bore the future King William IV two daughters, of whom neither survived infancy.

CHAPTER EIGHT

Gambling Ladies

Gaming is an enchanting *witchery*, gotten between *Idleness and Avarice*: an itching disease, that makes some scratch the head, whilst others, as if they were bitten by a *Tarantula*, are laughing themselves to death; or lastly, it is a paralytical distemper, which, seizing the arm, the man cannot chuse but shake his elbow. It hath this ill property above all other Vices, that it renders a man incapable of prosecuting any serious action, and makes him always unsatisfied with his own condition; he is either uplifted up to the top of mad joy with success, or plung'd to the bottom of despair by misfortune, always in extreams, always in a storm. *The Compleat Gamester* (1674)

Dr Johnson in his *Dictionary* observed a distinction between "gaming" and "gambling", which latter was "to play extravagantly for money". The emphasis was on the word "extravagantly". Everybody played for money, even children in the street markets if they had a groat or two. Parson Woodforde played backgammon, commerce, cribbage, loo, quadrille, sans prendre vole, vingt-et-un, and whist, for "fish" or small sums of money; never enough to embarrass him and his friends, but enough to add a little zest to the pastime. Lady Spencer, mother of the two most compulsive women gamblers of the 18th century, Georgiana, Duchess of Devonshire and Harriet, Lady Bessborough, enjoyed her gains or losses of a few pounds, while deploring the gambling excesses of her daughters.

The Georgian era was the zenith of the gambling mania. But it did not suddenly arise with the enthronement of George I or disappear with the interment of George IV. It started far earlier with royal example and continued far later in the involvement of King Edward VII, when Prince of Wales, in the Baccarat Scandal. The only difference was that in the case of the future Edward VII, Queen Victoria was far from being amused, whereas as early as the reign of Henry VIII, gambling was the province of the "Groom Porter", an officer of the Lord Steward's Department of the Royal Household. The Groom Porter saw the King's lodgings furnished with tables, chairs, stools, firing and rushes for floors, and provided cards, dice and other materials for play. He was a referee for disputes over games and gambling in the King's Household.

Pepys and Evelyn were shocked at the excesses of play at the Groom Porter's, especially by the ladies. In the reign of Queen Anne, the Groom Porter, Thomas Archer, by Letters Patent was given authority, with the aid of deputies he appointed, "to supervise, regulate and authorise (by and under the Rules, Conditions and Restrictions by the Law prescribed), all manner of Gaming within this Kingdom". The appointment was made as much to defend subjects of Her Majesty keeping Plays or Games in their houses from being blackmailed by unauthorised persons, as to regulate public Assemblies, where Quality gambled. But the fact that the office of the Groom Porter was a *Royal*, not a *Parliamentary* appointment, meant that the practice of gambling was given a royal sanction.

George I and George II played at the Groom Porter's at Christmas. How George II spent Epiphany was recorded in the first issue of the *Gentleman's Magazine*:

> Wednesday, Jan 5, 1731. This being the Twelfth Day . . . their Majesties, the Prince of Wales, and the three eldest Princesses, preceded by Heralds etc., went to the Chapel Royal, and heard divine Service. The King and Prince made the Offerings at the Altar, of Gold, Frankincense and Myrrh, according to Custom. At night, their Majesties etc., played at Hazard, for the benefit of the Groom Porter, and 'twas said the King won 600 Guineas, and the Queen 360, Princess Amelia 20, Princess Caroline, the Earl of Portmore and the Duke of Grafton, several thousands.

If the Groom Porter made a profit, there must have been heavy losses among other players. The office of Groom Porter was abolished during the reign of George III, probably in 1772.

Card playing, dice and other gambling games had for centuries been permissible for all classes during the twelve days of Christmas. But they were forbidden among artificers, labourers, servants, apprentices, etc., at all other times. The Royal family participated in this festive licence. The rest of the year was a sort of grey season, in which some people in some places were able to gamble. For the king to win six hundred guineas at Hazard on January 5 was splendid; for an apprentice to win six pence on January 6 was illegal. If gambling was a vice or a sin for the rest of the year, why should it be permissible for twelve days?

In street-markets all the year round, gambling was a pavement game with dice. At sweet stalls, children would be encouraged to gamble their farthings to get nothing in hope of getting more. At the fairs all over the country there were sharpers playing cards or ringing variations on spot the lady. Dice were loaded, cards marked, E.O. tables rigged and gulls plucked.

Eighteenth century gambling was a legacy from the past. The affluence and idleness, boredom and avarice of the Georgians brought it to a peak. But it had gripped earlier men and women. Mrs Centlivre's epilogue to *The Gamester* (1705) ended:

This Itch for Play, has, likewise, fatal been,
And more than *Cupid*, drawn the Ladies in
A Thousand Guineas for *Basset* prevails,
A bait when Cash runs low, that seldom fails;
And, when the Fair One can't the Debt defray,
In Sterling Coin, does Sterling Beauty pay.

The same sentiment was repeated with variations into the 1820s. The lady gambler, caught in her obsession would lose and lose until she was placed under financial obligations which she could not meet except with her favours. C. Dunne, writing under the pen-name of Charles Persius Esq., suggested in *Rouge et Noir* (1823) a variation of the technique. Instead of laying the lady under a debt of honour to himself which she settled in bed, the seducing gambler should *deliberately lose* to a lady a sum sufficiently large for her to give him in gratitude more erotic licence than she would have allowed him under duress. In Rowlandson's gaming scene in what is supposedly Devonshire House a young woman is being pressed to recoup herself. Sex and gambling were never far apart, when men and women sat around the card table. Nor for that matter were they absent, when men were gambling together. Mistresses were gambled for and lost. Complaisant husbands might even trade a wife's favours; parents pay gambling debts with children.

Steele complained also of the effect of gambling on a woman's looks.

There is nothing that wears out a fine Face like the Vigils of the Card Table, and those cutting Passions which naturally attend them. Hollow Eyes, haggard Looks, and pale Complexions, are the natural Indications of a Female Gamester. Her Morning Sleeps are not able to repair her Midnight Watchings. I have known a Woman carried off half dead from *Bassette*, and have, many a time grieved to see a Person of Quality gliding by me, in her Chair, at two a Clock in the Morning, and looking like a Spectre amidst a flare of Flambeaux. In short, I never knew a thorough paced Female Gamester hold her Beauty two Winters together.

The Spencer girls, Georgiana Devonshire and Harriet Bessborough, were, like their maternal grandmother, inveterate gamblers. Though they held their beauty many more than two winters, they sank deeper and deeper into debt. The fifth Duke of Devonshire played for high stakes, but the Cavendish wealth on which he drew was so great that he never needed to enquire whether there was money to meet his outgoings. His wife and sister-in-law had comparatively little money of their own to meet the extravagance of their dress, the generosities of their compassionate hearts and their losses at play. Georgiana borrowed indiscriminately from friends, lovers and financiers pledging, tacitly, her gracious favour and eventually her husband's credit. Worry drove her to increase her losses in the hope of reducing them.

Her rival beauty, Mrs Crewe, was more favourably placed. She had enough money of her own to avoid falling into the hands of money-lenders. Perhaps in consequence of this, we hear more often of her winning. She was not forced to make desperate bets. There is a story of a gentleman who presented Charles Fox with a sum to give Mrs Crewe in settlement of his losses. Fox went to the tables and lost the money forthwith. Mrs Crewe having hinted on several occasions to her debtor finally asked outright for repayment. On hearing that it had been given to Fox months before, she said, "Oh! did you, Sir? Then probably he paid me, and I forgot it." It was an act of generosity for which she has been repaid over the centuries by the repetition of this story.

Wherever play was high, the money-lenders were not far away, ready to advance more money on notes of hand to distraught gamblers. One member of White's fled to France to avoid the moneylenders. "That," remarked George Selwyn, "will be one passover not celebrated by the Jews!" Charles Fox's friends were half ruined by annuities they had given as securities for him to the Jews. £500,000 a year of such annuities of Fox and his "society" were advertised to be sold at one time. Such sums seem incredible. But if Walpole is to be trusted, on Tuesday, February 4, 1772, Charles Fox started the evening playing Hazard at Almack's. He played all night and lost £12,000, which he had recovered by 4 p.m. next day, but when they ceased playing an hour later he was £11,000 down. On Thursday, he spoke indifferently in a Commons Debate on the Thirty-nine Articles, went to dinner at 11.30 p.m. then to White's where he drank all night till 7 a.m., thence to Almack's, where he won £6000, before leaving for Newmarket in the afternoon. Two nights later his elder brother lost £11,000 and Charles a further £10,000 on February 13. The two brothers, the elder of whom was not yet 25, had between them lost £32,000 in ten days.

It is impossible to do more than speculate about this type of gambling. Henry Fox, 1st Lord Holland, had been paymaster-general from 1757 to 1765, the most lucrative post in Government. Four years after retiring he had not presented his accounts, and Beckford, Lord Mayor of London, petitioned the king against his ministers, charging Fox as "the public defaulter of unaccounted millions". Though Fox had blocked the petition with the plea that the delay in presenting the accounts was neither unusual nor illegal, it is generally admitted that the interest on the balances outstanding when he left office brought him a fortune (as some assert £250,000). The most indulgent of fathers, as well as the most self-indulgent of men, he would have been hypocritical to pretend that thrift was a virtue, when he had come by money so easily. He took Charles James from Eton when he was still a junior schoolboy, and initiated him in Paris to the gambling table and the bed, taking a pride in his precocious prowess at both.

Henry Fox, in Chesterfield's view, "had not the least notion of, or regard for, the public good or the constitution, but despised those cares as the objects of narrow minds, or the pretences of interested ones". But he commanded the loyalty of his sons. He had an endearing wit. When George Selwyn, whose morbid passion for executions, hangings and other violent endings were notorious, left his card at Holland House, Lord Holland, in bed with terminal illness, said,

"If Mr Selwyn calls again, show him up: if I am alive I shall be delighted to see him; and if I am dead he would like to see me."

A gambler of completely opposite temperament was William Douglas, 3rd Earl of March, 4th Duke of Queensbury. Born in 1725, he was old enough to be Charles Fox's father. He was beguiled by the charm of Charles, who in his extreme youth, gained entrance not only to White's New Club to which William had been elected years before, but also to White's Old Club, from which William was blackballed in his rakish middle-age. But Douglas was appalled by Charles Fox's bad gambling habits.

William Douglas was a Scotsman, as canny in his seduction of teenage girls, nymphettes who did not have to be necessarily virgin provided they were kittenish, as he was in his betting on near certain odds. Not for him the hazards of roulette, rouge et noir, hazard and other games of choice. He played such games of skill as picquet, or even whist. But he preferred wagers where the odds appeared against him, but were heavily in his favour. If he had not come to London as a sprig of a noble Scottish tree, with a competence of his own, he would have been written down as a professional gambler, if not sharper. There had been many such before him.

Old Q, to give William Douglas the nickname which he did not receive till towards the end of his life, but by which he is known to posterity, was a calculating adventurer. He thought out odd bets which could at the same time lose him no money and increase his fame in London Society. As ambitious as his junior, James Boswell, and as randy, he achieved his position with newsworthy bets which stood him in better stead with gambling society ladies and nymphettes who staked their charms than did Boswell publishing his newspaper articles, adventuring in Green Park, with or without armour and nursing his guilty clap.

Old Q's bets were works of scientific calculation compared to which his only female rival Mrs Thornton was the veriest amateur. The first of his famous bets was as creative as the sort of prizes offered by newspapers or industry for conspicuous achievement. It was accepted as an immutable law that a coach or post-chaise could only travel at four to six miles an hour and a light gentleman's carriage drawn by fast horses at a little more than ten miles an hour. Douglas wagered that he could produce a four-wheeled carriage which covered 19 miles in one hour, driven by four horses.

The main bet was for a thousand guineas, taken up with "Count" Taaffte, an Irish adventurer, and one Andrew Sprowle. Douglas enlisted his old Wykehamist friend, Lord Eglinton, to help cover the bet and plan the venture. They approached Wright the coach-builder of Long Acre to design a revolutionary vehicle, four wheels with a centre bar joining the two axles, the driver on a leather seat slung over the rear axle. The harness was made from silk and whalebone, and the traces were silk. The whole contraption had been reduced to just over three hundred pounds, strong but lighter than any known at this time.

In the training of the horses, seven died. Douglas cared only for the expense. His bet was more profitable in fame than money. When the proof came (August

29, 1750) on Newmarket Heath, with riders or postilions on all four horses, he was sure he would win his bet. He was only concerned lest he might win it too easily. He wanted to hold his horses back to lengthen the odds so that he could make side-bets while the race was on. Alas! the horses had been over-trained. The first four of the nineteen miles were covered in nine minutes, a record of nearly 26 m.p.h. The course was finished 6 minutes and 33 seconds under the hour.

When placed in a position that he had either to fight a duel, or admit that he had cheated, he chose survival. To recover his reputation, he made his second famous bet, to send a message fifty miles in an hour. Clubmen at White's thinking of every possible means of travelling fifty miles declared it impossible and he collected a little fortune when twenty cricketers threw a ball containing a message fifty miles round a circle in under an hour.

He was the most imaginative and successful of gamblers. Only once did he nearly overreach himself, in what was perhaps his most ingenious wager. Riding in his carriage one day, he noticed a journey-man coach-builder trundling a wheel at uncommon speed. Here he thought, was something which might be the basis of a bet to catch the ears of the town and rook a flock of gulls.

He got to know the coach-builder and timed him over a flat course with a stop-watch. Then he waited till conversation at White's came round to sprinting. Someone said a waiter at Betty's fruit shop in St James's had a wonderful turn of speed. Douglas went down to Betty's, bought some fruit and arranged to time the waiter on the same course he had used for the coach-builder. The waiter was not so fast.

Some days later he was sitting in the window at White's and he started to decry the speed of Betty's running waiter. Why, he said, he would bet he could find a man who could outpace Betty's waiter, trundling the hind-wheel of his coach (which was standing outside White's). He had no difficulty in finding takers; indeed he was besieged by gamblers whom he respected for being as shrewd as he was. And he did not realise how he had blundered until he approached the coach-builder, who pointed out that the hind-wheels of Douglas's coach were unusually small and he could not possibly keep up his normal speed, if he had to bend down.

Appalled that he might be injured both in pride and pocket, he took a fellow gambler Sir Francis Delaval into his confidence. Then he consulted a friend of his in the Board of Works and during the night before the race, an army of labourers erected a raised runway of Board of Works's planks along the course. There had been no mention of a runway when the bets were made; but when the coach-builder romped home, his opponents protested that they had been cheated. The matter was referred to the Jockey Club, who were forced to rule in favour of Douglas, since the use of a runway had not been forbidden in the bet. He had won without actually cheating, and those gamblers whose fingers had not been burnt were delighted.

Ladies did not gamble as unconventionally as men. The famous bet at White's as to whether a pedestrian run down outside the club would live or die (and the objection that if a doctor was fetched it would be cheating) would have been unthinkable at Almack's ladies club. But throughout the Georgian era, ladies were in the gambling business, not merely as players but as hostesses of gambling Assemblies or societies.

The Grub Street Journal, September 2, 1736, printed a letter of protest against the prevalence of gambling.

> I beg leave, through your Means, to make a few Remarks upon the great Encrease of a Vice, which, if not timely prevented, will end in the Ruin of the young unwary of both Sexes; I mean, Play in private Houses, and more particularly that artful and cheating *Game* of *Quadrille*. It is the constant business of the *Puffs* who belong to the Gaming Societies, to make a general Acquaintance, and, by a Volubility of Tongue, to commend Company and Conversation: to advise young People, or those who have but lately come to Town, to improve themselves in the *Beau Monde*. The young and unwary, thro' their inexperience, greedily swallow this Advice, and deliver themselves up to the Conduct of those Harpies who swarm in every Corner, where Visiting is in fashion: by whom they are introduced into these polite Families, and taught to lose their money and Reputation in a genteel Manner. These Societies consist mostly of two or three insignificant old Maids, the same number of gay Widows: a battered old Beau who, in King William's time, were the Pink of the Mode; The Master of the House, some decay'd Person of a good Family, made use of merely as a Cypher to carry on the Business, by having the Honour to be marry'd to the Lady, who, to oblige her Friends and People of good Fashion only, suffers her House to be made use of for these Purposes. In these places it is that young Ladies of moderate Fortunes are drawn in, to the infallible Ruin of their Reputations; and, when by false Cards, Slipping, Signs and Crimp they are stript of their last Guinea, their wretched companions will not know them.

In 1739 an Act was passed "for the more efficient preventing of excessive and deceitful gaming" throughout the kingdom. Fines of £200 were imposed on gambling house owners, £50 on gamblers and £10 on Justices of Peace refusing to act and convict under the Act.

With the sort of money gambling houses took, it must have been easy to pay Justices of Peace enough to keep them quiet. Six years later another Act was introduced against gaming and horse races. While it was in committee, the Chairmen of the Quarter Sessions of Westminster and Middlesex appeared at the Bar to report that the Ladies Mordington and Cassilis claimed "the privilege of Peerage" to prevent peace officers from suppressing their Gaming Houses.

The plea of "Dame Mary, Baroness of Mordington" for her assembly at her house in the Great Piazza, Covent Garden "where all persons of credit are at liberty to frequent and play at such diversions as are used at other Assemblys" sounded innocent enough. With a staff of fourteen, it was quite an establishment.

But the House ruled that Lady Mordington and Lady Cassilis, despite their rank, were just as subject to the law as the proprietors of the numerous other gambling houses in the neighbourhood of Covent Garden, Drury Lane, Sadler's Wells, Goodman's Field, etc.

This of course did not mean that gambling ceased, any more than the passing of the Volstead Act meant that Americans stopped drinking. Everybody in fact profited. The law-enforcement authorities got a larger rake-off. In illegal gambling houses, cheating, sharping, loaded dice, crooked E.O. or roulette tables, more violent bouncers became even more usual. Pacts were made with footpads and highwaymen to waylay gamblers who had been successful: and because forbidden, gambling added guilt to greed as an inducement to the giddy punter.

By the end of the 18th century, there were many society ladies living as Gambling Hostesses. There was Mrs Sturt; there was Lady Archer, a harpy hidden in carmine and dead white; there was Mrs Concannon who at the turn of the century found it wise to transfer her activities to Paris. Most notorious of all was Albinia, Lady Buckinghamshire, whose croupier, Martindale, held the Duchess of Devonshire in a state of terror for years through his collection of her notes of hand.

Horace Walpole preferred to waste his time not in play but in gossiping about those who did. On January 29, 1791, he wrote:

> Pray delight in the following story. Caroline Vernon, *fille d'honneur*, lost t'other night, two hundred pounds at faro, and bade Martindale mark it up. He said he would rather have a draft on her banker. "Oh! willingly"; and she gave him one. Next morning, he hurried to Drummond's, lest all her money should be drawn out. "Sir", said the clerk "would you receive the contents immediately?" "Assuredly." "Why, sir, have you read the note?" Martindale took it; it was "Pay the bearer two hundred blows, well applied." The nymph tells the story herself; and yet, I think, the clerk had the more humour of the two.

Lady Buckinghamshire and Martindale were a brace of crooks. It is hard to say who was using whom. Lady Buckinghamshire slept with a blunderbuss and a pair of pistols by her bedside to protect her Faro bank. Yet on January 30, 1797, Martindale announced that the box containing the Faro bank had disappeared. Things were growing hot for the Faro ladies. James Gillray had been satirising them for some years and Lord Kenyon, at a trial to obtain £15 won at gaming on a Sunday at a public house, had gone out of his way to censure the bad example set by the higher sort of people in the matter of gambling. "They think they are too great for the law;" he said, "I wish they could be punished . . . If any prosecutions of this kind are fairly brought before me, and the parties are justly convicted, whatever be their rank or station in the country, though they be the first ladies in the land, they shall certainly exhibit themselves in the pillory."

Two of Lady Buckinghamshire's staff were dismissed. But was this, one wonders, really a cover-up? Had Martindale decided that the Faro bank really belonged to him? Or had Lady Buckinghamshire reached the conclusion that the game was nearly up and she might as well pretend to rob herself before someone else robbed her?

The police failed to find the Faro bank; but on the very same evening they raided Lady Buckinghamshire's Assembly, on information laid by the servants whom Lady Buckinghamshire had dismissed. *The Times* reported the prosecution on March 13, 1797.

> PUBLIC OFFICE, MARLBOROUGH STREET.—FARO BANKS.—On Saturday came on to be heard informations against Lady Buckinghamshire, Lady Elizabeth Luttrell, Mrs Sturt, and Mr Concannon, for having on the night of the 30th of last January, played at *Faro*, at Lady Buckinghamshire's house, in St James's Square, and Mr Martindale was charged with being the proprietor of the table.
>
> The evidence went to prove that the defendants had gaming parties at their different houses in rotation; and that when they met at Lady B's, the witnesses used to wait upon them in the gambling room, and that they played at *E.O.*, *Rouge et Noir* etc., from about eleven or twelve till three or four in the morning. After hearing counsel the Magistrates convicted *Henry Martindale* in the penalty of £200, and *each of the ladies* in £50. The information against Mr Concannon was quashed, on account of his being summoned by a wrong Christian name.

The fines were the same as those imposed by the Act of 1739. Gillray, whose satire always had a double cutting edge, produced his comment on the Magistrates' fines and Lord Kenyon's previous threats with "Discipline à la Kenyon". Lady Buckinghamshire was tied to the tail of a cart on which was a placard "FARO'S DAUGHTERS BEWARE". Kenyon was shown flogging her with birch and cat-o-nine-tails, while Lady Luttrell and Mrs Sturt stood in the pillory, guarded by a police constable and pelted by a mob.

By the end of the century the wild days of gambling were over. Cotton was right. Idleness and avarice were the parents of that "enchanting witchery". But Britain during the French Revolution and Napoleonic Wars was not the prey to idleness. Society mothers were worried about their sons, and younger women about their husbands. The young men were serving in the navy and the army; the older men were more concerned with the calculation of political manoeuvres than of the hazards of play. Corresponding societies became more important than gambling societies, reform than roulette, votes than whist.

Avarice was finding other outlets. Wealthy landowners who had been content to live upon their rents were discovering the black gold hidden beneath their green acres. The ingenuity which had been expended on astute wagers was more profitably and interestingly employed in building bridges and aqueducts, canals and docks. The new generation of industrialists, of nabobs, merchants and bankers convinced the British aristocracy, both ancient and recent, that there were financial opportunities which they must not ignore. The new men were demanding more power because they had more wealth. The old families (aware that the aristocracy was based less on birth than money) were not to be outdone. Gamblers who had been rescued from the clutches of "money-lenders" discovered the virtues of bankers like Drummond and Coutts and married their children into the new rich.

There had been a terror of speculative investment since the bursting of the South Sea Bubble. But gradually confidence was established in the profitability of risk capital. It was more exciting than government stock and less ruinous than the turn of a card. A Mr Winsor had exhibited a single gas lamp in Pall Mall in 1803. Four years later he introduced the first permanent gas street-lighting in Golden Lane, London. Within three weeks, Lady Bessborough, that confirmed loser at the gaming table, wrote to her lover Lord Granville Leveson Gower (September 5, 1807), with the fever of a gambler turned speculator.

What can occasion such a ferment in every House, in every street, in every shop, in every Garret about London? It is the Light and Heat Company. It is Mr Winsor, and his Lecture, and his gas, and his patent, and his shares— these famous shares which are to make the fortune of all who hold them, and will probably involve half England in ruin, me among the rest, and prove a second South Sea Scheme. Yet it promises fair if it did not promise too much— *six thousand a year* for every seven guineas seems more than can be possible; but if it were hundreds instead of thousands it is immense. *17 thousand shares* have been sold within these ten days: they went first for a guinea, then 3, five, seven; they will be twenty, fifty, a hundred, for there is scarcely means of passing thro' Pall Mall for the crowds of carriages, and people on foot and Horseback. Ld Anson has 100, the D. of Athol 200, the Royal Family 200, Ld Choly 20—everybody some, and I five. There is no resisting it, and I love for you to have some. At first I dreaded its hurting the holders of coal mines, but now they say it will raise the coal trade, as, if it passes, all London will be lit from Coal instead of oil. . . . That Shining Lamp which has lit up Pall Mall for this year past has all at once blaz'd up into a comet that bears everything along with it. I only stipulate to know the amount of the forfeit in the case of a failure, and not answer for the debt of the Company. He only wants *a million* to begin with, and has almost got it already.

In the 19th century the gambling fever moved from the gaming room to the Stock Exchange. One can sense even now the excitement which Lady Bessborough felt about her five shares (and her fears in those days of unlimited liability companies that she might have committed herself to bankruptcy). But for a thrill, for such alternation between wealth beyond the dreams of Almack's and indebtedness within the bounds of the Marshalsea, stocks and shares were destined to surpass the turning of a card.

Horse-racing increased enormously throughout the Georgian era. For centuries there had been matches between individual riders and their mounts. Newmarket Heath was the original favourite course, then Ascot Heath, Epsom

Downs as nearer Windsor or London. Owners sometimes rode their own horses; sometimes their horses were ridden by friends, or professional jockeys.

It was unusual for women to ride as jockeys. So the feats of "Mrs Thornton" in 1804 became national gossip. Her real name was Alicia Meynell. She was given a courtesy title, because she was the mistress of Colonel Thornton, whose friend Mr Flint was married to Alicia's sister. One day riding in Thornville Park, Mrs Thornton and Mr Flint were discussing the merits of their respective mounts. Mrs Thornton on Vingarillo succeeded in outdistancing her brother-in-law on Thornville each time. And so Mr Flint challenged her for the last day of the York August meeting, 1804.

> A match for 500gs., and 1000 gs. bye—four miles—between Colonel Thornton's Vingarillo and Mr Flint's br.h. Thornville by Volunteer—Mrs Thornton to ride her weight against Mr Flint's.

The *York Herald* estimated the crowd to witness this challenge at 100,000, ten times the number that had appeared on the historic occasion when the unbeaten Eclipse (some thirty years before), had left the two best horses of the day 1½ miles behind on that four mile course. To aid the stewards in keeping the course clear, a detachment of the 6th Light Dragoons was enlisted, in addition to the usual personnel.

At the starting post the odds were 6 to 4 on the lady. She took the lead from the start and for the first three miles the odds lengthened from 7 to 4 to 2 to 1 in her favour. Then Mr Flint pushed forward, took the lead and held it to the winning post. Nevertheless the *York Herald* was ecstatic for the lady jockey. "Never, surely, did a woman ride in better style. It was difficult to say whether her horsemanship, her dress, or her beauty, were most admired—the *tout ensemble* was *unique*. Her dress was a leopard-coloured body, with blue sleeves, the rest buff and blue cap. . . . No words could express the disappointment felt at the defeat of Mrs Thornton. The spirit she displayed, and the good humour with which she bore her loss, greatly diminished the joy, even of the winners."

What diminished the joy of Mr Flint was that Colonel Thornton who had taken over his "wife's" bets maintained that the 1000 guineas bye had not been meant seriously, but was merely to attract larger crowds to the course. Mr Flint appealed to the Jockey Club who ruled in his favour. But by the next year's August races at York the debt was still outstanding.

This year the lady jockey was advertised as riding once again, against a Mr Bromford:

> For four hogsheads of Coti Roti p.p. and 2000 guineas h.ft.; and Mrs T. bets Mr B. 700 gs. to 600 s.p.p.; the 2000 gs.h.ft. provided it is declared to the Stewards four days before starting, Mrs T to have choice of four horses.
>
> Mr B. to ride Allegro sister to Allegranti.
>
> *N.B.*, Colonel T., or any gentleman he may name to be permitted to follow the lady over the course, to assist her in case of accident.

Colonel Thornton may have hoped, with the shrewd choice from four horses, to recoup himself enough to pay Mr. Flint and show a profit over the two years' meetings. But the day of the race Mr Bromford scratched and paid a forfeit, leaving Mrs Thornton to canter over the course.

In order not to disappoint the crowds a match was arranged instead between her at 9st. 6lb, and the well-known Newmarket jockey Mr Buckle at 13st. 6lbs. This year Mrs Thornton wore "a purple cap and waistcoat, nankeen coloured skirts, purple shoes and embroidered stockings". Again she took the lead, but when Mr Buckle came to challenge he took the lead for only a few lengths. Mrs Thornton came again and passed the winning post ahead by half a neck.

Great was the acclaim at Mrs Thornton's victory; but greater still the scandal in the stand. Two days before the race, Mr Flint had summoned Colonel Thornton for the 1,000 guineas. The day before Colonel Thornton had "recriminated" (i.e. brought a counter-claim). Now Mr Flint appeared with a brand new horse whip with which he belaboured the Colonel's shoulders. "Indignant at this gross and violent outrage", the gentlemen present "hissed and hooted" Mr Flint. He was arrested by order of the Lord Mayor and several magistrates, who were present, and given into the custody of the City runners, until he could find bail, himself in £1,000, and two sureties in £500 each. The Colonel was also bound over to prosecute the party for assault.

In the Court of King's Bench, Lord Ellenborough and his fellow judges were not very sympathetic to the colonel. They considered he should have accepted the judgement of the Jockey Club; but if he rejected it, he should prefer a Bill of indictment at the County Sessions.

It seems likely that the Colonel had more local influence than Mr Flint. At any rate, the latter became very poor and was reduced to managing a horse bazaar at York. There he "died from taking too large a dose of prussic acid as a medicine".

Mrs Thornton was exceptional as a woman rider. But in racing families women were as fond of the turf as men. Witness Lady Sarah Lennox, in the days when she was still married to Sir Charles Bunbury, writing from Newmarket to her friend Lady Susan O'Brien.

> There was a meeting of two days this time of year, to see the sweetest little horse run that ever was; his name is Gimcrack, he is delightful. Ld Rockingham, the D. of Grafton, & Genl. Conway kissed hand the day Gimrack ran. I must say I was more anxious about the horse than the Ministry, which sounds odd, for Sr. Charles loses £4,000 a year by the Secretary's pay.

Gimcrack, Eclipse, Diomed, names famous in the history of British racing and bloodstock, date from the 18th century, when the Sport of Kings was emerging from amateur to professional status. To the 18th century we owe the Jockey Club, Tattersall's, the idea of Classic Races, such as the Oaks and the Derby.

With the rise of the Stock Exchange in the 19th century, speculation in shares siphoned off money which otherwise would have passed over green baize tables.

WALKING, & MORNING DRESS.

I

You are Clean Fair Lady but our Ways and Means are Dirty.

London, Printed for R. Sayer and J. Bennett, Map and Printsellers N° 53, Fleet Street, as the Act directs 9 April 1781.

II

MORNING WALKING DRESS.

III

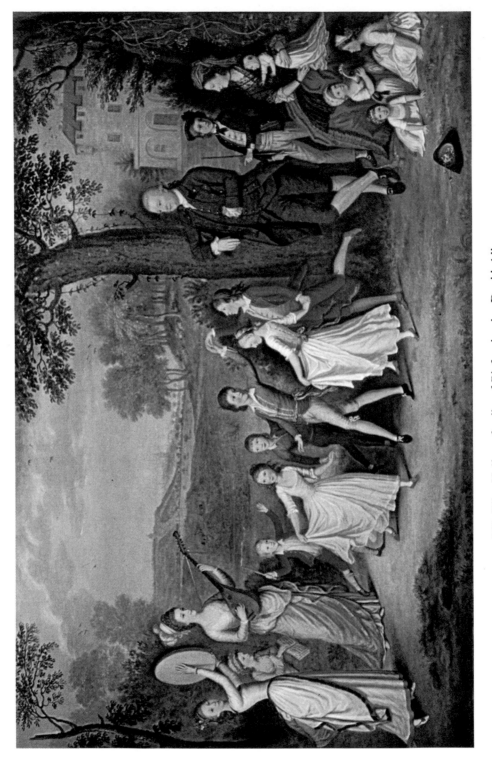

IV. The Halkett family of Pitfirraine by David Allan.

V. Courtship: accepted, rejected, preferred.

VI. Some fashionable dresses of 1800.

Evening Dress.

VII

VIII. Morning dress, 1799.

IX. Full dress, 1799.

X. Promenade dresses, 1802.

XI. Promenade dress, 1818.

But horse-racing did not decline. There was more to it than chance, or chicanery, the flutter of the punter and the welshing of bookies. It was, and is, a noble sport; the thunder of hooves on the turf; the empathy between horse and rider; the subtleties of form; the skill of timing; the state of the ground; the brilliance of the colours; and the beauty of horseflesh.

An eighteenth century cleric observed to a lady parishioner, over-fond of play, that card-games were a waste of time. "Yes," she agreed, "all that shuffling!" Horse-racing, they would probably have agreed, might be, for losers, a waste of money, but with the bustle and pageantry of the course, not of time.

CHAPTER NINE

Ladies on Canvas

The Georgian Era saw the birth of British schools of painting. The great portraitists had hitherto, with a few exceptions such as Samuel Cooper and Nicholas Hilliard, been foreigners. Holbein, Gheeraerts, Van Somer, Mytens, Van Dyck, Peter Lely, were the masters, who came from Europe, stayed for as much as forty years, and took pupils to help in their studios. But they were not interested in founding a school of Island painting. They executed their commissions and departed with their profits. The change came with Godfrey Kneller, who had studied in Holland, Rome, Naples and Venice. Like so many followers of William of Orange, Kneller made Britain his home; and in 1710 he founded the first London art school. When Thornhill took over from him, other rival establishments sprang up, under John Vanderbank, Louis Cheron and William Hogarth. British artists still went abroad to extend their training, but for the first time it was possible to study painting in England. In 1768, the foundation of the Royal Academy with its schools, its annual exhibitions, and its grades of R.A. and A.R.A., gave to painting and sculpture the royal acknowledgment of status. During the last half of the Georgian era, British painting became the finest in Europe.

Though the perfection of technique was due to the art schools, and the proliferation of commissions was the result of Georgians wishing to perpetuate themselves and their possessions, their Palladian residences, their lakes and parklands, their horses, dogs, goats, children and coloured servants, the contribution of Georgian ladies was outstanding. Visiting foreigners agreed that the women of the island were beautiful, not merely society ladies but those of all classes.

The style of female beauty, and its portrayal, changed during the era. Sir Godfrey Kneller painted Sarah Churchill several times. Even when painted in full robes she wore her hair unpowdered, used little make-up and did not mind having a shiny nose. His portrait of her when she had "cut off her hair in the Spleen" is magnificent for its boldness of spirit, the broad brow, flashing eyes, determined chin, full mouth and chunky nose; she is a splendid woman first, and only secondarily a great lady. The portrait of Henrietta Howard, Countess of Suffolk, the mistress of George II, was painted by Charles Jervas, enormous against a dark landscape in whose distance appears the Palladian house she built in Marble Hill Park, besides the Thames. She is obviously a great lady, superbly yet simply dressed, hair natural and unpowdered, complexion owing little to art, her pose so natural that one feels that any moment she might stand up and walk out of the picture.

What a contrast these make with Sir Joshua Reynolds's masterpiece, Jane, Countess of Harrington! The Countess herself is a delight, her exquisite neck, the poise of the head, the elaborately piled hair with the two white feathers continuing the line of the arm and balancing the right hand, the left sleeve drawing the eye down from the face to the rich drapery resting on the terrace wall. The classical clothes by the fall of their heavy folds reveal the legs and thighs more enchantingly than if she was nude. Yet one cannot imagine *her* walking out of the picture. She is held in a balance between nature and human artifacts. Her hand rests on a terrace wall, the vertical columns of which repeat the upward movement of her legs and knees, while the horizontal lines of the wall and the decoration of the classical urn beside her echo the horizontals of her sash and the fold of her left elbow. She belongs in the world of ancient architecture; but she belongs also to the world of nature. The shadowed side of the urn merges in with the trunk of the tree behind, whose branches not only repeat the movement of the hair across the countess's shoulder, but also link with the trees on the left, so that within their verdure her head and shoulders are framed against the sky, the cumuli of the clouds making a counterbalance to the fullness of the robes. This is not a portrait, but a picture; a composition which reconciles the beauty of the human form to the forms of nature and man's hand; an idea expressed in purely pictorial terms. The same formula was used by other artists; it was in fact a sort of artistic *cliché*. In Thomas Gainsborough's Penelope, Viscountess Ligonier, painted three years before, the composition was not dissimilar: a classical pediment on the right, supporting a small sculpture of the discobolus, a parkland vista providing the background left; the top of the pediment aligned with the sash, a billowing curtain top and middle right echoing the folds of drapery. But how different is the total effect! The face is not that of a beauty, but of the lovely and very self-reliant daughter of George Pitt, a woman of character. The landscape is the painting of a painting, the classical sculptures, which include the head and shoulders of a bambino and, still smaller, that of a bearded man, both propped on a book which is resting on a chair are props to carry the viewer's eye to the scallop shell on the pediment, up the left arm to the model's face. She is the centre of interest; all else is there to show her off.

At the same time that Sir Joshua painted the Countess of Harrington (1779), he also painted her mother Mrs Edwin Lascelles (afterwards Lady Harewood). Mrs Lascelles was then a woman in her forties, not to be treated in the same way as her daughter Jane. She is posed out of doors, seated before a wooden hill (which is a real hill, not a canvas one like Gainsborough's); but as with all portraits, the figure is the most important element in the picture and the head the most important element in the figure.

Thomas Gainsborough loved all the members of Thomas Linley's family and painted most of them. His picture of the grey-eyed Elizabeth (who became Mrs Sheridan) and her brown-eyed sister Mary (who became Mrs Tickell) shows his over-riding interest in their faces. Walpole placed Elizabeth "above all living beauties". But among Georgian portraits one cannot rate the Linley sisters so highly. An artist needs money to live and time is money. The background to his dual full length portrait is conventional; the painting of the dresses does not contribute much. This was a case where the painter would have been better advised to cut his canvas to show only the heads of the sisters and the bodies down to the lace of Elizabeth's right sleeve. But in cutting his canvas, he would have drastically curtailed his fee.

The case of Mr and Mrs Andrews was very different. The Andrews were clearly as interested in their estate as in themselves; and so was Gainsborough. The right half of the picture is a sunlit harvest landscape under a stormy sky: the left half shows a wealthy sporting squire with his flintlock and gundog in a pose of ease and complacence leaning against a wrought iron garden settee which is totally occupied by the elegant blue hooped skirt out of which the body of his wife emerges erect, fine-featured but curiously chilling. Behind them the stormclouds are noticeably darker than over the fields and woodlands. The two halves of the picture are linked by the lace on the squire's tricorne, the undulant line of his lady's hat and the distant hills, as well as by the arm of the green chair running towards the green spinney and the hedgerows in the middle distance.

The convention in most Georgian portraits whether of men or women was that the corners of mouths turned up. The mouth of Mrs Andrews is pursed, her husband's depressed. They are not happy: what unites them is the land. By a curious, (deliberate?) trick the face of Mr Andrews looks like a mask which, if removed, would reveal a different face underneath. I do not know whether the Andrews liked the picture. Perhaps they saw themselves as he saw them, together and yet separate on their private eminence, wanting no more than that superiority.

This and other conversation pieces were painted by Gainsborough while still in his native Suffolk, before he was 33. He was bored by people, in comparison with landscape: but whereas Richard Savage Lloyd and his Sister in an earlier conversation piece of his are unrelated either to one another or to their background, Mr and Mrs Andrews and their acres are joined in a relationship of incongruity; a sort of antithesis to Reynolds' Jane, Countess of Harrington.

Gainsborough left Suffolk and lived expensively in Bath for the winter season of 1760. He raised his prices from five guineas to eight guineas a head and ultimately to forty guineas a half and a hundred guineas a full length portrait. He painted no more conversation pieces, but there were many who did. Mario Praz analyses The Family Group in an Outdoor Setting into seven different types: in front of a porch or balustrade; in a courtyard or in the open air; against a screen of foliage or with a tree in the middle; with a view of a country house; with a view of a landscape; in a boat; and portraits of children. They can also be analysed according to composition. In some the figures are not related to one another. They are a collection of *tableaux vivants* or posed full length portraits in which the models are concerned not with one another but in looking at the artist.

Johann Zoffany was one of the most successful painters of conversation pieces, in which human figures were related to one another in consonance with the background. In The Three Daughters of John, Third Earl of Bute, his design is shaped like an hour-glass, the top of which is the frondage of a tree, the bottom the three girls, with their billowing skirts. They are of different ages, and different degrees of composure, but linked together in the fascination of the pet squirrel (?) on a chain which is on a low branch of the tree. Zoffany has caught a moment in time, which embraces a lasting family relationship; while the background with the noble portico on the right and the long vista on the left puts the young ladies in their social setting.

This was an early work. In his fifties, he spent six years in India (1783–9). Among the conversation pieces he painted there was The Auriol Family. It tells us little about the Auriols, except that there was little to tell, at least before the servants. There are three groups. The three Englishmen on the left are deep in conversation. The central group consisting of two ladies and one gentleman are either ignoring that they are being waited on by the handsome servant with the kettle or are watching what is taking place between the Englishman and the moustachioed Indian on the right. Whether deliberately or by chance the Indians are pictorially more interesting than the whites; and the ladies for all their finery the most out of place. It is one of the earliest views of the White Man's Burden and the White Woman's Boredom.

The Georgians not only loved dressing; they also loved dressing up, for amateur theatricals, for *tableaux vivants*, for allegorical impersonations. Angelica Kauffman, who was one of the founders of the Royal Academy and the only woman R.A. until the 20th century, was painted with Mrs Catharine Macaulay, Mrs Montagu, Mrs Sheridan and five other ladies in classical costume against an antic background as the Nine Muses of Britain. "Madam," said Sir Joshua Reynolds to Mrs Siddons as she entered his studio, "Ascend your undisputed throne, and graciously bestow upon me some idea of the Tragic Muse." Emma, Lady Hamilton, entranced the court of Naples and elsewhere with her classical poses, male as well as female. When Romney painted Lady Hamilton at Prayer, her contemporaries seem to have found nothing absurd in the pose, though Georgian gentlemen at least must have preferred Romney's more sensuous studies of that entrancing beauty with her Doric accent, warm heart and excellent mind.

There was a great vogue for theatrical pictures; attempts to capture on canvas performances which had been memorable on the stage. They seldom succeeded in being more than records of dramatic experience; as photographs of stage productions recall emotion to those who have seen them, but cannot give much to those who did not. The exceptions succeed because they are good pictures. Sir Joshua Reynolds' Portrait of Kitty Fisher as Cleopatra Dissolving the Pearl owes nothing to her performance on the stage; everything to her posing on the dais and his superb painting. What it tells us of Kitty's complexion is another matter. We know that she died of lead poisoning through over use of cosmetics. The skin beneath that white lead and rouge must have been very different.

It is hard to tell what people looked like from their pictures. The most pleasing portrait of Lady Caroline Lamb is that of her in page's dress: this must surely have been the aspect that for a time charmed Lord Byron. A portrait attributed to John Hoppner is more conventional, and with more melancholy eyes: while Henry Meyer's engraving changes the proportion of the head. The chin is similar, but the breadth of the cheekbones greater and the length from chin to cranium less. We cannot tell from portraits what she was like, but perhaps that was because she did not herself know. Similarly with Lady Elizabeth Foster, who married Lady Caroline's uncle, the Duke of Devonshire, as his second wife, there are so many different artists' visions of "dearest Bess", the "racoon" as they called her in Devonshire House nickname-code. Angelica Kauffman, Ozyas Humphreys, and Reynolds saw her in recognisably similar ways. Angelica made her more feminine, Ozyas more challenging, Sir Joshua more calculating. They all painted her with the billowing hair above and the billowing lace below, a face peering through a cloud of fashion. Sir Thomas Lawrence drew her in Rome, in 1819, when she, now the second Duchess, was aged 62. She looks younger than in Reynolds's portrait painted 31 years before. The first portrait Lawrence is known to have painted was when he was aged twelve; and his father, an innkeeper at Devizes, would ask his clients, "Here's my son. Will you have him recite from the poets or paint your portraits?" Mr and Mrs (later Lord and Lady) Kenyon sat for him, and he painted the lady in profile, "because her face was not straight". He only made one error when he grew up. It was to paint the Queen as she was. She was furious and he never repeated the mistake. This was, perhaps, the reason why he could command a price as high as fifteen hundred guineas for a portrait of Lady Gower and her child. He did more than paint; he cured the ills of nature.

Where there are many portraits, the inadequacy of portraiture is the more apparent the better the portraits are. Because each presents a different aspect, one becomes the more aware that the original must have had many more which have gone unportrayed. It is perhaps better to have one good portrait of a writer, to typify the author of the works. Edward Francesco Burney's portrait of his cousin Fanny is all I need to supplement the novels and Madame d'Arblay's *Diary and Letters*. One can follow her fortunes with that face. But if not a good portrait, it is better to have none. Cassandra Austen's pencil and water colour sketch of Jane tells us nothing of the author of *Pride and Prejudice* and *Emma* except that her sister couldn't draw.

CHAPTER TEN

Women and Medicine

There are many who look back to the eighteenth century as the age in which they would like to have lived—"provided of course one was a member of the aristocracy". There should be a further proviso, the enjoyment of perfect health. It was a terrible age in which to fall ill. Great advances were made in physics and chemistry, in botany and zoology, in engineering, in inventions, mining, transport and manufacturing. But in the theory and practice of medicine and surgery, there was comparatively little progress until the end of the century: and even then it was a very painful world for the mentally and physically sick.

In 1750 Voltaire remarked that doctors were pouring drugs of which they knew little into human bodies of which they knew less. The regular medical schools gave little training. The average medical student spent four to five years as the servant of a physician. He groomed his horses, drove with him to visit patients, compounded his pills, distilled his tinctures, but spent precious little time in study or by the bedsides of patients. If the teacher was a surgeon, he assisted at operations and robbed graves for the corpses necessary to study anatomy; and since the surgeon was a barber, also, he cut hair and shaved chins.

Not only were barbers considered qualified to perform operations, but even executioners; perhaps on the theory that if an executioner could kill a man quickly, he was as able as any surgeon-barber to kill him slowly.

After such an apprenticeship, wealthy students might spend a year or more, travelling to see different teachers or hospitals. This was very costly and it was considered a waste of money to train daughters for such a career. Yet the fact that there were no degrees in medicine or surgery meant that until the end of the 18th century women could, and did, practise medicine, though usually as gynae-cologists or midwives. This was a concession more to the modesty of middle class mothers than to the medical ability of the female sex.

Any woman who could afford it preferred to be confined at home. The con-ditions of Paris lying-in hospitals in the 1760s were no worse than those of hospitals in other capital cities. But before and after confinement, the mothers lay four in a bed. The sheets were soiled with discharges, and infected often with the germs of puerperal fever. By the end of the century, single beds were installed, the straw mattresses frequently changed and ventilation improved. English hospitals had a few bath-tubs and the walls were white-washed regularly, but there was no nursing care. Vinegar was sprinkled on the floor to keep down dust. Filth and vermin accumulated under beds. Street-walkers were brought in as night-nurses and accommodated the internees rather than the sick and dying. No wonder that in the villages mothers were delivered by the local wise-woman and nursed by relatives or neighbours.

Academic medicine was a closed profession. Most practitioners kept their secrets to themselves. Fathers passed on their knowledge to sons, teachers to paying pupils. Some medical textbooks were written by theorists, who were proud that they had never practised. A six-volume work on obstetrics was written by an authority who had never delivered a baby. Johann Kampf produced the "doctrine of infarctus", namely that the cause of most diseases was due to constipation. Reputable physicians had their specifics. Richard Guy, founder of Guy's Hospital, recommended "Plunkett's Caustic" for treating cancer. Sir Hans Sloane, president of the Royal College of Physicians, peddled an eye ointment. William Cullen, founder of the medical school of Glasgow in 1744 and the first lecturer in Britain ever to use English instead of Latin for his lectures, though inspiring as a teacher "did not add a single new fact to medical science".

Georgian women made a considerable contribution to medicine. The most famous is Lady Mary Wortley Montagu and her introduction of smallpox inoculation. Smallpox, endemic at all times and sometimes epidemic, killed or blinded or disfigured. Princess Anne was so pockmarked that her complexion was hideous except in portraits. Lady Mary lost her beauty and her eyelashes, so that she could not bear to look at herself in a glass. In Turkey, as Ambassadress, she discovered something already known in France, but not in England, and wrote to her friend Sarah Chigwell:

> The smallpox, so fatal and so general among us, is here entirely harmless by the invention of ingrafting, which is the term they give it. There is a set of old women who make it their business to perform the operation every autumn in the month of September when the great heat is abated. . . . They make parties for the purpose . . . the old woman comes with a nutshell full of the matter of the best sort of smallpox . . .

Lady Mary's brother had died of smallpox and she took the risk of having her own children inoculated. In England it was tried on three condemned prisoners who were promised pardon, if it worked. The Princess of Wales experimented on five charity children, before having Prince Edward and Princess Augusta inoculated. Variolation, as it was called, was mortal in about 4% of cases. But the normal mortality from smallpox was around 50%. It was not until 1796 that Dr Edward Jenner "discovered" vaccination and with the help of the Countess of Berkeley later succeeded in bringing this to the notice of humanity. Ironically the secret had been known to countrywomen probably for centuries. It was one of those true old wives' tales, like putting cobwebs on a cut or mouldy cheese on a festering wound. Any countrywoman knew that if you'd had cowpox, you never caught smallpox. Dr Jenner's genius resided in two very simple things. He did not despise the wisdom of his patients and he produced deliberately the effects of what they had observed as the result of chance. He had taken the first step in the course of controlled immunisation.

Smallpox was only one of the scourges of the 18th century. Typhus and typhoid (not then separated as separate diseases) measles and scarlatine (similarly confused), venereal diseases (in which gonorrhoea and syphilis were not clearly distinguished), diphtheria and influenza were almost as widespread, though they left less obvious traces on those who survived.

The causes and carriers of disease were not understood. John Howard, the penal reformer, was concerned with the plight of prisoners in rat-infested cells. He did not know any more than the doctors did that the plague was transmitted by fleas feeding on the blood of rodents and humans. Milk was regarded as a pure and nutritive liquid. There was no suspicion that cows might transmit tuberculosis or undulant fever even if milked under the most hygienic conditions. In St James's Park, dairymaids (with not too clean hands) milked not too clean udders for delicious (but insanitary) syllabubs. That typhoid might be transmitted by well-water into which had seeped the oozings of cesspits occurred to no one. It was not until the end of the century that doctors decided it would be better to confine fever cases to hospitals outside city limits rather than inside private houses. The fumigation of clothes and bed linen was initiated for the elimination of body-lice and bed-bugs as nuisances, rather than as vectors of disease.

Milk-vendors carried their wares on their heads more to preserve themselves from what came out of windows above than to preserve the purity of what was already impure from infected cows in unscalded receptacles. For babies it was recognised that breast-feeding was purer (unless the mother or wet-nurse was suffering from puerperal fever). Suckling continued as long as possible; in the case of a mother in the belief that a woman would not conceive while still nursing; in the case of a foster mother because the longer the job lasted, the longer she was paid. A special appliance of leather was fitted to protect the breast against baby teeth. Breast feeding might go on up to the age of two.

Professional wet-nurses, in order to ensure a continuous supply of breast-milk, tried to ensure that they would never run dry by becoming pregnant, if possible while still on the old wet-nurse job. There must have been lay-off periods. But as mistresses who needed to be serviced, they made small claims on the father for children who would be put out to foster-parents whose calculated neglect would be connived at. Professional wet-nurses must have been in demand. They were not whores: and their customers were not poxy soldiers and sailors, but eminently respectable shopkeepers, merchants or even noblemen, only too anxious to pay them modestly so that they could pursue their profession.

Great attention was paid to the mineral properties of different springs. Each spa advanced its therapeutic claims for its waters taken internally or externally. Tomes were written to guide the ailing from well to well throughout Britain and the continent. Brighthelmstone was launched as a watering place by Dr Russell, who advocated the use of sea water not only for bathing, but to be drunk, though not too near the edge. Yet doctors were not interested in non-mineral drinking water: or whether it was pure or contaminated. It was only in the early years after weaning that water was drunk. If toddlers survived, they were by then so fortified by anti-bodies that they had developed resistance to typhoid and enteric fevers.

Housekeepers were equally ignorant of the dangers of contaminated milk or water. It was not until 1786 that Mrs Charlotte Mason, in her *Ladies Assistant*, recognised the necessity of purifying water for drinking or cooking, whether from rainwater-butt, spring, well, pond or river by boiling it, in order to kill the animals and precipitate the other impurities (including "fuliginous particles, invisible seeds, mud, decayed vegetables and the spawn of vermin"). She considered Londoners fortunate in being able to draw drinking water from the river Thames rather than rely upon the pump; surprising since that river must have been heavily polluted by the sewer-drainage begun in 1766.

In the first three-quarters of the 18th century, sanitation was as primitive as it had been in Tudor times. Admittedly the first known valve water closet had been invented by a kinsman of Queen Elizabeth I and installed for her relief in Richmond Palace, a royal flush. The first Duke of Devonshire in the 1690s installed no less than ten at Chatsworth. The cost of four of these, with pots and cisterns made of Derbyshire alabaster and brasswork flushing gear, was near half as much as the demolition of the old North Front. But even one water closet was a luxury few could afford. Britain was a land of chamberpots, jakes and middens. Those with castles had an edge. Moats dug to keep the enemy without received the evacuations of those within, which sustained the fish which plenished their tables. For countryfolk without water, there was the garden. "I am very much offended," remarked Dean Swift, "with those ladies, who are so proud and lazy, they will not be at the Pains of stepping in the Garden to pluck a Rose, but keep an odious Implement, sometimes in the Bed-chamber itself, or at least in a dark Closet adjoining, which they make use of to ease their worst Necessities".

Utensils were kept in sideboards in the dining room and were used not only by Georgian gentlemen drinking after dinner when the ladies had withdrawn, but also by Georgian ladies when they were dining alone.

"Never empty the chamber-pots till they are quite full," Swift advised the housemaid, "if that happens in the night, empty them into the street; if, in the morning, into the garden; for it would be one endless work to go a dozen times from the garret and upper rooms, down to the back-sides; but, never wash them in any other liquor except their own: what cleanly girl would be dabbling in another folk's urine? And besides, the smell of stale urine, as I observed before, is admirable against the vapours; which, a hundred to one, may be your lady's case."

Smollett (whom Sterne nicknamed Dr Smellfungus) made Matt Bramble write from Edinburgh to his friend Dr Lewis of the Scottish custom of Gardyloo. "You are no stranger to their method of discharging all their impurities from the windows at certain hours of the night, as the custom is in Spain, Portugal and some parts of France and Italy . . . notwithstanding all the care that is taken by the scavengers to remove this nuisance every morning by break of day, enough remains to offend the eyes, as well as other organs of those whom use has not hardened against all delicacy of sensation."

In 1775 Alexander Cummings of London took out the first patent for a W.C. Others were invented by Samuel Prosser (1777) and Joseph Bramah of Pimlico (1778). None of the 18th century plumbers earned the immortality of Thomas Crapper, who provided the English language with new meanings to the word "crap" as noun and verb. At the turn of the century, the W.C. was familiar in many British homes. By the time that Lady Hamilton gave up Nelson's house at Merton, each of its five major bedrooms had a W.C. fitted in the adjacent dressing room, together with a washstand with fitted bowl, lead tank and tap, and a simple form of bath which was filled and emptied by servants. The only trouble was that the domestic drainage system was imperfect. Unventilated pipes running to the cesspit through ancient woodwork produced a stench which permeated the house.

Improvements in sanitation depended on Local Authorities and as late as 1832 open gutters were still the only means of disposing of sewage and household slops in the city of Exeter. But there was a gradual lessening of water-borne and fly-borne diseases from the 1760s onwards.

The comparative absence of mention of mice, rats, bed-bugs, lice and fleas in the literature of the time is because they were accepted as facts of everyday life. The Royal households of George III and IV included professional flea-catchers. That they were not always successful is seen from a letter written from Weymouth by Princess Elizabeth to the Prince of Wales about his little daughter Charlotte. "When she goes to Bed she always says, 'Bless Papa, Mama, Charlotte and friends'; but having been cruelly bitten by the fleas on the foregoing night, instead of *Friends* she introduced *Fleas*, Lady Elgin, being told of it, said 'We must make her says *Friends*'. Miss Hayman with much humour answered, 'Why, Madam, you know we are told to pray for our enemies, and surely the Fleas are the only ones H.R.H. has' ."

Women played a progressively smaller role as the insistence on medical training became more stringent. The career of a woman like Elizabeth Blackwell (1712–70) would have been impossible in the latter half of the Georgian era, when the possession of a university degree was necessary. Her husband Alexander Blackwell had graduated at Aberdeen University and set up as a printer and an apothecary. Elizabeth was taught botany and anatomy both by her husband and by James Douglas (1675–1742), who was famous as an obstetrician, surgeon and anatomist. She became so skilled in flower painting and copper-plate engraving that when Alexander was imprisoned for debt in 1737, she secured his release with her publication of *A Curious Herbal*, in two volumes, containing "five hundred cuts of the most useful plants which are now used in the practice of Physic". She made the drawings, engraved them on copper herself and painted them with her own hands. In this she was encouraged and assisted by Sir Hans Sloane and Mr Rand the curator of the botanical garden which Sloane had set up at Chelsea. When her husband was imprisoned in 1747 for conspiracy against the King of Sweden, this enterprising Scotswoman studied obstetrics under Dr William Smellie (the friend and teacher of Smollett). She was not able to save her husband, who before being beheaded apologised to the executioner for not knowing "where to lay his head on the block because this was his first experience". But she supported herself and her family for another 23 years as an obstetrician and general practitioner, a respected and wealthy colleague of Sir Hans Sloane and Dr Richard Mead.

Another woman to make a name in orthodox medicine was Mrs Martha Mears, friend of Dr Thomas Denman, the physician and medical writer, Dr John Armstrong, the poet of hygiene, and Dr Francis Willis, one of the gentler specialists in his treatment of George III's "insanity". Her *Pupil of Nature; or Candid Advice to the Fair Sex* (1797) dealt with pregnancy, child-birth and the diseases incidental on both. In some respects it was popularisation of Denman's *Introduction to the Practice of Midwifery*; but her German translator described it as the best book of its kind to have been published for fifty years. Mrs Mears was one of those instrumental in enabling women to study midwifery in the new lying-in hospitals on payment of a fee of five pounds.

Midwives in the 18th century were usually accompanied by nurses when they attended confinements. The nurse was responsible for washing the mother and baby; she assisted the midwife and then took over the feeding of mother and child, staying in after the labour as long as she was needed. Midwives had an arduous life, called out at any time of day or night, travelling on horseback or in spring-less carriages, often for small fees. The more fashionable midwives, however, made good money. Mrs Kennon who delivered George III in 1738 collected such a wealthy clientele that in 1751 she was able to commission Dr Frank Nicholls to write a satire against men-midwives for a fee of £500. It provoked *A Vindication of Man-Midwifery* in counter-argument. But both George IV and Queen Victoria were delivered by women. At the birth of George IV, William Hunter was standing by in case of complications, but Mrs Draper the midwife refused even to call him in to approve her handiwork, so he lost his fee.

Elizabeth Blackwell had been on the best of terms with Dr Smellie. But Mrs Nihell, wife of a surgeon apothecary, who herself had been trained in Paris in midwifery, fell foul of him for his saying that women practised only for money. She had a fashionable practice in the Haymarket, but had helped at some nine hundred deliveries in hospital, mostly without the use of forceps. She lambasted Smellie, who taught obstetrics with the aid of a wooden mannikin, a copper-belly and a uterus made from a bladder full of beer, in which a wax doll floated. It was only on his mannikin, she said, that Dr Smellie performed for nothing.

His celebrated implements, including the forceps he had invented, she regarded as instruments of torture.

Though women tended to specialise in obstetrics, there were some who distinguished themselves in other fields. Catherine Bowles was renowned for operations for hernia, stone in the bladder and hydrocele. Lady Reid, the widow of Sir William Reid, Queen Anne's eye-doctor, continued his practice with no less success than her husband; though this was not very great. Mrs Hutton, who practised general medicine in Shropshire, discovered the properties of the foxglove, digitalis, in the treatment of diseases of the heart; a secret which she sold to a Dr Withering who arranged it to be inserted in the new *London Pharmacopeia* (1785), taking the credit to himself.

Orthodox Georgian medicine could be considered quackery to-day; with its inordinate blood-letting, its emetics and purgatives, its clysters and leeches. The surgeon spread infection with his knife and with his clothes. The physician lowered resistance with his prescriptions, even when he rallied his patients with his charismatic presence. Women doctors claimed that they were more successful than men, because they were gentler in their methods; and it was even truer then than it is today that those doctors succeeded best who interfered least with the body's own curative processes. Pills often did more harm than placebos.

In consequence the Georgian quacks, abominated by their learned colleagues, often did more good, just because their panaceas were useless. Quassia cups tasted bitter, and on the puritan principle that anything unpleasant is good for you encouraged patients to get well of their own accord. Elisha Perkins of Connecticut produced his "magnetic tractor" in 1798. Shaped like a compass, with one sharp and one blunt-ended arm, made from combinations of copper, zinc and gold, or iron, silver and platinum, he effected remarkable cures, especially among women, by tractation (which was a solemn term for stroking). The theory was that it was analogous to galvanism or animal magnetism. It was exploded by a Bath physician who effected similar cures with wooden tractors. Perkinism was dismissed as fraudulent, since the cure was obviously wrought by faith. What was ignored was the importance of faith as a therapy.

James Graham (1745–94) was for a decade the most fashionable and successful quack of the Georgian era, appealing especially to ladies of society. He studied medicine in his youth under the great Scottish teachers of his day, Munro primus, Cullen, Black and Whytt; but he did not qualify. After two years spent in Philadelphia as an ear and eye specialist, he went to England in 1774 to begin a career which became progressively more sensational. The first patient to make his reputation was Mrs Catharine Macaulay who had taken his young brother as her second husband. His therapy was based on what he had learned of Benjamin Franklin's discoveries. He placed his patients either on a "magnetic throne" or in a bath through which electrical currents (at presumably very low voltage) were passed. These treatments could only be given under his supervision, for which he charged as high a fee as he could command. He also used "aetherial" and "balsamic" medicines, milk baths, and dry friction. Though denounced as a quack, he was received by Franklin in Paris, and at Aix-la-Chapelle, collected glowing testimonials from aristocratic patients, including Georgiana, Duchess of Devonshire, that amateur of frivolous novelty.

Equipped with these, he set up his Temple of Health in London in the autumn of 1779. On the Royal Terrace, Adelphi, facing the river Thames, it combined the attractions of a Catholic shrine of miracles, a Greek temple and a raree show. In the entrance hall was an array of crutches and other appliances, such as spectacles and ear-trumpets, said to have been left by those who had no use for them after being cured. The upper rooms were large and ostentatious. (The house and its equipment, he claimed, had cost £10,000.) There was the "great Apollo department", dedicated to that god as a temple of health. There were huge, elaborately decorated electrical appliances, jars, conductors and of course the "electrical throne". There was a lecture hall, with stained glass windows, paintings on the walls, sculpture in niches, a dais for musicians, the odour of oriental incense, and a posse of gigantic footmen (who were also employed, wearing huge cocked hats, in distributing advertisements to the houses of nobility, fashionable clubs and the better coffee houses).

Graham began with a course of lectures on health and procreation at two guineas a head, a price so outrageous that any wealthy nobody who wanted to be somebody could not resist. His lectures, delivered to mixed audiences, were salacious enough to attract, without being rude enough to repel. After he had finished, a concluding discourse was delivered by a beautiful young woman, described as the Goddess of Health. It was rumoured in the days when Lady Hamilton's affair with Nelson had become the talk of the town that as Emma Lyon, she had made her debut as the Goddess of Health. If Graham had not been dead by that time, he would not have denied the rumour, but it was probably unfounded.

When audiences at two guineas flagged, he dropped the price successively to a guinea, half a guinea, a crown and finally "for the benefit of all' to half a crown. Then he threw the temple open to visitors at a shilling.

Horace Walpole waited until the price had dropped to five shillings. On August 23, 1780, he wrote to the Countess of Ossory.

> In the evening I went to Dr Graham's. It is the most impudent puppet-show of imposition I ever saw, and the mountebank himself the dullest of his profession, except that he makes the spectators pay a crown apiece. . . . A woman, invisible, warbled to clarionets on the stairs. The decorations are pretty and odd; and the apothecary, who comes up a trap-door, for no purpose, since he might as well come upstairs, is no novelty. The electrical experiments are nothing at all singular; and a poor air-pump, that only bursts a bladder, pieces out the farce. The Doctor is like Jenkinson in person, and as flimsy as a puppet.

Whatever Graham's resemblance to Charles Jenkinson (later 1st Earl of Liverpool), he was by all accounts of handsome physique though pontifical in manner. His most extravagant property was his "Celestial Bed", standing on glass legs and provided with the richest hangings. Any sterile pair sleeping in this bed (on payment of one hundred pounds) would surely produce an heir. Despite reputed cases of success (and the cutting of the fee to fifty pounds) his property was seized for debt. For a time he subsisted on marketing an Elixir, the taker of which could live for 150 years.

This was followed by Fangotherapy (solemn for mud-baths). For one hour daily (for a payment of one guinea, descending finally to one shilling) the Doctor and the Goddess of Health "in their first suits" could be seen buried up to the neck in warm earth. A spectator described the two, the doctor with his hair full dressed and powdered, and the goddess fashionably coiffeured, as looking "not unlike two fine full-grown cauliflowers".

The two most famous women quacks flourished in the first half of the 18th century. Mrs Mapp today would be described as an osteopath, and still be frowned on by the medical profession, even though resorted to surreptitiously. In the 1730s, she was described more straightforwardly as a bone-setter. Her father was also a bonesetter in Hindon, Wilts; but she left home as the result of a family quarrel; and after wandering round the country pretending to be mad, as Crazy Sally, she settled at Epsom, Surrey. She was strong, fat, masculine and fond of drink. She began by frequenting fairs, where she healed the bones broken or dislocated in drunken brawls. Her fame so spread that wealthy patients came from London to be treated by her brawny hands. The story goes that even Sir Hans Sloane sought her out to treat his niece whose back had been broken nine years and stuck out two inches, and that the people of Epsom were so grateful for the trade she brought them that they offered her a hundred guineas to stay there. She is said to have earned twenty guineas a day and have driven in a coach and four with liveried servants. In his Consultation of Twelve Physicians, Hogarth portrayed Mrs Mapp holding a humerus in place of the canes in which the doctors concealed their smelling salts. She was the subject of a comedy, *The Husband's Relief; with the Female Bonesetter and Worm-Doctor*, the first night of which she attended. At the peak of her success, she married Hill Mapp, the footman to a Ludgate Hill mercer. Within a week, her husband ran off with her fortune. But she did not repine. To get rid of the rogue was cheap at the price and next month she was reported as having waited on Her Majesty.

Her claims were remarkable, if vague. "A man of Wardour Street" was cured of a broken back. "A gentleman who went with one shoe heel six inches high, having been lame twenty years of his hip and knee; whom she set straight, and brought his leg down even with the other", could not deny the miracle, since he was not specified by name. But Thomas Barber, tallow-chandler of Saffron Hill, published his protest:

Whereas it has been industriously (I wish I could say truly) reported that I had found great benefit from a certain female bonesetter's performance, and that it was from a want of resolution to undergo the operation that I did not meet with a perfect cure. This is to give notice that any persons afflicted with lameness (who are willing to know what good and harm others may receive, before they venture on desperate measures themselves) will be welcome any morning to see the dressing on my leg, which was sound before the operation, and they will then be able to judge of the performance, and to whom I owe my present unhappy confinement to my bed and chair.

Mrs Mapp moved from Epsom to Pall Mall, but she did not forget her Epsom friends. She gave a plate of ten guineas to be run for at Epsom and went to see the race. In those days horse-races were run in heats and culminated in a final. The winner of the first heat was a mare named "Mrs Mapp". The lady bone-setter gave the jockey a guinea and promised him a hundred if he won the plate. Unfortunately neither she nor the mare had staying power. Whether because of the exposure of her preposterous claims or her addiction to alcohol, which success enabled her to satisfy, she was soon deserted alike by patients and friends and died on December 10, 1737, at her lodgings near the Seven Dials, so destitute that the parish was obliged to bury her.

As a bone-setter, Mrs Mapp may have possessed some skill, when sober. Jane Stevens was a quack of different plumage. In the age of gout, stone in the bladder was a common ailment. Ladies and gentlemen flinched at the prospect of an agonising, and dangerous, operation. How much better to dissolve the stones so that they could be passed, or better still to prevent their formation in the first place! Mrs Stevens came forward with two specifics, a pill to dissolve the stones and a decoction to prevent their formation. Skilfully advertising, she made a large fortune from their sale as proprietary medicines. Such was her success that an Act of Parliament was passed in 1736 to purchase the formulae of her prescriptions for the sum of £5,000, for the benefit of the poor. Her merits were vouched for by Sir Caesar Hawkins, inventor of the cutting gorget and William Cheselden, the most rapid of all the pre-anaesthetic operators (54 seconds for the removal of a bladder-stone). Benjamin Franklin, who was in London at the time the Act was before Parliament, also approved in principle of Mrs Stevens' pills, but revised his opinion when he learnt of their composition. The pills were made from soap and calcined egg and snail shells, and the decoction from herbs, honey, burnt swine's cresses, burdock, hips and haws. Even after that revelation, the Reverend Stephen Hales, author of *Haemodynamics*, on the mechanical relations of blood-pressure, saw no reason to doubt the efficacy of Mrs. Stevens' specifics.

Mrs Stevens lived happily ever after and a number of ladies and gentlemen suffered less pain from the stone as a result of taking her soap-shell pills and drinking her decoction, until post-mortem examinations showed that all the people she had "cured" still had stone in their bladders. Then the agonies recurred.

44. *A Harlot's Progress*, plate 2, by William Hogarth. The series was substantially the story of Moll Flanders, published by Defoe ten years before. Hogarth in this new genre described himself as "the author" rather than "the artist". Here the Harlot distracts her keeper's attention while her lover escapes.

Discipline à la Kenyon.

45–47. Playing cards, or faro, for money, or "fish", was almost universal in society throughout the Grand Century. Only in rare cases did it result in addiction and ruin. (*Lower right*) Mrs Thornton as a jockey was unique.

48–52. The Duchess of Devonshire ruined her health and peace of mind by gambling debts (minor compared with those of her father and husband) – Walpole called her "the Empress of Fashion" and the feathers of her headdress were the highest in Europe; (*lower right*) Jane Austen, the genius of a later simpler age, flourished among fashions simpler and more flowing; (*centre*) no one would think, looking at this charming miniature of Lady Mary Wortley Montagu that she was so disfigured with pock marks that she refused to have a looking glass in her house; (*lower left*) Catherine, third Duchess of Queensberry, after C. Jervas, beautiful, witty, generous and eccentric, she dressed to the day of her death in 1777 in the fashion of her youth, refusing "to cut and curl my hair like a sheep's head, or wear one of their trolloping sacks"; (*top right*) Mrs Laetitia Pilkington, the diminutive poetess in distress, by Nathaniel Hone.

53-54. When painting Mr and Mrs Andrews, Thomas Gainsborough recognized the equal importance of them, their sports and broad acres. The Linley sisters shon better forth deprived of the backcloth of lands they never owned. Mary, Countess of Howe, however, improbably dressed for the countryside, is beautifully, if not the dryad, the lady, of the silver birch.

55. Jane, Countess of Harrington, Sir Joshua Reynolds' masterpiece of the heiress of Time and Place.

56. For Mrs Lascelles (later Lady Harewood), mother of the Countess of Harrington, the light of sky and youth is behind, almost obscured by the wooden hill, but survives in the repose of mature beauty.

57. Gainsborough's Penelope, Viscountess Ligonier, is a study of temperament. One can almost hear the impetuous question, "How long, Mr Gainsborough, do you expect me to hold this pose? The carriage is waiting."

58. (left) Fanny Burney (aged 30) protested, "Never was Portrait so violently flattered. I have taken pains incredible to make him" (her cousin Edward) "*magnify* the Features, & darken the complection . . . it really makes me uneasy to see a Face in which the smallest resemblance to my own can be traced looking almost *perfectly* handsome." It was true, if not to Life, at least to her Art: as much a dramatisation as, (59 *lower right*), Mrs Siddons as the Tragic Muse.

60. *Marriage à la Mode*, "The visit to the Quack Doctor": it was hard to determine where medicine ended and quackery began, when "for a kind of paralitic attack in the head" Mr Linley had his pate shaved and "a blister applied" and Lady Susan Lennox recommended for cancer and "violent humours" "the juice of crow's stomack."

61. Constipation obsessed the Georgians as much as it did Victorians. In November 1817, Queen Charlotte, accompanied by the Duke of Clarence (later King William IV), took the waters at Bath. The Old Tom proffered as a specific was Strong Gin.

THE OLD MAIDS PETITION

CHAPTER ELEVEN

Old Maids

"Where there's marriage without love," wrote Benjamin Franklin in *Poor Richard's Almanac* for 1736, "there will be love without marriage."

Yet if there was one principle accepted generally throughout the Georgian period by men and women, young, old and middle-aged, it was that a marriage based simply and solely upon love, in the sense of sexual attraction, was almost certain to end unhappily. "He who marries a wife because he cannot live chastely," observed the ill-favoured Alexander Pope, "is much like a man who finding a few humours in his body, wears a perpetual blister." And Johnson told Boswell that it was a weak man who married for love.

At the age of 25, a year after Franklin published his dictum, Johnson himself had married Mrs Porter, a widow twenty years older than himself in what he later told Topham Beauclerk was "a love marriage on both sides". To outsiders Samuel Johnson and his middle-aged wife were a ludicrous couple. But widow Porter, like many another lady after her death, recognised in the physically monstrous Samuel Johnson the "most sensible man" she had ever met. Johnson was living more or less from hand to mouth and widow Porter had if not wealth at least a competence.

Dr Johnson respected wealth, provided that it was not hoarded. "Go into the street and give one man a lecture on morality and the other a shilling, and see which will respect you most. If you wish only to support nature, Sir William Petty fixes your allowance at three pounds a year; but as times are much altered, let us call it six pounds. This sum will fill your belly, shelter you from the weather, and even get you a strong lasting coat, supposing it to be made of good bull's hide. Now, Sir, all beyond this is artificial, and is desired in order to obtain a great degree of respect from our fellow-creatures. And, Sir, if six hundred pounds a year procure a man more consequence, and, of course, more happiness than six pounds a year . . ."

About six hundred pounds in all was Elizabeth Porter's fortune; but it enabled Johnson to start up a little school, consisting of David Garrick, his brother George and one other student, "young rogues" who "used to listen at the door of his bedchamber, and peep through the key-hole, that they might turn into ridicule his tumultuous and awkward fondness for Mrs Johnson, whom he used to call by the familiar appellation of *Tetty* or *Tetsy*, which, like *Betty* or *Betsey*, is provincially used as a contraction for *Elizabeth*, her Christian name, but which to us seems ludicrous when applied to a woman of her age and appearance . . . very fat, with a bosom of more than ordinary protuberance, with swelled cheeks, of a florid red, produced by thick painting, and increased by the liberal use of cordials; flaring and fantastic in her dress, and affected both in her speech and her general behaviour."

To his boyhood memory of Mrs Johnson in bed, David Garrick added his genius for mimicry. The young always imagine the ardours of sex as impossible, or at least, obscene in the older. At seventeen Jane Austen's Marianne Dashwood could not imagine the 35 year-old Colonel Brandon as marrying anyone except a nurse to tend his death-bed.

But others were more realistic about marriage and the partners whom they chose, or who were chosen for them. "Don't marry for money, but marry where money is," was a maxim I used to hear in the nineteen twenties. But in the early 18th century, the money was even more important than the name of the bride. In the early volumes of *The Gentleman's Magazine*, founded by "Sylvanus Urbanus" (Edward Cave) in 1731, the Marriage entries for each month frequently mentioned the sums of money involved and sometimes omitted the name of bride or bridegroom.

> 25th March 1735, *John Parry, Esq.*, of *Carmarthenshire*, to a daughter of *Walter Lloyd, Esq.*, member for that county, a fortune of 8,000 *l*.
> *Sir George C*, to widow *Jones*, with 10,000 *l* a year, besides ready money.
> *The Lord Bishop of St Asaph* to Miss *Orell*, with 30,000 *l*.

One wonders who stood to gain by the publication of such financial intelligence. There must have been a number of knights or baronets christened George whose surnames began with C and a battalion of widows Jones. And what of the announcement in *The Gentleman's Magazine* of 1731.

> Married, the Rev. Mr Roger Waind, of York, about twenty six years of age, to a Lincolnshire lady, upwards of eighty, with whom he is to have 8,000 *l* in money, 300 *l* per annum, and a coach-and-four during life only.

The most remarkable matrimonial notice of all was printed by Sylvanus Urbanus, I imagine, purely for its gossip value.

> The son of Mr *Graves* of Baldock in *Hertfordshire* (a lad of 14 years of age) to Mrs *Luke*, Daughter to Sir *Samuel Luke*, a Maiden Lady, aged 70.

It is impossible to decide the truth about any human situation. Was Samuel Johnson, who drank either nothing or to excess, really in love with a fantastic widow twenty years older than he, who herself was overfond of liquor? Or was it a sort of *mariage de laideur*, the discovery by two physically unendowed people of spiritual qualities which neither of them might have found if the other had been beautiful? Tetsy Johnson was his wife for eighteen years and her death plunged the Doctor deeper into the melancholy to which he was constitutionally prone. "To argue from her being much older than Johnson, or any other circumstance that he could not really love her, is absurd," Boswell wrote, with an insight not at all astonishing in a century of arranged marriages which were disarranged, of liaisons, elopements, frigidities, impotencies, bastardies and other symptoms of the failure of the human passions to be subjected to the principles of family business. "Love is not a subject of reasoning, but of feeling, and therefore there are no common principles upon which one can persuade another concerning it. Every man feels for himself, and knows how he is affected by particular qualities in the person he admires, the impressions of which are too minute and delicate to be substantiated in language."

Boswell was frank about his own marriage. Having for many years cherished a system of marrying for money, and having sex with women to whom he was drawn physically or sentimentally, he chose his first cousin, Margaret Montgomerie, poor and two years his senior, not a beauty, but sexually very attractive, "a heathen goddess". Like Henry de Montherlant's Costals, however, he wished to settle the details of the separation before the marriage. "I bargained with my bride, that I should not be bound to live with her longer than I really inclined; and that whenever I tired of her domestic society, I should be at liberty to give it up. Eleven years have elapsed, and I have never yet wished to take advantage of my stipulated privilege. Children no doubt connect man and wife most agreeably, and we have some fine ones, whom we love with mutual fondness." (Boswell, *The London Magazine*, April 1781.)

Like most 18th century males, Boswell thought and wrote about love with little regard for what women might feel. The Georgian man had a wide variety of choice. Before marriage, the sowing of wild oats was accepted as something naturally following the descent of the testicles and the voice breaking. Caution must be observed to gain experience without contracting disease. So matronly ladies would counsel not pre-marital chastity but initiation through women of mature years rather than ladies of the town, *grisettes* or *filles de chambre* (which sounded sexually more attractive than whores, shop-girls or maidservants).

The feminine point of view was infinitely more varied, delicate, vulgar, pathetic or tragic. Love played a greater part with daughters than it did with sons, and in more tortuous ways. Marriage was the ambition of most girls, even when not achieved. Each girl was dealt a different hand. This was assessed by the girl herself and by her parents or guardians. In *Evelina*, Mr Villars, who regarded his ward, as "innocent as an angel, and artless as purity itself", warned Lady Howard (to whose care he entrusted Evelina for a country visit) against exposing her to the temptations of the "circle of high life" in London.

Evelina, Fanny Burney's darling, beautiful dream girl, was fortunate enough to attract the attention of Lord Orville, an aristocrat at the same time so rich that he did not need to wed a fortune, so fastidious that he could not endure the attentions of ambitious mothers and their designing daughters and finally so discerning that he could distinguish the gold of Evelina's gifts from the dross of her acquaintance. He was prepared to contract what his, and Fanny Burney's "circle of high life", would consider a misalliance, until, to the gratification of all, Evelina's position was discovered to be socially and financially sound. Romantic love was reconciled with social status.

In real life, things happened rather differently. Consider the case of Betsy Sheridan (1758–1837). She was the youngest of Thomas Sheridan's four children by his wife Frances Chamberlain, who died in 1766. The Sheridans were of an Irish family who as a result of Jacobite sympathies were distinguished more by talent than wealth. Thomas's father had been a schoolmaster and friend of Dean Swift. Thomas spent his early years of manhood as an actor and stage manager in London and in Dublin, and his later in teaching, lecturing and writing about elocution. His circle of friends was distinguished. He commanded at one time so much influence that he persuaded the Earl of Bute to offer Dr Johnson a pension of £300 a year for his services to literature. Dictionary Johnson had written under Pension, "In England it is generally understood to mean pay given to a state hireling for treason to his country." But he accepted the pension provided no political strings were attached. A year later, Thomas Sheridan himself obtained a pension of £200 a year to write a pronouncing dictionary. "What! Have them given *him* a pension?" asked Johnson. "Then it is time for me to give up mine." He gave up Thomas Sheridan instead.

Sheridan's daughter Betsy had a vagabond upbringing. Her father's pension and other activities did not keep the duns from the door. As a child she commuted between Dublin, London, Blois and Bath until she and her sister Alicia landed back in Dublin, dependent on her elder brother Charles who had married and become a corrupt Irish MP. Her father, snobbish, tetchy and tiresome, and her brother Dick, romantic, witty and ambitious, remained in England. Life for Betsy became even more humiliating when Alicia married Joseph Le Fanu, who was a Dublin Customs Officer, leaving Betsy to the untenderness of her brother Charles and his hard wife.

Her father quarrelled first with Charles, because he failed to promote the study of elocution in Ireland. He quarrelled next with Dick because he sacked him from the business-management of Drury Lane Theatre, at the request of the actors. At this point Betsy was summoned from Ireland to look after the old man. She was young and more than pretty. The portrait of her in a Spanish hat shows her style: she had a witty mouth, shrewd eyes, a determined chin. Thomas Sheridan expected her not so much to nurse his declining years, as to forward his undeclined ambitions.

The *Journals* which she wrote for the amusement of Alicia give a vivid picture of the life she led. The first journal lasted from autumn 1784 to summer 1786, when she kept house in London or visited Bath and Tunbridge Wells. The second, resumed after a 20-month visit to Dublin with her father, described the months leading up to her father's death, her life with Dick Sheridan and his wife, in London and the country, and the early months of her marriage to Henry Le Fanu, younger brother of Alicia's husband.

Betsy had met Henry Le Fanu at her sister's house in Dublin before she went to look after her father in 1784. He was a Captain in the 56th Foot and had distinguished himself in the Siege of Gibraltar in 1779. As an officer on half-pay, Henry depended on an allowance from his father, a banker of great probity and small generosity. Betsy and Henry had reached an understanding. If Henry had been wealthier, Betsy would probably have married him and left her father to be tended in his old age by William Thompson, his family retainer. If there had been no understanding, Betsy would willingly have gone into English society and so furthered her father's ambitions.

Her *Journals*, though addressed to Alicia, were designed to be read by Joseph, Henry and perhaps "good old Mr Le Fanu", whose blessing was necessary if she and Henry were ever to marry. This secret purpose gives a subtle twist to what appear straightforward accounts of every day events. For good Mr Le Fanu it was useful to make him aware that the Sheridans mixed in fine society. For Henry, it was necessary to assure that she was heart-whole, though not for lack of admirers. For them all, it was pleasant to be amusing.

In London, Thomas Sheridan gave public and semi-private readings. He was assisted by John Henderson whose rendering of John Gilpin afforded relief to her father's weightier stuff. Betsy reported how they crammed eleven hundred people into a hall calculated for a thousand. At Mr Vesey's *conversationé* [sic] were Lords, Ladies, Bishops, "Miss Pulteney—Heiress to £30,000 a year", "Soame Jenyns the most hideous mortal I ever beheld" and Miss Hannah More "exactly *de ces figures dont on ne dit rien*".

The passage which follows might be from the pages of *Evelina*, but was designed to assure Henry Le Fanu that this grand company was none of Betsy's choosing.

> I had little pleasure from the party—conscious that I was the only person in the room who had not some consequence in life, from fortune, rank or acknowledg'd abilities, I felt alone in the crowd and could not wholly banish the mortifying ideas this consciousness necessarily brought with it. . . I never coveted the honour of sitting at great people's tables and feel the difference the world makes between a man of talents and the women of his Family unless these are at least independent.

This was the cry of countless women in similar position, without fortune, outstanding birth or artistic genius. "My own wish would be to spend the remainder of my days in that middling state of society where people are sufficiently raised to have their minds polish'd though not enough to look down on a person in my situation." What could a young woman do outside filial duty or marriage, except become a governess or lady's companion? At 27, Betsy Sheridan had fears of being left an old maid and also fears that Henry might come to look on her as such, because she had had no proposals. She wrote from Tunbridge Wells—

I am struck with a great difference in the treatment of single women here and in Ireland. It seems as in France, to be an *état*, no ridiculous jokes on *Old Maids*, no anticipation of young ones becoming so. No Man here thinks of marrying without money and, as tolerable fortunes are so much more general than in Ireland a Man finds little difficulty in uniting interest and liking. Now as the Men in Ireland who have the means of supporting a wife are very ready to overlook the want of money in a Woman who pleases them, it seems as if a girl was totally without merit, or foolishly ambitious, who remains upon hands, as they phrase it, and so I account for the disregard generally shewn there to Maiden Ladies.

Betsy succeeded in convincing her Henry. A year after her father's death they settled down to a middling state of matrimony in Ireland. But was she right in saying that ageing spinsterhood was not despised in England?

In 1673, the author of *Lady's Calling* had written "An old Maid is now . . . look'd on as the most calamitous creature". But nearly a century later Oliver Goldsmith, an Irishman existing in London as a Grub Street hack, wrote in *The Citizen of the World: or Letters from a Chinese Philosopher residing in London to his Friends in the East:*

"As for old maids," continued I (the Chinese Philosopher), "they should not be treated with so much severity, because I suppose none would be so if they could. . . . No lady could be so very silly as to live single if she could help it. I consider an unmarried lady declining into the vale of years, as one of those charming countries bordering on China that lies waste for want of inhabitants. We are not to accuse the country, but the ignorance of its neighbours, who are insensible of its beauties, though at liberty to cultivate the soil."

"Indeed, sir," replied my companion, "you are very little acquainted with the English ladies, to think they are old maids against their will. I dare venture to affirm that you can hardly select one of them all, but has had frequent offers of marriage, which either pride or avarice has not made her neglect. Instead of thinking it a disgrace, they take every occasion to boast of their former cruelty; a soldier does not exult more when he counts over the wounds he has received, than a female veteran when she relates the wounds she has formerly given: exhaustless when she begins a narrative of the former death dealing power of her eyes. She tells of the knight in gold lace, who dies with a single frown, and never rose again till—he was married to his maid; of the squire, who being cruelly denied, in a rage flew to his window, and lifting up the sash, threw himself in an agony—into an armchair; of the person who, crossed in love, resolutely swallowed opium, which banished the stings of despised love by—making him sleep. In short, she talks over her former losses with pleasure, and like some tradesmen finds consolation in the many bankruptcies she has suffered."

The assumptions of this diatribe against the excuses of unfortunate old maids are almost incomprehensible today, when there are so many opportunities of careers for women who for one reason or another have found no men they would want to have for husbands or who would want them for wives. Goldsmith could be written off as "a male chauvinist". But he was describing types recognised by his readers, when marriage was the only way out.

Miss Squeeze was a pawnbroker's daughter; her father had early taught her that money was a very good thing, and left her a moderate fortune at his death. She was so perfectly sensible of the value of what she had got, that she was resolved never to part without an equality on the part of her suitor: she thus refused several offers made by people who wanted to better themselves, as the saying is; and grew old and ill-natured, without ever considering that she should have made an abatement in her pretensions, from her face being pale, and marked with the small-pox.

Rather than the rule, old maids in Goldsmith's day were the exception; and smallpox was so prevalent that among men and women its incidence was commoner than acne among adolescents. Daughters of pawnbrokers inheriting their father's business could profitably choose a clerk of ability, or if their fathers were still living buy social preferment among the better born and worse endowed.

In most classes marriages were equal. Manservant married maidservant. Tradesman's daughter married rival tradesman's son or the industrious apprentice. Ploughman or cowherd married dairymaid. Clergyman's son married, if possible, canon's or bishop's daughter. But the younger daughter of a squire or landowner possessing a living could choose a clever, charming or handsome husband who would take the living for a dowry and influence for his advancement. So Goldsmith was right, in his man-dominated world, to detect some element of perversity in old maidship. He went on:

Lady Betty Tempest had beauty, with fortune and family. But fond of conquest, she passed from triumph to triumph; she had read plays and romances, and there had learned that a plain man was no better than a fool: such she refused, and sighed only for the gay, giddy, inconstant, and thoughtless; after she had thus rejected hundreds who liked her, and sighed for hundreds who despised her, she found herself insensibly deserted: at present she is company only for her aunts and cousins, and sometimes makes one in a country-dance, with only one of the chairs for a partner, casts off round a joint-stool and sets to a corner cupboard. In a word she is treated with civil contempt from every quarter, and placed, like a piece of old fashioned lumber, merely to fill up a corner.

Lady Tempest is the least typical of Goldsmith's old maids. He was no expert on marriage, never embarking in his lifetime on that hazardous voyage. He died in fact an "old youth" from whose head an actress who loved him as much as, but no more than he loved her, besought a lock of hair, the cause of his death being, in proportions indeterminate by *post mortem*, fever and debt.

No Lady Betty Tempest possessed with fortune and family need have been ignored in the 18th century even after her beauty had faded. There was never an age in Britain when money and the value of rank and power counted for more. Lady Betty Tempest spinster would have been courted at her deathbed by bishops, nephews, nieces and servants, provided that her fortune was not entailed.

Goldsmith's final category of old maid was the educated woman, the blue-stocking, that rarity in an age when children of both sexes shared governesses and tutors until the boys went off to Eton, Harrow or Westminster and then to the University and the Grand Tour, leaving their sisters to be taught only those maidenly arts which led to the altar.

Sophronia, the sagacious Sophronia . . . was taught to love Greek, and hate the men from her infancy; she has rejected fine gentlemen because they were not pedants, and pedants because they were not fine gentlemen; her exquisite sensibility has taught her to discover every fault in every lover, and her inflexible justice has prevented her pardoning them: thus she rejected several offers, till the wrinkles of age had overtaken her; and now, without one good feature in her face, she talks incessantly of the beauties of the mind.

Goldsmith's *Letter on Old Maids* was a newspaper essay tossed off in a day, calculated to flatter feminine frivolity and masculine philistinism. Georgian ladies were preferred to be seen and not heard, admired for beauty and even wit, but not for intellectual achievements which put to shame men whose pride was in drinking, gambling, riding and whoring hard.

Yet most of the blue stockings were married women, Mrs Montagu, Mrs Carter, Mrs Chapone and Mrs Boscawen. Lady Mary Wortley Montagu was learned enough, but no hater of men. Miss Hannah More, in Johnson's opinion the most "powerful versificatrix in the English language", never married but this was not for lack of opportunity. At the age of 22, she accepted the hand of a Mr Turner, a wealthy man twenty years older than she. Mr Turner kept putting off the marriage for six years, unable to bring himself to the altar rail. When their mutual friend, Sir James Stonehouse, tried to bring him to the point, Turner begged off, suggesting he should give Miss More an annuity of £200 a year as compensation. Hannah refused, but Sir James took the money as trustee without her knowledge, and Miss More was at last induced to accept this honorarium for the loss of her most marriageable years. Turner continued to admire her without the ties of matrimony and left her £1,000, which enabled her to go to London and shine with lunar grace reflected from Garrick, Reynolds and the Dictionary Doctor.

Hannah's father was a schoolmaster and her sisters school mistresses. Her precocious accomplishments were terrifying. Before she was four, she could say her catechism so well that the clergyman of the parish was astonished. At eight she listened to anecdotes from Plutarch. When her father started her on Latin and mathematics, he was "*frightened* at his own success" (my italics). Perhaps Mr Turner was equally frightened, knowing as well as the powerful versificatrix that More rhymed as well with Bore as Lore.

Miss Maria Edgeworth was born in 1767, twenty-two years after Hannah, and died thirteen years after her, in 1849. She was the daughter of Richard Lovell Edgeworth by the first of his four wives (not counting the daughter of his schoolmaster whom he mock-married after a dance). Maria, in an age when almost everyone was painted, never sat for a portrait. Not only was she not beautiful, but she was so short that to make her taller she was submitted as a child to a number of mechanical devices including hanging by the neck. Her eyesight was so bad that Thomas Day, author of *Sandford and Merton*, a moral tale which held the palm for boringness until it was superseded by Dean Farrar's *Eric or Little by Little*, dosed her with tar-water. Maria, versed in French and Italian, a favourite among schoolmates for her story-telling, was treated by her father with a confidentiality rare at any time.

There was a moment in 1798 when Maria betrayed resentment at her father marrying a fourth wife. But soon she and Mrs Edgeworth the fourth were the best of friends, and remained so for the next 51 years. It is very difficult to think of Maria Edgeworth as an "old maid". As well as being a prolific writer for the young and old, she was her father's literary collaborator, a woman of business and foster-mother of the children begotten by her father on her evanescent step-mothers. She was too needed by her immediate family ever to be spared to marry, even if with her natural diffidence and her physical singularity she had wanted to. Her life was full and devoid of the hates and envies of Goldsmith's Sophronia.

The span of Jane Austen's life was short. Born in 1775, eight years after Maria Edgeworth, she died thirty-two years before Maria, in 1817. All her novels end happily in the marriage of heroine and hero. Yet she herself never married. Across a life of domestic serenity among her family and friends flits the shadow of a lover. Her nephew Austen Leigh considered that he was a gentleman met at the seaside who later died suddenly. Her great-nephew, Edward, Lord Brabourne, admitted the shadow but did not think it was cast by any gentleman at the seaside. It matters little. We do not think of her as Miss Austen, an old maid pining for matrimony, but as Jane Austen one of the greatest novelists of her age and ours. Her genius flourished in surroundings less urbane than Fanny Burney's and less raw than Charlotte or Emily Brontë's. Like one of those con-cave or convex mirrors, which in her day hung over mantelshelves, it encompassed in small the immediate world at large. Though she did not publish a novel until she was 36, she spent the greater part of her life writing. Four novels were pub-lished in her lifetime, and two, *Northanger Abbey* and *Persuasion*, in the year after her death. But all of them, including *Emma* (which in its final form was written between January 1814 and March 1815), had been worked on in one form or another for many years. She was the most conscious and fastidious of artists, reaching in *Emma* a subtlety that is unsurpassed.

Jane Austen was more emotionally fulfilled by literary creation than most women by conjugal love and procreation. Yet it is from her that we learn most movingly of the "dreadful propensity for being poor" found among single women. After the death of her father in 1805, Jane, her sister Cassandra and her widowed mother, though never poverty-stricken, were dependent on the generosity of the Austen brothers for their livelihood. (Jane's literary earnings during her lifetime brought her only £700.) The spectre of poverty was more constant than the shadow of any girlhood lover. Jane Fairfax in *Emma* says, "There are places in town, offices, where inquiry would soon produce something—Offices for the sale—not quite of human flesh—but of human intellect." And later, "I was not thinking of the slave-trade . . . governess trade, I assure you, was all that I had in view; widely different certainly as to the guilt of those who carry it on; but as to the greater misery of the victims, I do not know where it lies."

This bitter comparison had been made in the previous century by Lady Mary Pierrepoint to her lover Mr Edward Wortley Montagu *à propos* of her father's higgling over a marriage settlement. "People in my way are sold as slaves, and I cannot tell what price my Master will put on me." For Jane Austen, marriage was never a slave market. This was partly because in her section of society it was not a question of the unions between great estates so much as how much money a year was necessary for the happiness of the married parties. For Elinor Dashwood wealth was £1,000 a year and she married Edward Ferrars on £850 which was as much "as was desired, and more than was expected", though "they were neither of them quite enough in love to think that three hundred and fifty pounds a year would supply them with the comforts of life." Her sister Marianne, the creature of "sensibility", who does not think money matters supposing that she has a competence of £2,000 a year, prefers to her first love Willoughby, who would have had only £750 a year for their dashing way of life, the 35 year-old "ninny" Colonel Brandon, who, "because he has two thousand a year himself, he thinks that nobody else can marry on less".

This was the arithmetic of marriage among the upper middle class in Jane Austen's day. Elinor the girl of "sense" made a marriage of "sensibility". Marianne the girl of "sensibility" made a marriage of "sense". Jane Austen, the marital mathematician, was not concerned with praise or blame. Both marriages, as calculations, were right.

In all her novels, Jane Austen remains, unmarried, in equipoise, like someone in the centre of a seesaw, able by bending a little this way or that to change the balance. In *The Watsons*, which was an earlier version of *Emma*, Emma Watson says, "Poverty is a great Evil, but to a woman of Education and feeling, it ought not, it cannot be the greatest.—I would rather be Teacher at a School (and I can think of nothing worse) than marry a Man I did not like." To which her sister answers, "I would rather do anything than be a Teacher at a school. *I* have been at school, Emma, and know what a life they lead; *you* never have."

This was why Jane Austen was literally a "balanced" writer. She was always on the brink, but never forced to take the plunge. She did not have to earn a living by writing. She never had to compromise her reputation, or expose her private life to prevent the duns clapping her into the Fleet. She never needed to tout for subscriptions or employ a pen for blackmail. She never found herself a penurious celebrity who accepted drudgery as a royal lady's maid as a means of livelihood. She never hacked for the theatre or in Grub Street. She did not struggle to teach or governess or indulge in politics. She never became pregnant and tried to commit suicide. She never made herself an object of ridicule and contempt. She was not concerned with the vindication of women's rights or the salvation of souls.

She was tall and slender, graceful and delighted to dance. She had brown hair, which caused her no difficulty with papering, the long hair plaited under her cap and the short naturally curly. She had hazel eyes, fine features and zest for ordinary things. She loved family jokes like calling mutton chops "chutton mops". Her humour was so amiable that one gets a slight shock when reading, "Mrs Hall, of Sherborne, was brought to bed yesterday of a dead child, some weeks before she expected, owing to a fright. I suppose she happened unaware to look at her husband." It indicates her limitation.

She was incapable of tragedy. Life in her novels was as neat and demonstrable as the theorems of Euclid. Instead of writing at the bottom of the last page Finis or The End, one feels that she might have written Q.E.D. She was completely honest about the people of whom she chose to write. But there were many other Georgian ladies, who were outside her concern yet must be ours.

CHAPTER TWELVE

Marriages of Convenience

Talking of marriage in general, he observed, "Our marriage service is too refined. It is calculated only for the best kind of marriages; whereas we should have a form for matches of convenience, of which there are many." Boswell, *The Life of Johnson*.

The marriage of convenience was the inevitable result of family entail, a custom generally accepted among families of title and great fortunes. The head of the family was half way between a feudal lord and the proprietor of a great business. As well as wealth, he had influence. He could command seats in Parliament, as a result of which he could secure for himself political power and for others sinecures or royal places. He owned livings, the income from which could support political parsons who might give an elegance of style, and an appearance of impartiality, to the views he wished to promote. The wealth and happiness of his other relatives was subject to his whim.

Mrs Elizabeth Montagu, a blue-stocking whose husband mined and marketed vast reserves of coal found under his estates, was one of the few to criticise the system of entail; though being childless she could not induce her husband to exemplify a more rational scheme of inheritance. Writing to her clerical brother in 1762, she observed:

I suppose you have heard of the death of Sir Edward Dering, which was sudden. He has entailed everything on his grandson, and left but very small fortune to his younger children. People seem to think that by making one person in their family very rich, they can make one very happy; but, alas! happiness cannot be carried beyond a certain pitch. Competency will make every one easy: great wealth cannot make one happy. It is strange, parents should feel only for one child, or, indeed, that the heir should be dearer than the child; for it is as heir they show their regards to one of the family. No personal merit, no tender attachment, no sympathy of disposition can over-rule that circumstance. Sir Edward Dering dyed very rich . . .

The head of the family looked upon his sisters and his younger brothers if not as employees, at least as assistants who should be rewarded proportionately to their obedience to his aims. For the men, politics or the church, the courts of law or royalty, the Army or Navy and as the century proceeded the service of the East India Company offered careers, whose rewards could be supplemented or furthered by suitable marriages of convenience. Where there was more than one marriage, it was usual that the first wife should be nobly born and the succeeding wives richly endowed: though of course both were always preferable. It was pardonable for any young man to fall in love with a beauty of a lower station, provided that he did not marry her. If he did, he could expect no further favours from the head of his house.

Girls had their roles allotted to them; one to marry a fortune, another to ally two political families, a third to merge landed estates, a fourth to serve in a royal household. In some cases they had a latitude of choice, according to their preference. But woe betide them, if they demeaned their social status. Boswell relates how Dr Johnson pronounced to Mrs Thrale:

Were I a man of rank, I would not let a daughter starve who had made a mean marriage; but having voluntarily degraded herself from the station which she was originally entitled to hold, I would support her only in that which she herself had chosen; and would not put her on a level with my other daughters. You are to consider, Madam, that it is our duty to maintain the subordination of civilised society; and when there is a gross and shameful deviation from rank, it should be punished so as to deter others from the same perversion.

Mrs Thrale was all for mildness and forgiveness, Boswell tells us. Her first marriage, to Henry Thrale, had been undertaken to please an uncle, who threatened to disinherit her if she refused, and then promptly disinherited her by marrying another lady. After Thrale's death, she fell in love with the Italian pianist Piozzi and to the disgust of her daughters and her dear young friend Fanny Burney, married him. As an Italian and a musician, Piozzi was considered doubly undesirable for the widow of a wealthy brewer.

When he wrote his life of Dr Johnson, Boswell took every opportunity he could to denigrate Mrs Thrale who, as the author of *Thraliana*, had appeared as the closest friend of the great Doctor. In this passage, Boswell went on to emphasise his own agreement with Johnson.

It is weak and contemptible, and unworthy, in a parent to relax in such a case. It is sacrificing general advantage to private feelings. And let it be considered, that the claim of a daughter who has acted thus, to be restored to her former situation, is either fanatical or unjust. If there be no value in the distinction of rank, what does she suffer by being kept in the situation to which she has descended? If there be a value in that distinction, it ought to be steadily maintained. If indulgence be shown to such conduct, and the offenders know that in a longer or shorter time they shall be received as well as if they had not contaminated their blood by a base alliance, the great check upon that inordinate caprice which generally occasions low marriages, will be removed, and the fair and comfortable order of improved life will be miserably disturbed.

The contamination of blood by base alliances is immoderate language to describe the "misalliances" of Lady Sarah Lennox and her friend Lady Susan Fox Strangeways. Lady Sarah, fourth daughter of Charles, 2nd Duke of Richmond, the young love of the infatuated King George III, was married at the age of seventeen to Charles Bunbury, owner of Diomed, the first Derby winner. Sir Charles was more interested in breeding horses than children. When Lady Sarah conceived a daughter by her cousin Lord William Gordon, she left her husband and went to live for twelve years in Goodwood Park, unreproached by her brother, the third Duke of Richmond. She was divorced by Sir Charles Bunbury after he had made several attempts to win her back; and then she committed the social blunder of marrying the Hon. George Napier, second son of Francis, 5th Baron Napier. Napier was a professional soldier who had served all through the American War. His only crimes were that he was poor and honest. Lady Sarah had £500 a year and Napier's army pay was slightly less. When he was made Deputy Quartermaster-General to the army in Holland in 1794 and controller of army accounts in Ireland in 1799, he could have made a fortune, as Lady Sarah's brother-in-law Henry Fox, 1st Lord Holland, had done when pay-master general. But because he preferred uncommon probity to common corruption, he and his wife were despised as poor relations.

Similarly her friend Lady Susan Fox Strangeways could have made a brilliant match. The Duke of Gloucester and Charles Fox were among her admirers: but she chose William O'Brien, an Irishman of good family, that had been impoverished through adherence to the Jacobite cause. His two crimes were that he was poor and he had chosen the stage as a profession. Lord and Lady Ilchester, Lady Susan's parents, behaved towards their daughter in the way which Johnson and Boswell approved. Because the O'Briens desperately needed help, they were denied it. If biblical authority was needed for such behaviour, it lay to hand. "From him that hath not, even that which he hath shall be taken away."

Though Dr Johnson approved of arranged marriages, he thought the method of arrangement could have been bettered. "I believe marriages would in general be as happy, and often more so, if they were all made by the Lord Chancellor upon a due consideration of the characters and circumstances, without the parties having any choice in the matter."

The lady who in her old age was known as Mrs Delany, and whom Burke pronounced "the fairest model of female excellency of the days that were passed" would have agreed with him. She was born in 1700. the daughter of Bernard Granville, who was younger brother to Lord Lansdowne. Her paternal aunt, Ann, was maid of honour to Queen Mary. Mary Granville grew up expecting to be taken into the household of Queen Anne. But when the last Stuart queen died, the Granvilles suffered the same reversal of fortune as other Jacobite Tories.

Lord Lansdowne was imprisoned in the Tower for eighteen months. Her parents were arrested on suspicion of trying to escape to France; and when they were released, they retired to the country, subsisting on a small allowance from Lord Lansdowne.

While there, Colonel Granville became involved in an abortive Jacobite plot. Among his fellow conspirators was a young man called Twyford, who had expectations of wealth.

When Mary was sixteen, Twyford asked her father for her hand in marriage. The Colonel told Twyford that he must get his parents' approval, which he feared would be withheld from a girl without dowry or prospect of advancement in the Hanoverian court. Before he left, Twyford took Mary aside and begged her to marry him secretly, if his parents disapproved. She replied that she was no actress. She was prepared to marry him, but not without parental consent. She was an obedient daughter, but if she was in love with anyone, it was with Sarah Kirkham, the daughter of a neighbouring clergyman. The proposal came to nothing.

When her uncle, Lord Lansdowne, was released from the Tower, he invited the Colonel and his daughter to stay at Longleat, the estate which his 27 year-old wife had inherited from her first husband. Gay, fashionable and luxury-loving, Lady Lansdowne planned to celebrate her 50 year-old husband's release with country parties that would compensate for their exile from London. So when Bernard asked his brother to increase his allowance, he was told to cut down his expenses. Mary, on the other hand, was invited to prolong her stay indefinitely. A charming young poor relation appeared a useful asset to the hostess of Longleat.

It was not so long, however, before the residents of Longleat separated into two factions. On the one side were Lady Lansdowne and her sister, descendants of Barbara Villiers, the Duchess of Cleveland, "at once the fairest and the lewdest of royal concubines"; on the other the poetical Lord Lansdowne and his niece, with Henry Villiers, Lady Lansdowne's brother as a sort of go-between. Old Lansdowne found in Mary someone who liked books as much as he did. He would take her off to the library, where in her husky, beautiful voice she read him from Shakespeare, Milton, Pope and Prior, while in some chamber perhaps thirty yards away his young wife, the centre of all attention except theirs, listened to music, played cards, exchanged scandal and received compliments.

Lady Lansdowne decided that the best way to rid herself of Mary and rid her husband of his brother's requests for money would be to marry her to a fortune. And what better opportunity was there than when Alexander Pendarves, Lansdowne's old crony, wrote to say that he was going to London to alter his will, and might he break his journey at Longleat?

Mr Pendarves, the owner of Roscrow Castle in Cornwall, was rich, but even by the standards of an unfastidious age he was unattractive. He was 60, a heavy drinker, plagued by the gout, testy, snuffy and malodorous. A bachelor who had let himself go, he had quarrelled with Francis his nephew and heir, because the whippersnapper refused to change his name from Bassett to Pendarves, if he inherited. The Lansdownes talked it over. Mary was a dutiful daughter. What did filthy habits and a hasty temper matter in a husband who had not long to live, provided he had the fortune to sustain his young widow and relieve her indigent parents?

Mary was not forewarned. Mr Pendarves arrived, as she said, "like Hob out of the wall", one evening in the middle of dinner. He was sopping wet after a hard day's riding and was shown straight into the dining room. His wig was askew. His boots were plastered with mud. His complexion, florid with years of drinking, was empurpled with wind and rain. Mary caught the eye of Henry Villiers and they became so convulsed with laughter that they had to leave the room.

Pendarves had intended to stay only one night. But the fondness of his old friend's reminiscences and the excellence of his port induced the Cornish squire to stay on. Mary and Henry Villiers were delighted, because they had never seen anything so exquisitely absurd as his grotesquery.

Mary suspected nothing, until she noticed the way Mr Pendarves, old enough to be her grandfather, followed her every movement and Henry suddenly stopped joining in her mockery. As she realised the obscene plot afoot, she became alarmed. In her room, she could not keep from tears. In company with him and others, she was cold, curt and indifferent. If he came into a room where she was alone, she walked out. Her only defence was to make it obvious that she loathed him.

When Henry Villiers started to pay her exaggerated attentions, she responded. Henry invited her to go with him on excursions which her gouty old suitor could not undertake. She accepted, hoping that this would shake him off. But it only egged the randy sexagenarian on. One evening over the port, Mr Pendarves proposed—not of course to Mary, but to her uncle. And on her behalf, Lord Lansdowne accepted.

How drunk Lord Lansdowne was that night we do not know; nor how he was bullied by his wife in the following days. But it was not till several evenings later that he asked Mary to join him before dinner in the library where she had so happily read to him. Then he laid before her the splendid prospect of becoming mistress of Roscrow Castle. He explained what a compliment it was that his old friend Mr Pendarves, so rich, so generous, so respected in the Duchy, should offer his hand to a dowerless girl. He expatiated on the advantages of a young girl marrying an older man, who could set her up for remarriage according to her choice, while she was still in full beauty. He used reason, persuasion and all the appeals of family loyalty and obedience to which any dutiful young lady should accede. Then, when she said nothing, he accused her of still loving Twyford. She began to weep, thinking that perhaps she had been wrong in not accepting a clandestine marriage with a personable young man whom she did not love. "If Twyford ever shows his face at Longleat," he shouted, "I'll have him dragged through the horsepond." He stormed and he threatened. But it was not until he said that if Mary did not marry, she would have to leave Longleat, that she finally gave way. She would marry Mr Pendarves, she said, on condition that she was excused appearing that evening before his guests. Lord Lansdowne gave his permission and she retired to her room.

He hurried to Pendarves to assure him of his victory. But his old friend was not content. He demanded that Mary should be exhibited to the assembled company as his bride-to-be, rather as captive chieftains were led in triumph through the streets of Rome.

Her parents' delight decided Mary to make the best of so repulsive a match. Two months spent at Longleat after the wedding were passed in company, and the old man, having secured his prize, was more anxious to exhibit than despoil her. During that un-honeymoon, news came that Twyford had been stricken with palsy. Mary wondered if she was to blame.

Mary won her husband's consent to take her brother to keep her company at Roscrow Castle. They spent two weeks on the journey, stopping at every friend's house for Pendarves to show off the bride he had bought. The Cornish castle proved as decrepit and the staff as slovenly as its master. But Mary enjoyed exploring the countryside with her brother.

After he left, Pendarves insisted on taking Mary to stay with Francis Bassett and his wife to show how much he had lost by refusing to change his name to Pendarves. The nephew took revenge by paying such court to Mary that the old man was filled with jealousy. "Take care of Francis," the old man warned Mary. "He is a cunning treacherous man, and has been the ruin of one woman already who was the wife of his bosom friend." Pendarves was haunted by the resemblance of his marriage to that of the Pinchwifes in Wycherley's comedy. But when Mary suggested they leave at once for home, he insisted on staying with the Bassetts another ten days.

Mary was in fact a constant wife. She refused the advances of other men; and spent her time on improving Roscrow Castle, since her husband was so little capable of improvement. Three years passed without disaster. When Mr Pendarves had to visit London to see about his investments in the South Sea Scheme, he allowed the Granville parents to keep his wife company. They were impressed by the castle, visited tombs of Granville ancestors in the neighbourhood and Colonel Granville even flirted with the idea of a little Jacobite sedition. For the first time in her married life, Mary was happy. Grass widowhood became her.

Then Pendarves summoned her to London. The South Sea Bubble was about to burst. She found him living in Rose Street, Hog Lane, Soho, with his sister and her husband, "a cunning Scot". The sister ran the household, regardless of Mary while Mr Pendarves, frantic with worry, devoted himself to drinking and gambling between attacks of gout. Aged twenty and now a beauty, Mary was launched in London society by her aunt Ann, Lady Stanley. She gave up hurrying home from the opera, from dinners or masquerades, when she found her husband did not come home till dawn, often carried in insensible.

Mary Pendarves was regarded as fruit ripe for the picking. The Hanoverian Ambassador, M. Fabrici, pursued her, when Pendarves moved from the squalor of Soho to a rural slum in Windsor. He engaged the King's mistress Lady Walsingham (the erstwhile Melusinda de Schulemberg) to act as his procuress and would have raped her in Windsor Little Park, if Mary had not threatened to appeal to the King, who could be seen through the windows as he dined.

George I had proved less severe on Jacobites than had been feared. The Lansdownes, who had gone into self-exile, returned to London. Lady Lansdowne, less beautiful but more vicious than when she had plotted Mary's marriage to Pendarves, tried to wreck that marriage by aiding her discarded lover Lord Clare to take Mary by force, if he could not seduce her by assiduity. Rather than take a lover, Mary decided to give up the Lansdowne circle and devote herself to the old man, now so riddled with gout he could not drink or gamble.

Now came the twist that Restoration dramatists loved. Pendarves, once the jealous husband, thought that by nursing him, his wife was neglecting important social and financial contacts. He made her go back, where Lady Lansdowne was waiting to set Lord Clare upon her behind locked doors, while she sat watching. It was the sort of scene which Casanova played successfully with more sophisticated performers. But Mary was too modest, Lady Lansdowne too shameless and Lord Clare too aware of being the puppet of his old mistress for him to win a new one.

When Pendarves recovered from his gout, he returned to his old life and she to hers: until one evening returning home from a mask, to her surprise she found her husband already home. He said many kind things of her having been so good a wife. Next day he would alter his will. He was so gentle that, perhaps for the first time, she realised that this gross sot had loved her in a way he could not express because of the burdens of age and habit he had acquired before he arrived, drenched, filthy and bespattered during the elegant dinner at Longleat.

She put him to bed and went in beside him. His breathing was not that of a drunken man. It was hours before she slept.

When she woke at seven, she pulled the curtains from the bed. His face was black. What uncle Lansdowne had prophesied seven years before was true. She was a young widow.

But she was not a rich widow. Mr Pendarves had not squandered his whole fortune, but there was no will in her favour. All she inherited was her jointure, bringing in not thousands, but a few hundred a year. As a matter of convenience, the marriage had proved as much a failure, as in other ways.

Mary Pendarves was now free to choose a husband who pleased her. Charles Calvert, Lord Baltimore, courted her for five years, but when she hesitated, he transferred his affections to another lady. Shaken by this and by the death of her aunt, Lady Stanley, she went to stay with a friend in Dublin. There she met Dean Swift and the Reverend Patrick Delany, whom she married in 1743, to the indignation of her brother, the dear Duchess of Portland and other aristocratic friends. She who had hesitated was determined not to be lost a second time. They spent a quarter of a century happily married; and when Dr Delaney died in 1768, she lived on for another twenty years, watching the new generations growing up, marrying for convenience or love, breeding, flirting, divorcing. She became an institution regaling her juniors with stories of the five reigns through which she had lived. At the age of 74, she started to make flowers in paper mosaic with such an accuracy and skill that they are now preserved in the British Museum. When she was presented to the royal family, King George III called her his "dearest Mrs Delany" and Queen Charlotte accepted a specimen of her flower work as a "lowly tribute of her humble duty and earnest gratitude". When the Duchess of Portland died, the King gave Mrs Delany, by then nearly blind, a house in Windsor and a pension of £300. Nearly seventy years had passed since his grandfather the first George had arrested her parents and imprisoned her uncle on the suspicion of treason. She was a woman rewarded for the integrity with which she accepted the social rules of her times.

Lord Chesterfield never achieved marital happiness for himself. He saw it as an equation between wealth and merit; a marriage of true minds and full purses. As he put it in his letter congratulating his friend Baron Torck on his wedding.

> If marriage can be happy, which I believe possible, yours ought to be. If I should find a match in which the appearances were as good as yours, I should take the step also . . . feminine merit without money would not suffice, and money without merit would be a turbulent mixture.

Lord Chesterfield himself never found so happy a combination. Mlle du Bouchet gave him a son, Philip Stanhope, on whom he lavished paternal advice, at the same time austere and hedonistic. He did not marry until he was 39, and then he chose the illegitimate daughter of George I and Countess Ehrengard Melusina von der Schulenberg, Duchess of Kendal. Petronella, Countess Walsingham, was aged 40 and her portion was £50,000, with £3,000 a year payable out of the civil list revenue in Ireland. They lived next door to one another; and to celebrate his marriage, Lord Chesterfield took a new mistress. The marriage was financially very successful. Instead of prosecuting George II for destroying a will leaving the Countess of Walsingham £40,000, bequeathed to her mother by George I, he settled out of court for half that sum.

The reconciliation of sexual desire and marital convenience was a major concern of the century. Two great comedies played on this theme. In *She Stoops to Conquer*, Marlow rejects the heiress of his father's choice but falls in love with her when he thinks she is an innkeeper's daughter. In *The Rivals*, Lydia Languish, a Marlow in petticoats, falls romantically in love with the penniless ensign Beverley, and is nonplussed to find he is the wealthy Captain Absolute in disguise. Both Goldsmith and Sheridan satisfied the needs of love and money.

There was a precedent in real life. A noble lord, married for convenience, as a boy never lived with his bride. But several years later, meeting a ravishing beauty at the theatre, he made advances to her, which he discovered were not improper, because she was his wife.

Revolt against the marriage of convenience led to hasty and impetuous elopements. But in the annals of galloping lovers none matched the absurdity of Lady

Mary Pierrepoint's cautious elopement with Mr Edward Wortley Montagu.

Her father had been born Evelyn Pierrepoint; but he succeeded to the title of Marquis of Dorchester and was created Duke of Kingston by George I. Mary was his eldest child. Her mother died when she was eight and she became prematurely her father's hostess. At the Kit-Cat Club, her father nominated her as the toast for beauty, and when his Whig club mates demanded to see this enchantress, a message was sent and the eight year-old child in her best dress was produced and dandled on the knees of wits and poets. Or so legend goes; and Lady Mary was not one to discourage legend. Her education was not as assiduous or as terrifying as Hannah More's or Maria Edgeworth's. She had the run of her father's libraries. (He had five seats, at Arlington St., in London, at Acton outside, at Thoresby, Holm Pierrepoint and West Dean.) She educated herself, by and large. She devoured poetry, though she despised the pastorals.

While she was supposed to be reading romances, she spent two years teaching herself Latin, to such good purpose that she was able to send Burnet, Bishop of Salisbury, her translation into English of a Latin rendering of the *Enchiridion* of Epictetus, accompanied by a long letter, touching on the education of women, ("My sex is usually forbidden studies of this nature, and folly reckoned so much our proper sphere we are sooner pardoned any excess of that than the least pretensions to reading or good sense"), while not venturing to assert an equality between the sexes, ("God and nature have thrown us into an inferior rank," etc.) The young lady who subscribed herself "Your Lordship's most respectful and obliged" was no ordinary young lady, and well she knew it.

She was not just a bookworm. Later in her life she kept poultry, taught her Italian neighbours how to make butter and initiated them into the delights of "custards, cheesecakes and minced pies". When she was old enough, she carved for her father's guests at Thoresby and played his hostess. It was not until after Lady Mary married that her father troubled to marry again. With Mary as his housewife, he had more time for his mistresses.

Mr Edward Wortley, or alternatively Mr Edward Wortley Montagu, the man with whom she was eventually to elope, was aged 25 when he first met Lady Mary with his young sister Anne. Lady Mary was only fourteen, and we are told he was so impressed at her knowledge of Latin and her ignorance of Quintus Curtius, that he sent her a handsome copy of the works of Curtius inscribed upon the fly-leaf:

> Beauty like this had vanquished Persia shown,
> The Macedon had laid his empire down,
> And polished Greece obeyed a barb'rous throne.
> Had wit so bright adorned a Grecian dame,
> The am'rous youth had lost his thirst for fame,
> Nor distant India sought through Syria's plain;
> But to the Muses' stream with her had run,
> And thought her lover more than Ammon's son.

Lady Louisa Stuart, to whom we owe the preservation of these verses, adds:

How soon this declaration of love in verse was followed by one in prose does not appear; but Mrs Anne Wortley grew more eloquent in Lady Mary's praise, and more eagerly desirous of her correspondence. No wonder; since the rough draft letter of a letter in her brother's hand, indorsed "For my sister to Lady M.P." betrays that he was the writer, and she only the transscriber of professions and encomiums that sound extravagant as addressed by one woman to another.

Lady Mary was as aware that Anne Wortley's letters to her were written by Mr Wortley, as Henry Le Fanu was that Betsy Sheridan's letters to her sister Alicia were written, if not *to*, at least *for* him. She replied in a manner the more ardent, for being oblique. "I shall certainly love you, do what you will." "My dear, dear, adieu! I am entirely yours and wish nothing more than that it may be some time or other in my power to convince you that there is nobody dearer than yourself." "I cannot help answering your letter this minute, and telling you I infinitely love you . . ."

The first two of these excerpts were from letters written in 1707, the last from one dated 1709. The affair had begun in 1703 or 1704 and was obviously quickening towards a proposal of marriage. Not by the standards of the time, any too soon. Lady Mary was aged twenty, and many girls of her class were married at 16 or 17.

Then suddenly Mrs Anne Wortley died.

Mr Wortley sent Lady Mary some copies of the *Tatler*, in acknowledgment of which Lady Mary wrote:

Mr Bickerstaff has very wrong notions of our sex. I can say there are some of us that despise charms of show, and all the pageantry of greatness, perhaps with more ease than any of the philosophers . . . I carry the matter yet farther; was I to choose of 2,000 *l.* a year or twenty thousand, the first would by my choice.

By the death of his elder brother, Mr Wortley had expectations of a great fortune, if he survived his father. But meanwhile his income was less than the lowly figure Lady Mary declared acceptable. Her notion of a competence exceeded his wealth. Nor was she satisfied with what must have been his declaration of love. She wrote:

Give me leave to say it, (I know it sounds vain), I know how to make a man of sense happy; but then that man must resolve to contribute something toward it himself. I have so much esteem for you, I should be very sorry to hear you was unhappy; but for the world I would not be the instrument of making you so; which (of the humours you are) is hardly to be avoided if I am your wife. You mistrust me—I can neither be easy, nor loved, where I am distrusted. Nor do I believe your passion for me is what you pretend it; at least I am sure was I in love I could not talk as you do . . . I wish I loved you enough to devote myself to be for ever miserable, for the pleasure of a day or two's happiness. I cannot resolve upon it. You must think otherwise of me, or not at all.

I don't enjoin you to burn this letter, I know you will. 'Tis the first I ever wrote to one of your sex, and shall be the last. You may never expect another. I resolve against all correspondence of the kind; my resolutions are seldom made, and never broken.

Mr Wortley did not burn the letter: and, though it was unmaidenly for a young lady to write letters to a gentleman without permission from her parent or guardian, Lady Mary continued to do so, when she found that Mr Wortley could not be provoked into asking her father for her hand in marriage. Their protracted correspondence reads less like love letters, than despatches between high contracting parties, seeking a *detente*.

While Anne Wortley was alive, it had been easy for Mr Wortley to meet Lady Mary. Now the house of Mr and Mrs Richard Steele became their clandestine meeting place. Letters were conveyed secretly by orange women and servants. But their association was bound to be discovered sooner or later.

In the spring of 1710, Evelyn Pierrepoint, now Lord Dorchester, was made aware of the correspondence; and there was a series of violent scenes between father and daughter, father and lover, lover and lover, which culminated in Mr Wortley finally asking her father for Lady Mary's hand in marriage. This formed the climax of Lady Mary's unpublished romance entitled *Sebastian and Laetitia* (of which "not a *sillable*" was "fictitious except the names".) But in real life it was merely the prelude to a new phase of fencing courtship.

Lord Dorchester accepted Mr Wortley's proposal: on one condition. Mr Wortley should entail his estate on his eldest son. This was the established practice: but Mr Wortley thought that a man who entailed his estate did not know that two and two made four; and wrote so to his friend Addison, who duly published an essay on entailing estates in the *Tatler*. It made good sense to many people, but not to the Marquess of Dorchester.

From being a niggling duologue, the marital negotiations became a niggling triologue. Lady Mary took sides with Mr Wortley against her father on the question of entail. But their old battles raged. Neither would confess to a passion which might have inspired a passion in the other. This was the age of Reason, which in affairs of the heart proved irrational.

Two years passed and thousands of words, arguing every which way by clandestine correspondence, with an animation and repetitiousness as if they had been married for years, instead of never having exchanged a kiss. A lady's reputation resided not in what she did, but in what she might be considered to have done. The arrangement of rendezvous was a matter of endless niceties, with the delicacy of Lady Mary and the jealousy of Mr Wortley confounding confusions.

Underlying all this was on Lady Mary's side, the possible attractions of a Mr D. and Mr K: and on Mr Wortley's side, whether he might take her without any marriage settlement, rather than accede to the marquess's demands. It might, thought Wortley, a shrewd Yorkshireman, prove less expensive in the long run.

This might have gone on forever, if Mr K. (who was rich and had estates in Ireland) had not put up a proposal which the Marquess of Dorchester was prepared to accept on Lady Mary's behalf. Menaced with this, Lady Mary preferred to accept Mr Wortley with all his imperfections. Her father threatened to leave her only an annuity of £400 a year unless she married Mr K. Lady Mary said she would prefer to live single. Mr Wortley's name she did not dare to mention.

The Marquess of Dorchester was beginning to grow impatient. Earlier in 1712 he had got rid of his second daughter, Evelyn, on John, Earl of Gower. Two years before, he had married off his son, Lord Kingston, while he was still under age. Lady Mary was 23 and it was high time he was shot of her. Mr K. was the obvious solution, as even Mr Wortley agreed. Unless Lady Mary really meant (of which he was not assured) she did not want to marry Mr K.

There was never a more reluctant eloper than Mr Wortley, nor was there a more reluctant elopee than Lady Mary. Lady Mary brought him to the point of saying that if she would fix time and place, he would be there with a coach and six. But he warned, after nine years of correspondence with the lady, the best thing to do would be to avoid speaking until they were married, lest they started to quarrel again.

Continental visitors were always surprised at the *mauvaise honte*, the bashfulness of the British. Lady Mary and Mr Wortley in their courtship were supreme examples of this. But once their resolve to elope was made, barriers were down on both sides. Or at least on Mr Wortley's. "I will only be yours, and I will do what you please," he wrote. "Love me and use me well."

Even then Lady Mary hesitated. As a female wit, she hated Mr K. Mr Wortley was the most sympathetic man she had met. Their elopement from Acton was foiled by her father. But the second attempt succeeded; and after the arguments, the frustrations and bargainings of years, they found a wonderful release.

Though this appears a comedy of non-committal, the reluctant elopers were proved right. Their heir, Edward Wortley, turned out a wastrel, on whom Wortley's estate would have been squandered, if entailed. Lady Mary Wortley Montagu, after having accompanied her husband to Turkey, as the British Ambassador's wife, returned to begin a career that put her husband's in the shade.

She became the friend of Pope and later with Lord Hervey, Pope's enemy. Then at the age of 47, she met Francesco Algarotti, a handsome young Italian adventurer, who arrived in London with a letter of introduction to Lord Hervey from Voltaire. Lady Mary had collaborated with Lord Hervey in satiric verse; but over the affections of the ambisextrous Francesco, they fell into rivalry. Lady Mary left Mr Wortley and went to live in Italy so that Francesco could enjoy her charms without scandal. When he failed to join her, she did not return. Though she corresponded with Mr Wortley, she never saw him again in her life.

Lady Louisa Stuart was a grand-daughter of Lady Mary Wortley Montagu on her mother's side. She was also the niece of another Lady Mary, whose inconvenient marriage to Lord Coke, the only son of the Earl of Leicester, was a scandal far more resounding than the elopement of the Wortley Montagus. Lady Louisa wrote about them both for the instruction of her family. Her memoirs derived from the gossip of the earlier Georgians. Though tempered for the sensibilities of those who were to become the eminently respectable Victorians, they provided a sense of what family tradition was, when almost any lady of quality was related remotely to any other, and the follies, eccentricites, *amours* and *bêtises* of ancestors beguiled the evenings of their children and succeeding generations.

For Lady Louisa, Lady Mary Wortley Montagu was positively remarkable, but Lady Mary Coke was superlatively eccentric:

> . . . a study for the observers of human character as a rare plant or animal would be for the naturalist. Her beauty had not been undisputed. . . . Some allowed, some denied it; the dissenters declaring her neither more nor less than a white cat—a creature to which her dead whiteness of skin, unshaded by eyebrows, and the fierceness of her eyes, did give her a great resemblance. To make amends, there were fine teeth, an agreeable smile, a handsome neck, well shaped hands and arms, and a majestic figure. She had the reputation of cleverness when young, and, in spite of all her absurdity, could not be called a silly woman; but she was so invincibly wrong-headed—her understanding lay smothered under so much pride, self-conceit, prejudice, obstinacy, and violence of temper, that you did not know where to look for it, and seldom indeed did you catch such a distinct view of it as certified its existence. So also her good qualities were seen only like the stars that glimmer through shifting clouds on a tempestuous night; yet she really had several. Her principles were religious. She was sincere, honourable, good-natured where passion did not interfere, charitable, and (before old age had sharpened economy into avarice) sometimes generous. For her friendships, they were only too warm and too zealous for the peace of the mortals upon whom they were bestowed—I am afraid I might say inflicted.

Lady Louisa Stuart found Lady Mary as wrong-headed as Don Quixote, except that he was mad, and she merely wrongheaded. "If she could have been committed a close prisoner to the Tower on a charge of High Treason, examined before the Privy Council, and of course gloriously acquitted, by the House of of Lords, it would have given her more delight than any other thing physically possible." She was one of those self-dramatising women, who, denied the stage, enacted her own plays in private and public life.

Youngest daughter of John, Duke of Argyll and Greenwich, by his second wife, she was born in 1726. When she was of marriageable age, the Earl of

Leicester's family made approaches to the Duchess of Argyll on behalf of his heir Lord Coke (pronounced Cook). After long haggling, it was agreed that for her £20,000, she should have £2,500 a year jointure and £500 a year pin money, which was a better rate than could be secured from the City. The financial terms were so good because the bridegroom's morals were so bad. Lord Coke was as dissolute and violent as his father. The Duchess hesitated until young Coke displayed his charm and his friends assured her that, having sown his wild oats, he would settle down and reap good harvests.

Lady Mary had shown that she liked young Coke, before ever the conveyances set to work. But as Lord Coke wooed her mother to acceptance of the match, Lady Mary drew further away. Lord Coke did not worry. He was as proud as she and when the marriage was celebrated he intended to take his revenge.

Lady Betty, Lady Mary's sister, begged her to call the marriage off, when she found Lady Mary weeping all the morning above stairs and in the evening sunk in the gloom below stairs. "No," said Lady Mary, "it will be time enough at the altar."

But when they came to the altar, instead of saying "No!", Lady Mary said "Yes." And when the moment came to consummate the marriage, Lord Coke, unwilling to take by force what she was too proud or frightened to surrender voluntarily, "begged she would make herself easy, and wished her a very good night."

It was an inauspicious start. Lady Mary could have borne the indignity of being raped by her husband. But Lord Coke's unwillingness to attempt it was humiliating. He reverted to his old habits of gaming and drinking. When they were alone together, he gave his wife pretty coarse language, though before company it was nothing but "My love! My life! My angel!" He abused her dead father, mocked her mother and lost no opportunity of taunting her. According to her lawyers, "she ever comported herself in a courteous and obliging manner . . . being of a sober, modest, chaste and virtuous conversation, and of a meek mild and affable temper and disposition." Lady Louisa thought this might in fact be true, observing, "We must remember that Lady Mary's teeth and claws were not yet fully grown; besides, people who, like her, fairly love a grievance, always support real evils better than those fabricated by their own imagination. As heroic sufferers they are in their proper element; it is exactly the character they aspire to exhibit, and it inspires them with a sort of self-satisfaction calculated to produce apparent equanimity."

Lord and Lady Leicester did not discover the state of the marriage until three months later, when they called early one morning to take them down to Holkham in their coach and six. Lady Mary was ready, but Lord Coke had not yet returned from the tavern. Finding that this was his son's regular practice, Lord Leicester berated him for so treating his splendid young bride. For a time Lady Mary rode high in the esteem of Lord Leicester, who wanted an heir to the estates, which otherwise would pass to his nephew Robert Wenman, and to the earldom which would become extinct.

But his favour turned to fury when Lady Mary announced that she had made a vow never to cohabit with Lord Coke. Lady Mary went to live with her mother in Bruton Street; and her husband returned to his parents' house. Both were suffering from illnesses, mental, physical or diplomatic. Lord Coke called a number of times at Bruton Street to enquire after the health of his beloved wife, but never gained admittance. Lord Mary's uncle, Archibald Duke of Argyll, gained admittance to the Leicester home but failed to persuade Lord Leicester or his son that the best thing would be a formal separation. All he got was the assurance of father and son that Lady Mary would be treated more kindly in future.

Reunited, husband and wife went to drink a mineral water at Sunninghill, accompanied by Lady Betty, Lady Mary's unmarried sister. Her presence did not prevent hostilities being resumed. Lord Coke told Lady Mary that he intended to take her to Holkham, there to make her as miserable as he could. She answered he would have to take her by force; but somehow or other, she went to Holkham, where if we are to believe her she was subjected to every sort of insult from the family and the servants. She remained there a twelve-month, withdrawing into the citadel of her own apartment, which, she declared, she was too ill to leave. Despite attempts to intercept her letters, she remained in contact with the outside world, smuggling out reports on her brutal captivity, with the assistance of her maid or the apothecary. A guest at Holkham, Lady Cecilia Johnstone, told Lady Louisa that she went to see Lady Mary in her room, where she received her, muffled in a night-cap and sick-dress, but in the merriest of spirits. A good hate was a tonic to Lady Mary: and as the fight grew more and more bitter (the dismissal of her maid, the banishment of her apothecary, because she would not pay his bill out of her pin-money and so on), she kept her spirits up with instructions to Mr MacKenzie, Lady Louisa's father, on how to bring the law to her aid.

The powers of a husband in those days were extensive: and the Leicesters were careful not to exceed those powers, until they refused to allow her mother to see Lady Mary. The Duchess called witnesses and promptly obtained a writ of Habeas Corpus, enjoining Lord Coke to produce his wife before the Judges of the King's Bench on the first day of Term in November. Brought up, Lady Mary swore the peace against Lord Coke and instituted a suit for divorce on the grounds of ill usage. The Chief Justice declared her under the protection of the Court and ordered that her near relations, her lawyers and physicians should have free access to her. The Court was crowded with adherents of the rival factions; the Argylls mustering a fine array of relatives and noble friends, Lord Coke cheered on by fellow gamblers and drinking companions. The Duchess of Argyll wept copiously and Lady Strafford, one of Lady Mary's sisters, swooned at intervals. Least afflicted was Lady Mary herself, who stood forth "feeble, squalid, dressed almost in tatters", which the Leicesters pointed out was her own choice, since they had never withheld her pin-money of £500 a year.

After the case, the mob, surging to catch a glimpse of the unfortunate plaintiff, now blasphemously nicknamed "the Virgin Mary", broke the glass of her sedan-chair. "Take care!" said her tyrannous husband, as he handed her out of it. "My dearest love! Take care and do not hurt yourself!"

While the suit was pending, Lady Mary resided at the Leicesters' town house, insisting on living in a garret to convince those who toiled up the flights of stairs how cruelly she was used. But when her lawyers asked for instances, Lady Mary was evasive. "It is enough to say that in every respect my usage was barbarous". "But how and in what precise respect? Cannot your ladyship state some one act on some one day?" "Oh! a thousand acts every day." Apart from their barring her mother the house, the direst accusations Lady Mary could produce were that once Lord Coke in a passion struck her on the arm and tore her lace ruffle and that seeing her reading Locke upon the *Human Understanding*, he said she could not understand a word of the book and was an affected bitch for her pains.

Her suit was hopeless and if the Leicesters had wished they could have held her captive as long as they wanted. However at Lord Hartington's suggestion, they agreed, provided that she withdrew her suit, paid its expenses, undertook not to set foot in town and was content to live on her pin-money, she could reside at Sudbrook, unmolested. Perhaps for Lady Mary, the cruellest condition was one unstated, that she was deprived of any persecution about which she could complain.

For three years Lady Mary lay at Sudbrook, becoming more and more like a white cat in beauty, tooth and claw. She did not even have to become a mouser. Lord Coke died of dissipation and the Leicesters were left heirless. Triumphant, Lady Mary advanced on London, secure in £2,500 a year for life, in search of persons superior to the *canaille* into which she had been forced to marry without loss of virtue.

Nothing less than royalty would satisfy her. She became an intimate of Princess Amelia and also of George II's German mistress, Lady Yarmouth, whom Lady Mary was certain was "really married" to his Majesty.

Her career was long, as full of fantasy as devoid of fulfilment. See the sexagenarian Lady Mary in December 1792 in a letter from her niece to the Duchess of Buccleugh, raging against the French Jacobins:

Poor Aunt Mary is really . . . wild and possessed. She has been doing all that was necessary to raise an uproar, had the people been so inclined; haranguing in the bookseller's shops, lecturing the tradespeople, examining the walls for treason, threatening the *démocrates* with the Mayor, calling monsters, villains, atrocious wretches, etc., in short, everything that could provoke honest John Bull's surly disposition, and all in a riding-habit of the King's *dressed* uniform shining with so much gold, I am amazed the boys do not follow her.

Marriage of convenience must obviously have worked better than worse, in most cases. Whomever she had married, Lady Mary Coke would probably have been frigid. Lady Mary Wortley Montagu was too intellectual a woman to invite a tempestuous lover and in middle age became too tempestuous a wooer to win a younger man. In any form of marriage, they would probably have proved misfits.

Most women were conformists and accepted the standards of the time. Dr Johnson was a good eighteenth century Christian, but he believed that there were different standards of chastity for men and women.

> Confusion of progeny constitutes the essence of the crime; and therefore a woman who breaks her marriage vows is much more criminal than a man who does it. A man, to be sure is criminal in the sight of GOD; but he does not do his wife a very material injury, if he does not insult her; if, for instance, from mere wantonness of appetite, he steals privately to her chambermaid. Sir, a wife ought not greatly to resent this. I would not receive home a daughter who had run away from a husband on that account.

Dr Johnson, being a conversationalist rather than a comprehensive moralist did not think of the chambermaid and her rights, as either a virgin or an unmarried mother. This was left to Samuel Richardson.

CHAPTER THIRTEEN

Mean Marriages

I must caution you particularly against my lord's eldest son: If you are dextrous enough, it is odds you may draw him in to marry you, and make you a lady: if he be a common rake, or a fool, (and he must be one or the other) but, if the former, avoid him like Satan, for he stands in less awe of a mother, than my lord doth of a wife; and, after ten thousand promises, you will get nothing from him, but a big belly, or a clap, and probably both together.

Dean Swift, *Instructions to Servants*, The Waiting Maid

On November 10, 1739, Samuel Richardson, a wealthy printer aged 50, sat down and began writing a novel in letter form. He finished it two calendar months later, having written over 225,000 words. The theme of *Pamela, or Virtue Rewarded*, according to Richardson, was based upon a story he had heard from a friend. It is summarised by the quotation above.

But the originality of Pamela consisted in the intensity of its narration, the psychological subtlety, the sustaining of suspense, the authenticity of Pamela Andrews as a person about whose character readers could argue among themselves and disagree with the author. Indeed it seems likely that the middle-aged moralist was not fully conscious of what he had achieved in this, the first modern psychological novel.

Born in 1689, Samuel Richardson, as a "bashful and not forward" schoolboy, had compensated for his failure at games by telling stories. One, he remembered, was about "a fine young lady" who preferred a virtuous "servant man" to a "libertine lord". As a prig of eleven he wrote a letter to a widow in her forties, reproving her, with Biblical chapter and verse, for scandalmongering. As a young man, he wrote love letters for illiterate girls. There was not enough money to train him for the church and so he was apprenticed to a printer. At the age of 30, he set up on his own and within five years was reckoned "a high-flyer". He married the daughter of an equally "high-flyer", secured the lucrative job of printing the journals of the House of Commons and bought a moiety of the patent of law printer to the king.

Samuel Richardson had no financial need to turn author. One can only imagine that the booksellers Rivington and Osborne proposed that he should write a series of familiar letters as a sort of primer for semi-educated country correspondents, because he had told them it had been an ambition.

But once he started, all these conflicting elements in his life came together in the form of a novel: the moralist, the "high-flyer", the story-teller and the letter-writer united in a variation of the mean marriage theme. In this case, it was not the lady of quality who married a virtuous manservant rather than a libertine lord. It was the maidservant, who resisted a libertine, converted him to goodness and then was rewarded by marrying him.

There had been earlier essays in the epistolary form. The *Letters* of Alciphron give a brilliant series of vignettes of Attic country and urban life. Montesquieu's *Lettres Persanes* published in 1721 formed a satirical commentary on society. But Richardson was the first to attempt a complex, dramatic novel, told in the form of letters (and a journal). He confined himself to the letters of Pamela, the lady's maid trained by her mistress above her station, and her two poor and pious parents, gifted with a prescience of the sexual dangers threatening their daughter. This imposed technical problems on him which militated against his depiction of Pamela as a perfect heroine, but which deepened her interest as an imperfect one. Since there was no other correspondents, the reader could not know all the tributes paid to Pamela's charms, talents and virtues, except through her own letters. In retailing them, she ceases to be the demure and modest girl her author intended. The reader cannot help the suspicion that just as we never know what Mr B. was really like, since he is always seen through Pamela's eyes, so we can never be certain of what Pamela is really like, because we have only her words for it. Her capacity for fainting, for example, for two hours when Mr B. put his hand in her bosom (Letter XV) and three hours when he made his second attempt (Letter XXV)! Could such vertiginous records be sustained without some dissimulation?

Perhaps it was the ambiguous quality of the heroine's virtue that made *Pamela* so universal a success. Methodist preachers chose it as a basis for sermons. One writer placed it next to the Bible. Ladies at Ranelagh flourished it to their friends. It was so lifelike that a Grub Street hack produced a sequel *Pamela in High Life* to counter which Samuel Richardson produced two further volumes, which demonstrated how very dull Mr B. and Pamela became after their marriage.

The book was translated into Dutch, French and Italian. M. Voltaire admired *Pamela* as a novel, while disapproving of Pamela as a paragon of virtue. Lady Mary Wortley Montagu considered it had "Met with very extraordinary (and I think undeserved) success . . . it was all the fashion at Paris and Versailles, and is still the joy of chambermaids of all nations." In her opinion, *Pamela*, and the later *Clarissa Harlowe* would do "more general mischief" than the lewd works of Lord Rochester. Yet she confessed "This Richardson is a strange fellow. I heartily despise him, and eagerly read him, nay, sob over his works in a most scandalous manner."

Pamela Andrews is a *trompe l'oeuil*. Look at her one way and she is a heroine too good to be true; in another, and she is a designing minx. Lady Mary Wortley Montagu's cousin Henry Fielding took the second view. He produced an anonymous parody *An Apology for the life of Mrs Shamela Andrews*. In *Pamela* Mr B. proposed marrying her off to his chaplain so that she could be his mistress. In *Shamela*, Parson Williams proposes that Shamela, who had already borne him a bastard, should marry Squire Booby so that they can continue their liaison in comfort. Shamela is a shameless Pam.

But Fielding had not done with Richardson in this *jeu d'ésprit*. The moral argument of *Pamela* was that Mr B. raised Pamela by marrying her, whereas if his sister married her groom she would debase herself. Mr B. says:

> Now, Lady Davers, see you not a difference between my marrying my dear mother's beloved and deserving waiting-maid, with a million of excellencies, and such graces of mind and person as would adorn any distinction; and your marrying a sordid groom, whose constant train of education, conversation, and opportunities, could possibly give him no other merit, than what must proceed from the vilest, lowest taste, in his sordid dignifier?

In *Joseph Andrews*, Fielding proposed the male equivalent to *Pamela*. Lady Booby, the rich widow of Sir Thomas Booby, and her chambermaid Mrs Slipsop, both set their caps at Pamela's brother, the virtuous and handsome footman Joseph Andrews, whose only desire is to marry the milkmaid Fanny. His moral is directed against Lady Davers; so far from wanting a lecherous, rich widow, wouldn't the groom prefer a sweet young maid of his own class?

Though *Joseph Andrews* launched Fielding as novelist to rival Richardson, it lacked the moral drive of Richardson's masterpiece, which had the repercussions which Lady Wortley Montagu foresaw. Indeed while she was in self-imposed exile at Lovere, the plot of *Pamela* was re-enacted in real life between a pious and beautiful young serving maid and Count Jeronimo Xosi, who having failed to to seduce her proposed marriage:

> . . . he would have proceeded immediately to the church; but she utterly refused it, till they had each of them been at confession; after which the happy knot was tied by the parish priest. They continued their journey, and came to their palace at Bergamo in a few hours, where everything was prepared for their reception. They received the communion next morning, and the Count declares that the lovely Octavia has brought him an inestimable portion, since he owes to her the salvation of his soul. He has renounced play, at which he had lost a great deal of time and money. She has already retrenched several superfluous servants, and put his family into an exact method of economy, preserving all the splendour necessary to his rank.

So Life follows the trails blazed by Art.

But majority opinion remained opposed to marriages between social inequals, however matched in temperament or accomplishments. Far greater tolerance was observed towards mistresses. In 1748, Horace Walpole took an urbane delight in seeing Dr Blackburne, the Archbishop of York, at dinner where "his mistress, Mrs Curwys, sat at the head of the table, and Hayter, his natural son by another woman, and very much like him, at the bottom, as Chaplain." Parson Wood-forde, an unaverage because unsensual clergyman, felt no moral qualms about meeting the wealthy "Mr Custance & his Mistress, Miss Sherman" in the parish where he was paid to perform compulsory marriages of handcuffed men to pregnant brides. Nor was he shocked by another parishioner, "an oldish man Sandall", keeping a mistress though he had a wife living. This was thirty years after the publication of *Pamela: or Virtue Rewarded*. The chaste, but poly-philoprogenitive George III had already begotten ten of his fifteen children. But the old tradition of George II was still stronger than the methodistical morality of Samuel Richardson. His consort Queen Caroline, having given George II a mere novenary of progeny, urged him to take another wife. "Non," replied his Majesty, as he watched her fade, "J'aurai des maitresses." "Ah! Mon Dieu!" she replied, wittier in death than she had been chaste in life, "çela n'empêche pas."

In *The Provoked Wife* Sir John Brute gave as his reason for marriage, "Why, I had a mind to lye with her, and she would not let me." But many mean marriages were the product not of frustrated lust but of genuine affection. Take the example of Mrs Armistead. There is so little known of her early life that we cannot be sure that there ever was a Mr Armistead. She began her career as lady's maid to Perdita Robinson, the first of the Prince of Wales's mistresses and the most successful in blackmailing him. Among the established lovers of Mrs Armistead were the Duke of Dorset, Lord Derby and the Prince of Wales himself. "She lived in splendour, kept two sets of horses for her carriages, a proportional estab-lishment of servants; her table was the constant resort of all the young men of fashion in the kingdom; yet no one ever heard of any person being ruined by his attachment to her, which is more than can be said of any other woman who has been fashionable for many years." Somehow along the way she acquired enough education to be accepted as a scholar by Charles James Fox, whom in 1783 she took to live with her at a little house she had bought or leased at Chertsey, St Anne's Hill, tastefully built on a slope with the Surrey hills before and the river Thames behind. She and Fox were both getting on in years and they lived together for the remainder of his life. It was a scandal that Charles Fox should thus flaunt his mistress and many doors were closed to her that remained open to him. Mrs Armistead did not mind this treatment in England, where she had her own circle; but she resented the cuts she received when Fox took her abroad in 1788. In 1794, when there was the prospect of another continental journey, Fox married Mrs Armistead. But he did not announce the marriage until eight years later, before they went to Paris in 1802. For those eight years, secretly husband and wife, they were socially considered master and kept mistress. Even Lord

63. Ema Hart (later Lady Hamilton) was the inspiration of George Romney from 1782, when Charles Greville commissioned a portrait of his mistress Emma, until 1785, when Greville offloaded her on his widowed uncle Sir William Hamilton, Ambassador in Naples. Romney refused commissions and reduced the number of his sitters to devote himself to the celebration of her beauty, both in her own person and in impersonations as Cassandra, Joan of Arc, the Magdalen, etc. "The Spinstress" is the most famous of these.

64. *Marriage à la Mode*, "The Contract". While the Father negotiates the terms of the Marriage Settlement, demonstrating the splendour of the family tree in order to increase the bride's dowry, the bored bridegroom takes a pinch of snuff, oblivious of the attentions being paid to his lovely fiancée. Note the father's swathed foot, resting on the gout-stool.

65. *Marriage à la Mode*, "The death of the Earl" at the hands of his wife's lover (escaping through the window). On the floor lie the masques, worn by the Countess and her bien-aimé. (*Top left*) a saint cranes curiously forward from the canvas as the beadle summoned by a manservant bursts in at the door.

66–67. In 1744, Joseph Highmore (1692–1780) painted twelve scenes from *Pamela*, which were engraved by A. Benoist and L. Truchy and sold in large numbers. (*Above*) Here the attempted seduction scene in the summer house, to which Pamela has been lured by the housekeeper (visible through the right window). (*Left*) While the housekeeper's back is turned, Pamela shows the worthy Mr Williams a hiding place for letters. Secret correspondence had to be resorted to by all sorts of lovers, true or untrue.

68–69. Flirtation and compliments were the common currency of polite society. They provided a smokescreen for serious intrigues. Those who were most intimate in private were most distant in public. The Fop and the Country Bumpkin were stock figures as popular as John Bull and Farmer George in print-sellers' shops.

70. Richard Samuel, "The Nine Living Muses of Great Britain". The first painting recognizing that women could not merely inspire but also practice the arts. Comparatively few could earn their livings by it, except by writing for, or acting on, the stage. But women's achievements in the last quarter of the eighteenth century were considered more than lady-like accomplishments.

MRS. JOHN ADAMS.

71. Mrs Abigail Adams. Fired by the writings of the Englishwoman, Mrs Catharine Macaulay (Graham), the wife of John Adams, is famous for her "Remember the Ladies" letter pleading for votes for women to be included in the Declaration of Independence.

72. Lady Caroline Lamb in pageboy's dress (from a miniature in possession of John Murray). Wife of William Lamb, second Viscount Melbourne, she conducted openly (and unsuccessfully) intrigues which her mother, the Countess of Bessborough, and her aunt, the Duchess of Devonshire, had conducted successfully (and privily) in the previous generation.

74. Mrs Fitzherbert, wife of George IV in the eyes of the Church but not in law: the woman whom the inconstant Prinny loved most constantly.

73. Mrs Charlotte Charke, after Gravelot, the unfortunately self-willed daughter of Colley Cibber: actress, puppeteer, sausage-seller, transvestist, publican and valet.

75. Mary Wollstonecraft Godwin, by John Opie. Disciple of Mrs Catharine Macaulay, advocate, practiser and victim of Free Love.

77. Hariette Wilson (drawn by Birch and engraved by Cooper), described by Walter Scott as a "smart, saucy girl with good eyes and dark hair, and the manners of a wild schoolboy," she practised "paid love"; and when her looks faded, she made more by the sale of her saucy revelations than she ever had by that of her charms.

76. Self-portrait by Angelica Kauffman, the only woman Royal Academician prior to the twentieth century.

78. Mary Shelley, daughter of Mary Wollstonecraft and William Godwin, wife of Percy Bisshe and mother of Sir Percy Florence Shelley, who, according to her wish, never had an original thought.

Holland, his beloved nephew, was kept in the dark about the ceremony, though Fox wrote him of his affection.

The Lady of the Hill is one continual source of happiness to me, I believe few men, indeed, ever were happier in that respect than I. I declare my affection for her increases every day. She is a comfort to me in every misfortune, and makes me enjoy doubly every pleasant circumstance of life; there is to me a charm and a delight in her society, which times does not in the least wear off, and for real goodness of heart, if she ever had an equal she certainly never had a superior.

On his fiftieth birthday, Jan 24, 1799, he gave his secret wife at breakfast this present of three couplets.

Of years I have now half a century passed,
And none of the fifty so blessed as the last.
How it happens my troubles thus daily should cease,
And my happiness thus with my years should increase,
This defiance of Nature's more general laws
You alone can explain, who alone are the cause.

It has been suggested that Fox knew too well the ways of the world. When at last the marriage was made public, Lady Bessborough remarked, "The odd thing is that people who were shocked at the immorality of his having a mistress are still more so at that mistress having been his wife for so long."

The life of the 5th Countess of Berkeley demonstrates how much more complicated the pursuit of virtue was in fact than in fiction and how bitter-sweet its rewards. She was the third and youngest daughter of William Cole, who kept the Swan Inn at Wotton, just east of Gloucester. William was also a small farmer, a grazier and butcher; and his wife Susannah earned a little money on the side by nursing the sick and young.

Born in 1767, Mary was sixteen when her father died and the family broke up. Ann, the eldest sister, was married to a man named Farren who took over the butcher's shop. Susan and Mary, who were both beauties, travelled to London to seek positions in domestic service. Before they found them however, they were taken by their landlady to a masquerade at the Pantheon, "the new winter Ranelagh in Oxford Road". There Mr John Perry, the young editor of the *Gazetteer*, struck up acquaintance with them. He continued to see the two girls when they found service with a Lady Talbot in Berkeley Square. The work was hard. Susan stayed in service for only a fortnight and Mary not much longer.

Mary was worried about her elder sister, who had more appetite for pleasure than decorum. She asked Mr Perry for advice and he said that they ought both to go home to Gloucester. Mary obeyed, but Susan, glad to be rid of Mary's restraint, went to visit relatives in Lincolnshire.

Back in Gloucester, Mary found the Farrens established in Butchers' Row,

Westgate. Ann Farren was too busy breeding to pay much attention to those she had bred. The home was slovenly, the butchery running down; and the modest Mary was disconcerted by the numbers of militia officers, released from leading their men to defeat in America, seeking conquests in Butchers' Row. One especially embarrassed her. Old enough to be her father, he was 5th Earl of Berkeley, Lord Lieutenant of Gloucestershire, Master of the Rolls of the county and the cities of Bristol and Gloucester, Constable of the Castle of St Briavel, Warden of the Forest and Colonel of the South Gloucesters. He was a huntsman whose coverts ranged from Berkeley in Gloucestershire, through Andoversford in the Cotswolds, Nettlebed on the Chilterns, Gerrards Cross in Buckinghamshire, Cranford in Middlesex, as far as Wormwood Scrubs on the outskirts of London. He was also a lady-killer, whose companions included the Prince of Wales and his philandering brothers.

When Mary Cole was addressed by this grandee not once but on several occasions and when she saw him hanging about opposite the Farrens' house, she decided it was high time to find herself another domestic situation well away from Gloucester.

She found a splendid position with Mrs Foote, a clergyman's lady, at Boughton Malherbe, Kent, 46 miles east of London. As lady's maid, she was paid £6 a year and shared a bedroom with the housekeeper. And so from March 1784 till the end of December in that year, Mary led a contented existence, learning how to play her part in a well-run household of a grandeur greater than she had experienced. Mrs Foote and the housekeeper were well-satisfied: Mary Cole was as demure and modest a lady's maid as ever Pamela Andrews was to Samuel Richardson's Mrs B.

But then a letter came from Susan, now Mrs Turnour, of Charles Street, Berkeley Square, telling Mary that she couldn't bear to think of her in an inferior position and begging her to give in her notice to Mrs Foote and join her loving sister. Mary immediately gave a month's notice, booked a seat on the London coach and wrote Susan to send the fare, because she had no money saved.

Before the four weeks had elapsed, Mrs Foote received a letter from Mrs S. Turnour, begging the immediate release of Mary, because she Mrs Turnour was going out of town. It ended, "Beleave me I am with real humility your humble Sivnt." So before the year was out, Mary was aboard the coach for London, having borrowed the fare from the housekeeper.

The house in Charles Street in which Susan lived as Mrs Turnour had been furnished by Mr Turnour with luxury. Mary was an intelligent girl but we do not know how quickly she realised that her sister was not married and that Mr. Turnour was a complacent protector who did not object to his mistress entertaining other gentlemen at lavish parties during his frequent absences. At these parties a frequent guest was the Earl of Berkeley. Had the Earl connived at the establishment of Susan in the street off Berkeley Square? We cannot be sure. But there is no doubt that Susan's sudden desire to have her sister Mary with her in London was prompted by his lordship.

This simple plan failed. Mary was not interested in the advances which he made her. Her heart was pure. And it was through this purity of heart that she was finally ensnared, in a Richardsonian melodrama devised by his lordship and Mrs Turnour.

One evening the two sisters were together, having supped off roast fowl, sausages and a bowl of punch, when there was a row in the passage and "two ruffians" burst in and seizing Susan declared that they would take her to the "spunging house" unless she paid a debt of a hundred guineas.

With a sensibility worthy of Pamela, Mary swooned and when she recovered consciousness, there was Lord Berkeley, appeared from nowhere. On her knees Mary begged his help. She had no money, but if he would save her sister "he might do whatever he would with her own person". His lordship promptly produced a hundred guineas, the duns unhanded Susan and Lord Berkeley took Mary off to lodgings in Mayfair.

Whether Mary had Pamela's gift for reducing her lover to impotence by protracted fits is not certain. But she became so ill that the wicked earl could not take her maidenhead. He was in a position similar to that in which the Prince of Wales was to find himself with Mrs Fitzherbert later in the same year. Prinny pretended to commit suicide and was driven to bribe a young curate, the Rev. John Burt, incarcerated in the Fleet Prison for debt, to perform a bogus marriage service in return for £500 down and the vicarage of Twickenham. His lordship did not have to hire a curate from the Fleet. At the vicarage of Berkeley, he had the Rev. Augustus Thomas Hupsman, who as his domestic chaplain was ready to enact the farce. Before breakfast on March 30, 1875, a ceremony took place in Berkeley Church which was to become known in legal history as "The First Marriage". In Mary's eyes, she was married to Lord Berkeley, even though she was willing to agree with his condition that the marriage should remain secret, in view of her own humble, and her sister Susan's disgraceful, position in society. In Lord Berkeley's eyes, he had done only what was necessary to accomplish his end. They returned to London, spent a few days at Kew and Hampton Court and then Mary, still ailing, was packed off to stay with her sister Ann Farren for five months.

In September Lord Berkeley recalled her and set her up in lodgings off Brompton Road, where he came to visit her from time to time. And in the following spring, the crisis came. Mary was pregnant. Though Lord Berkeley had had many women in is life, he does not appear to have begotten any children by them. He was pleased at this evidence of his fertility, rented her a furnished house in Park Street, gave her a carriage, and three months before the child was due had Mary's mother to live with her, as a sort of unpaid housekeeper. On December 26, a son was born. As he was illegitimate, there was some difficulty about the christening, but Lord Berkeley persuaded his old friend the Rev. John Chapeau to do it at St. George's, Hanover Square. Lord Berkeley did not attend the ceremony, but sent his friend Admiral Prescott, who stood godfather and provided the information for the baptismal register. "January 23rd, 1787.

William Fitzhardinge, son of the Earl of Berkeley, by Mary Cole."

Not long after this, Lord Berkeley took Mary, her son and her mother into his household. Mary now became his acknowledged mistress, mother of William Fitzhardinge or "Fitz" as he was nicknamed; but she was given a new surname Tudor, perhaps because Lord Berkeley could not bear that people should know that his mistress was daughter of that vulgar old soul, Mrs Cole, who occupied a sort of mezzanine position between the servants' and the dining hall. First in London, then in the red-brick Cranford House on the edge of Hounslow Heath and finally in Berkeley Castle, Mary Tudor became the mistress not merely of her lord but also of his households, introducing into their economy the discipline and order which she had learnt during her nine months as lady's maid in Boughton Malherbe Vicarage. She was kindly, efficient and practical, where Lord Berkeley was selfish, uninterested and negligent. At Berkeley she took over the management of the estate, repairing the neglect of years: rather as Mary Pendarves had at Roscrow Castle.

She continued steadily to breed; seven illegitimate children in the course of eight years, of whom four were still living in 1796. But though Lord Berkeley was a devoted father, adoring especially Fitz his first born, there was one question on which he and Miss Tudor could not agree, a question which became more and more urgent as the children began to grow to an age when they wondered why their father was an Earl and their mother a Miss Tudor. Mary recognised that though she was married in her own eyes and those of God, she was not married in the eyes of the Church and State. Though she had twined herself, like ivy, into the fabric of Lord Berkeley's life, she was so aware of her equivocal position that whenever they moved from Berkeley to Cranford, Cranford to London, even only for a matter of weeks, she had trunks crammed with all her own and the children's clothing for fear that she and her brood might be suddenly abandoned.

Lord Berkeley believed in never doing today what could be put off till tomorrow: but even he recognised finally that surrounded as he was by the fruit of his loins, he did not possess a legal heir. In the event of his death, his titles and the estates thereto pertaining would pass to his brother, Admiral Sir George Cranfield Berkeley. So on May 16, 1796, Mary once again being pregnant, the Right Honourable Frederick Augustus Berkeley, Bachelor, and Mary Cole, Spinster, were married at Lambeth Parish Church. The marriage was still kept secret and Admiral Berkeley was not informed until Thomas Moreton Fitzhardinge (Lord Dursley) was born in the autumn of that year.

So far from being angered at a marriage which, if Thomas Moreton survived, dispossessed him of title and inheritance, the Admiral congratulated his brother on the choice of one who would prove herself not unworthy of the high situation he had raised her to. Mary had honour, religion, a most attentive love to his children, and to all his interests and affairs she had proved a most zealous and watchful guardian. "If you had chosen from a throne you might perhaps not have met a better. I have admired and loved her for those qualities and for her own sake; I shall now love her, if possible, more for yours and by every attention in my power make her feel towards me as an affectionate sister."

Mary Cole's was in real life a more convincing case of Virtue Rewarded than Pamela's in fiction. Swift had warned the Lady's Maid that the eldest son must either be a rake or a fool. Lord Berkeley proved to be both. By signing themselves as bachelor and spinster in the Lambeth wedding, they had personally attested the invalidity of the first wedding. Three attempts were made to have Fitz recognised as the legitimate heir. But it was ruled that Thomas Moreton, the eldest of the six legitimate children whom Mary Countess of Berkeley bore her husband, had the only valid claim.

It shows much for the affection which bound these brothers together that Thomas Moreton refused to claim his earldom, even after his eldest brother Fitz had been created in his own right Baron Segrave and Earl Fitzhardinge.

CHAPTER FOURTEEN

Notorious Ladies

The Georgians were gossips and scandalmongers. It was as easy to lose a reputation as a handkerchief. It was not what a lady did which mattered so much as what she was said, or suspected, to have done. Conversation was oblique, and to us appears stilted. Simple language was considered inelegant; though Mrs Montagu, the blue-stocking, exceeded elegance when she insisted on saying "the silver Cynthia held up her lamp in the heavens" when she meant that the moon shone. Direct language might be all very well for the Quakers, whose morals were as sound as their habits were thrifty. But for all those whose practice fell short of the high standards publicly professed, ambiguity was a touchstone. "Hypocrisy," wrote de la Rochefoucauld, "is the homage which vice pays to virtue." Indirection was the litmus paper which distinguished between the righteous and the errant.

It could on occasion produce embarrassment. For instance, Lord March (later known as "old Q") was, like Wilkes, in the habit of making indecent proposals to every decent-looking woman he met, though in politer language. When Lady Mary Coke emerged from Sudbrook retirement with her jointure of £2,500 a year, Lord March hinted at the possibility of a little dalliance. Thereupon, Lady Mary wrote to his uncle and aunt, the Duke and Duchess of Queensberry, the happy news that she was going to marry their heir.

Lord March, "the most brilliant, most fashionable, most dissipated young man in London, the leading character at Newmarket, the support of the gaming table, the supreme dictator of the Opera House, the pattern whose dress and equipage were to be copied by all who aimed at distinction", was appalled. The Queensberries were the two people on earth whose respect he most valued and he was too polite a gentleman to point out to Lady Mary her ridiculous *bêtise*. When the Queensberries invited the prospective bride and groom to tea, Lord March did not address a word to Lady Mary, hoping that his coldness would say enough. Lady Mary ignored it.

His current mistress was Madame Rena, the prima donna. He had hitherto maintained the connection modestly; but now he flaunted it. You couldn't drive in the Park or down St James's Street without meeting him and the Rena in his chariot. The Rena sat at the head of his table and hung on his arm at Ranelagh. When the Rena was on the opera-stage, his enthusiasm was plain for all to see, and if Lady Mary happened to be present, vociferous.

The Duchess of Queensberry tried to sort the matter out. She asked Lord March what Lady Mary must think of the Rena remaining in his house. "The Rena, ma'am? The Rena? Pray what has Lady Mary Coke to do with the Rena's living in my house, or out of it?" The Duchess mentioned decency and propriety. "My dear Madam," he answered, "leave propriety and Lady Mary to protect themselves. She is no girl: she will act as she pleases, I dare say, and so shall I." Fond of Lady Mary, the Duchess tried to warn her against so volatile a husband. But Lady Mary was imperturbable. She could not by any means permit herself to doubt of Lord March's honour. Nor had he given her any cause of offence.

Lord March's friends at White's followed the entanglement with delight. That a philanderer to whom the word marriage was blasphemy should be caught between the stately white cat and the respected Queensberries was vastly diverting. Nothing which he did within the code of polite behaviour could secure his release.

At last in desperation, Lord March called on Lady Mary Coke one morning. What he did or said was never known. But Lady Mary boxed his ear and forbade him ever to see her again.

He drove straight to the Queensberries and explained that to his sorrow he had, for some reason he could not fathom, incurred Lady Mary's displeasure. He had tendered his apologies, but Lady Mary capriciously would not accept them: so, alas, he must accept his rejection as final!

Nobody's reputation was ruined by this misunderstanding. Lord March gained by being confirmed as a loving but non-marrying man. Lady Mary was so imperious that she did not notice if anyone laughed at her.

Most women, however, had to be constantly vigilant. A lady did not walk abroad alone. If unaccompanied by a man, she took a friend or her maid. There was danger from pickpockets, foot-pads or rakes; and there was danger from gossip, slander and malice. In the Georgian world, disasters, natural or man-made, were uncommon. The human instincts, of curiosity, prying and eavesdropping, were not sublimated, as they are today by radio and television serials and soap-operas. So neighbours and relatives filled the curiosity gap. Letters relayed the most trivial information throughout the islands and over the seas: juicy scandals, instead of making a headline one day and being wrapped round fish and chips the next, were passed down from generation to generation.

The only insurance against the loss of reputation was money. A lady might lose her maidenhead and gain a coach and six. She might, like Elizabeth Vassall, abandon her husband for another man and be shunned by decent society but as Lady Holland she became the centre of her own circle. Even the disreputable Queen Caroline maintained a court, which numbered some respectable if scheming politicians among its numbers. She had money, and with it, power.

Not every flighty society gal was as lucky as Miss Kitty Hunter. In March 1762, Miss Hunter (a maid of honour, at that!) scampered off to the continent with the Earl of Pembroke, who resigned his commission and his place of Lord of the Bedchamber and wrote his wife that Miss Hunter was irresistible, that he never intended to return to England and he would pay Lady Pembroke £5,000 a year. A month later, he wrote his wife from Holland, proposing that she join them, with her guitar, two servants who played on the French horn, and his dog Rover. His good lady would have made a *ménage à trois*, if the Duke of Marlborough had not dissuaded her. Before long the errant earl wrote that he was coming home. He could never be happy without his wife (and, gossips added, he had advised Miss Hunter to turn nun).

Miss Hunter did nothing of the sort. In 1763, Mrs Montagu wrote her brother in Naples, "Miss Hunter has come back in the character of the Fair Penitent. Her lover was soon tired of an engagement which had not the sanctions of virtue and honour. Shame and a fatherless babe she has brought back. I hope her miserable fate will deter adventurous damsels from such experiments." Alas for morality! No miserable fate awaited her. Her father was rich and soon she was married to a Captain Clarke, who ended his career Field Marshal Sir Alured Clarke, and the scandalous maid of honour of the 1760's died a venerable old lady of fashion in 1810.

It was those without capital who were at risk. A kept woman milked her protector and took lovers in his absence to save money against the day she was turned off at a moment's notice. An actress had far better stay single than marry a wastrel husband who had a legal right to all her earnings. At least she had fairly good wages and benefits, while her looks and talent lasted. The only form of writing which was rewarding was for the theatre. The copyright of books was purchased outright (aside from subscriptions, of which more later). But for a play, the author received recurrent benefits. In the seventeenth century, Mrs Aphra Behn had supported herself by books and plays; and in the eighteenth Mrs Centlivre and Mrs Inchbald made competences by writing for the stage. But for most women depending on the exploitation of their bodies or their minds, life was precarious, haunted by poverty, starvation, disease or the shades of the sponging house and the debtor's prison. It was a maxim of the Georgian gallant, Never kick a woman unless she's down. Some ladies were driven to desperate measures, fighting back. "Con Phillips", whom Walpole coupled in iniquity with Catharine the Great of Russia, was driven to blackmail.

She was born a lady, the eldest daughter of an Army captain, belonging to an old Welsh family. In 1717, when Teresia Constantia was aged eight, Captain Phillips took his family to London, where through the kindness of her godmother, the first Duchess of Bolton, Teresia was put to complete her education at Mrs Filler's boarding school in Prince's Court, Westminster. She is the sole authority for most details in her career. She boasted that in 1721 (when she was aged thirteen) she was seduced by "Thomas Grimes" (as Philip Dormer Stanhope, later 4th Earl of Chesterfield, liked to call himself for erotic purposes).

Lord Stanhope was then aged 27, a libertine who may have found some fascination in a schoolgirl, though it was denied in *Defence of the Character of a Noble Lord from the Scandalous Aspersion contained in a malicious Apology* which was published in 1748. Certainly in June 1721, Lord Stanhope left London for a mission in Paris: and Con Phillips was soon in new scrapes. At the age of fourteen, to avoid being arrested for debt, she married a bigamist, with whom she never exchanged a word. Her amours were "as public as Charing Cross", according to Chesterfield's apologist, but within three months of her invalid marriage to the bigamist, she wed a wealthy Dutch merchant, called Muilman.

Her career was a succession of lamentable episodes. Within a twelve-month Muilman secured an annulment of his marriage, but agreed to pay her £200 a year. The agreement lapsed when she went to live with a Mr B. in Paris. She traipsed through France and the West Indies and back to London, the inconstant, and one suspects, incompetent mistress of many. Her claim to notoriety was her *Apology for the Conduct of Mrs Teresia Constantia Phillips, more particularly that part of it which relates to her Marriage with an eminent Dutch Merchant* (1748). Its literary quality was owed to her "ghost", Paul Whitehead a political satirist, who had earlier issued his verses from the Fleet Prison and who later became secretary to Sir Francis Dashwood's "mad monks of Medmenham". Con Phillips paid him in kind. She published the Memoir in parts at her own expense. Later these were issued in three volumes and went through four editions in her lifetime. This did not prevent her being imprisoned for debt more than once in the Marshalsea. But it induced Mr Muilman to send her back to the West Indies in 1754 as "a remittance woman".

In Jamaica, she went into the legacy business. She first wed a well-to-do Irish surveyor whom she induced to leave her his fortune; then an ailing but affluent Scot; and finally, as a doubly endowed widow, a Frenchman. When she died on Feb 2, 1765, she was "unlamented by a single person" and without having given much happiness to anyone except her heir. This lady was a tramp.

Mrs Laetitia Pilkington, who compiled her *Memoirs* in the same year as Con Phillips, was more talented, as desperate, but less successful. She was born in Dublin in 1712. Her father was a Dutch man-midwife, but on her mother's side she could trace herself back to the Meades and the Earls of Kilmallock, which bolstered her pride as a child and supported her boasts when she became a *divorcée*. At eighteen, she induced her parents to consent to her marriage to the Reverend Matthew Pilkington. They were both poets, both tiny, and though Matthew brought to her as bridal gifts only a cat, owl and harpsichord, he loved her to the point of swooning. Very flattering in a 30 year-old clerical gentleman, in the eyes of a teenage girl. They had only £100 a year, but her father allowed her use of his coach.

Dean Swift met them through Dr Delany (the same Dr Delany who was to introduce Mrs Pendarves to him later). Less critical in his Irish exile, the creator of Lilliput described them as:

... a little young poetical parson, who has a little young poetical wife. ...
And the young parson aforesaid hath very lately printed his own works, all in
verse and some not unpleasant in one or two of which I have the honour to be
celebrated, which cost me a guinea and two bottles of wine ...

"The young parson aforesaid" was ambitious for preferment. The Dean had
not abandoned the political activities which he had shared with Mr Pope, but for
which in Dublin he suspected that he received less money and glory than Mr
Pope did at Twickenham, so handy for London. In July 1732, two years after
Pilkington's marriage, the Dean obtained for him the chaplaincy to the Lord
Mayor of London as a personal favour.

Swift had his own fish for Pilkington to fry, but he did not tell him how they
were to be done. Pilkington was only too pleased to be paid for arranging the
publication of Swift's poems anonymously, but was dismayed when Swift dis-
owned them. The chaplain did not appreciate that a mere poem could be charged
as treason.

After Pilkington had been in London a year, Laetitia went to join him, with a
woman friend, smuggling more Swiftiana. She found the Reverend Matthew
sadly changed. He was consorting with Mrs Heron the actress and plotted unsuccessfully to throw Laetitia into the arms of his friend, the painter Worsdale.
She returned to Dublin when Pilkington and three others were imprisoned for
publishing Swift's anonymous poems.

Pope wrote to Swift complaining of "the intervening, officious impertinence
of these goers between us, who in England pretend to intimacies with you, and
in Ireland to intimacies with me ..." Swift did not answer. Laetitia continued to
visit him with Dr Delany and read to him her poetical effusions. When Matthew
Pilkington was released from prison, he went home to Ireland and turned over a
new leaf. For an obsequious ode to George II on his Birthday, the Lord Lieutenant of Ireland gave him £50. A letter from Pilkington to Dr Delany survives,
explaining the agony this payment had given him, because it might have alienated
him from his patron, the Dean.

But it was not until 1737, three years later, that Swift washed his hands of
them both. "He proved the falsest rogue, and she the most profligate whore in
either kingdom," he wrote the friend in London who had procured Pilkington
the Lord Mayor's chaplaincy. "She was taken in the fact by her own husband."

The grounds on which the Consistorial Court gave the Reverend Matthew
divorce and secured for him the custody of their children were that Laetitia had
been reading a book late at night with a Mr Adair in her room. She wished to
finish the book and Mr Adair refused to leave it with her. In those days (and even
two hundred years later) this was considered valid proof of adultery (as if that sin
could be committed only at night). When Matthew turned her out, she took
refuge with Mr Adair and when she left his protection, ill women pursued her
with proposals of introducing rich gentlemen, who abused her when she repelled
their advances.

The divorce was never made absolute; but the scandal in Dublin was so resounding that Mrs Pilkington fled to London. She had become a woman of notoriety and if she had been "the most profligate whore in either kingdom", she could at the age of 22 have plied her trade very profitably. But in her own mind, she was a "little Irish muse" whose husband had been jealous of her superior talent. She determined to earn her living as a poetess, not a prostitute. It was not very long before, greatly daring, she set up in a fashionable first floor apartment in St James's Street, bang opposite White's Club. For this she paid a guinea a week, a high rent compared with the half a guinea a week George Selwyn, man of fashion, paid for his room up two flights.

Things started well. Dodsley published *The Trial of Constancy* and gave her five guineas or more. Colley Cibber read it and came bounding up her stairs, full of praise and sympathy and offers of help. The Poet Laureate wept when she read her poem *Sorrow* and then hurried across to White's to raise a subscription to publish it. This the gentlemen of White's, intrigued by the pretty little lady who appeared at the windows of the first floor opposite, were not averse to doing, provided they were given an introduction. Cibber, her patron, was in a fair way to becoming her pandar.

Gentlemen called at her apartment. Colonel Duncombe sent over a bottle of wine from White's and came to see her with Cibber. Colonel Duncombe was "a pleasant droll gentleman . . . so old that he had been page to King James when he was Duke of York".

He said a thousand witty things in half an hour, and at last, with as great gravity as his comic face would admit of, said that he wished I would take him into keeping. I answered I had never really seen any person with whom I was better entertained, and therefore, if he would make over to me all his real and personal estate, and dispose of his regiment, and give me the money, I would keep him . . . out of it. He swore a good oath, he believed me, and liked me for my sincerity. . . . I could relate a number of pleasant stories of this old gentleman; but, as his wit generally bordered on indecency, and sometimes on prophaneness, they are not proper for a female pen.

Laetitia enjoyed talking bawdy, though she was too genteel to write it. The love letters which Colonel Duncombe paid her to send him so that he could show them around White's as proof of his still being a young man were probably no more saucy than lines she addressed him when he refused to add his guinea to those of Lord Weymouth and Lord Augustus Fitzroy. Laetitia was a gay rattle when there was company around to rattle with. But she had only moderate success in her pleas for subscriptions.

Dryden had made £1,200 from the subscription to his Vergil (1697) and Pope £5,000 for his Iliad (1715–1720), but by Laetitia Pilkington's day, subscription had become a racket. Thomas Cooke, who made his name by translating Hesiod (1728), lived for twenty years on subscriptions for his Plautus, of which he finally published only one volume. There were more impoverished writers touting for subscriptions than coxcombs willing to pay to see their names in subscribers' lists.

Poor Mrs Pilkington wrote a poem, copies of which she sent to members of the nobility, hoping for subscription. Sometimes she received a guinea; from Samuel Richardson, to her surprise, she got more. From most she received nothing. She revived her old family connections, Colonel Meade and his wife the daughter of the Earl of Kilmallock, hoping that her shabby gentility would win hearts untouched by her Muse. Colley Cibber advised her never to call on a dark or foggy morning or take umbrage at a first refusal, as she might be luckier next time.

Mrs Montagu, who would certainly have had no time for Con Phillips, had a soft spot for Laetitia's "talent, pleasant audacity and suffering" and kissed her on both cheeks. But London emptied in mid-summer and did not fill again until September. She tried everything in the literary line, down to hack journalism and ghosting, on the one hand, and to vainly importuning respectable Meade relatives on the other. One evening she resolved on suicide in St James's Park. "The moon apparent Queen, unveiled her peerless light, and I waited in the silent shade, resolved to execute my dreadful purpose as soon as I could do it without observation, when a young lady and an old one both very well dressed, seated themselves besides me." The ladies took her home, where the young one begged her to stay, to the disapproval of her husband, an ex-footman who was fond of beating her, despite the fortune of £20,000 she had brought him. In 1742, she was imprisoned in the Marshalsea for debt and held for nine weeks, until at Colley Cibber's instancy sixteen Dukes contributed a guinea apiece to her enlargement.

With Samuel Richardson's aid she scraped together some money with which to open a print shop. In the window she placed a card: LETTERS WRITTEN HERE ON ANY SUBJECT, EXCEPT THE LAW. PRICE TWELVE PENCE. PETITIONS ALSO DRAWN AT THE SAME RATE. Mem. READY MONEY; NO TRUST. One of her first customers was a man, very badly dressed, with a greasy leather apron, who paid her a guinea for a print. Then he asked her to write a love letter for him, with which he was so pleased, that he sent out for a flask of champagne. While they drank together, he spoke of Homer, Horace and Milton and sang an Italian song. When she taxed him with a being a fine gentleman in masquerade, he smiled and said he was a house-painter named Thomas Brush.

> This put me in mind of an adventure I once had in Ireland, when one of the finest gentlemen in it came to visit me in a grazier's coat, and told me his name was Tom Long, the carrier, though he happened to be an English baronet, with a large estate and a great employment.

It puts us in mind that Con Phillips had already published the instalment of her *Apology* in which Lord Chesterfield wooed her as Thomas Grimes. Mrs Pilkington was determined not to be outdone.

Mrs Pilkington's *Memoirs* do not rank high as literature. Into them she bundled her poems, her anecdotes, her animosities against clergymen in general and her little husband in particular, her many misfortunes and few triumphs. But they brought her considerable success. At their publication, she returned to Dublin, perhaps the better to savour her husband's discomfiture. Two volumes of memoirs were published during her lifetime, and a number of polemical pamphlets and broadsheets written by Laetitia herself, by her husband, his partisans and gentlemen who considered themselves libelled in her pages. Young Lord Kingsborough took Laetitia up and sent her £20 bills in return for which she had to write him diverting letters; the Little Theatre, Dublin staged a comedy by her. She died in 1750 and a third volume of memoirs appeared the following year. She believed that as a poet she was among the great; perhaps it was a blessing that she did not live to see even her notoriety fade into insignificance.

What of her raffish, ambitious husband? He immediately married again and then faded away till he reappeared as the distinguished author of the *Dictionary of Painters*. Thomas Seccombe in the *Dictionary of National Biography* twice warned his readers that Matthew Pilkington author of the *Dictionary of Painters* should not be confused with Laetitia's scallywag husband. It was not until 1912 that the will of the second Mr Matthew Pilkington, author of *The Dictionary of Painters*, revealed him as the same mean little man Mrs Pilkington had married. As the aggrieved party, he had had custody of his two children by Laetitia, John Carteret and Elizabeth. To his second wife he left all his estate apart from three bequests.

> To my son William Pilkington, who never felt a filial affection for me (to the utmost of my observation) I give the sum of five pounds sterling and to those two abandoned wretches John Carteret Pilkington and Elizabeth Pilkington I give the sum of one Shilling if Demanded within 12 months, and I should abhor to mention them in any Deed of Mine, if it were not to prevent all possibility of Dispute or litigation.

Matthew, named after the first evangelist, had had the custody of their children, but Laetitia, christened for Joy in Latin, retained their love. John Carteret, her son, wrote a book in her defence.

Mrs Charlotte Charke published *A Narrative of her Life* in 1755. In so far as it had any purpose other than to raise money by publicising her adventures and misfortunes, it was designed to shame her father Colley Cibber into forgiveness. Though the Poet Laureate had taken pity on Laetitia Pilkington, Charlotte's behaviour had been so scandalously unladylike that her family wished to be shot of her. On his mother's side Colley claimed descent from William of Wykeham, but his father, though an eminent sculptor, could not be accounted a gentleman: and he himself was in an ambiguous position. As an actor-manager, writer of indifferent tragedies but amusing comedies, adapter of Shakespeare and Corneille and butt of Pope's *Dunciad*, Colley Cibber was rather a friend of gentleman, than a gentleman himself.

Shameless Charlotte was his last child and, if we believe her, unexpected and unwanted. She was a tomboy, loving horses, riding and shooting. She preferred gardening to housework or sewing. She had a broad, if brief, education (including French, Italian and the globes). At the age of thirteen, after staying a couple of years with a doctor for her health's sake, she decided to set up practice on her own. She ordered a stock of physick from the Uxbridge apothecary patronised by her family, and dispensed medicines gratis to the elderly sick in the neighbourhood. When the apothecary's bill was sent in, her bewildered father paid it, but gave orders that Dr Charlotte should not be given further credit.

I was resolved not to give up my Profession; and, as I was deprived of the Use of Drugs, I took it into my head, to conceal my Disgrace, to have recourse to Herbs. But one Day a poor old Woman coming to me, with a violent Complaint of rheumatick Pains and a terrible Disorder in her Stomach, I was at dreadful Loss what Remedies to apply, and dismissed her with an Assurance of sending her something to ease her, by an inward and outward Application, before she went to Bed.

It happened that Day proved very rainy, which put it into my strange Pate to gather up all the Snails in the Garden; of which, from the heavy Shower that had fallen, there was a superabundant Quantity. I immediately fell to work; and, of some Part of 'em, with coarse brown Sugar, made a Syrup, to be taken a Spoonful once in two Hours. Boiling the rest to a Consistence, with some green Herbs and Mutton Fat, I made an ointment; and, clapping conceited Labels upon the Phial and Gallipot, sent my Preparation, with a joyous Bottle of Hartshorn and *Sal Volatile* I purloined from my Mother, to add a Grace to my Prescriptions.

In about three Days Time the good Woman came hopping along, to return me thanks for the extreme Benefit she had received . . .

Charlotte was a girl determined to have her own way. When a violinist named Charke asked her to marry him, she did not rest until she won her parents' consent. Charke was very hard up, and hoped to be given a job at Drury Lane, of which Colley Cibber was at that time the patentee. It was only after marriage that Charlotte discovered that the violinist was a whoremonger, to find whom she had to search the Hundreds of Drury. When she gave birth to a daughter, Charlotte ceased to care about her husband. "I seldom had the Honour of his Company but when Cash run low, and I as constantly supplied his Wants; and have got from my Father many an auxiliary Guinea, I am certain to purchase myself a new Pair of Horns."

She ceased to live with Charke and went on the stage. With her father's influence and her own talent, she made rapid progress in straight female and in breeches' parts.

But she had a bias towards failure. In her second season, she offended her father by undertaking the part of Fopling Fribble, a satire on Colley Cibber in *The Battle of the Poets, or the Contention for the Laurel* which Fielding wrote in as a new act for his *Tom Thumb*. As a woman, she needed more, but displayed less discretion than her fellow actors. She took too active a part in the rebellion against the manager Fleetwood and wrote a spiteful play against him *The Art of Management*, which was never performed because Fleetwood bought it up. Her father came to her aid and made some sort of peace between them. In the following two seasons she appeared at the Haymarket and at Lincoln's Inn Fields. But after 1737, her name disappeared from theatre bills.

Charlotte's narrative is without dates. It is impossible to determine exactly what happened or why or when. The narrative was first published in eight instalments in March and April 1755. It is plain that the manuscript of each instalment was whisked away by the printer as soon as it was finished. The writing is of a woman distraught, pouring out her story incoherently, in the desperate need for money even making fun of what to her was tragic.

What does emerge is the hopeless insecurity of a talented woman trying to support a child after she had run into debt. As an actress, her livelihood depended upon public appearances under her own name; but as a debtor, her liberty depended upon her disappearance. She set up shop in Long Acre as a grocer and oil dealer without the first idea of commerce. She ran a puppet show over the Tennis Court in James Street, Haymarket. There she could display her histrionic talent without being discovered. But she fell ill and had to sell for twenty guineas the puppets which had cost her nearer £500. When Charke died in the West Indies she formed an alliance with another (unnamed) gentleman. But it was not long before *he* died, leaving her with debts she had no means of paying. Arrested for seven pounds, she was bailed out by the ladies keeping coffee houses in and about Covent Garden. She had by this time resorted to the disguise of male dress. Her brother, the scapegrace Theophilus, secured her the post of valet to a nobleman, for a time. She appeared anonymously in low theatres in male parts. Her daughter suffered from convulsions; but when she was well, they made sausages and sold them in the streets. Even here Fate struck. A dog ran off with her stock. She became a waiter at the King's Head Tavern in Marybone and the proprietress fell in love with her and wanted to take her as her husband. She borrowed some money to start a pub of her own and went broke in a night. She managed a brief comeback playing Macheath at the Haymarket; but she failed in a production of *Pope Joan* owing to the interference of her father.

Through it all, she was sustained by the desire to protect her child. This was the thread on which were strung the bizarre beads of her life. In jail or out, wandering as a strolling player, settling down as a pastrycook, a hog-merchant, a baker, only to move on to avoid the duns, she was sustained by the need to play mother. Inevitably the daughter became an actress and as inevitably she married a man of whom Charlotte disapproved. There followed a friendship with a woman, which perhaps was the satisfaction which she had unconsciously sought when she took to male dress. Like everything else in Charlotte's life, it did not last very long.

The *Narrative of the Life of Mrs Charlotte Charke* did not soften the heart of Colley Cibber, who died two years later, in 1757, or of her brother Theophilus who perished the following year in a ship-wreck off the coast of Scotland. She died in squalor, vague as always. Was it 1759? or 1760? We can't be sure. But her hectic little autobiography has stood the test of time better than her father's ponderous *Apology*.

Con Phillips, Laetitia Pilkington and Charlotte Charke, though very different in character, had much in common. They were desperately in need of money. They wanted to redress their wrongs with the world, to get their own back, to prove that they were morally right, the victims of misfortune. They felt the need to *apologise*.

Harriette Wilson was a bird of different plumage. She was saucy, impudent, shameless and out to get as much money as she could by the publication of the first volume of her *Memoirs* and the threat of publishing more. The reader's interest is engaged from the very first sentence, "I shall not say why and how I became, at the age of fifteen, the mistress of the Earl of Craven." Seventy years separate her *Memoirs* from Charlotte Charke's autobiography. We are in another social and moral age, closer to that of Anita Loos's *Gentlemen Prefer Blondes* than to *Pamela* or *The Adventures of Fanny Hill*.

She was born Harriette Dubochet at 2, Carrington St, Mayfair on February 22, 1786. Her father was a Swiss clockmaker, her mother the natural daughter of a gentleman named Cheney. So unhappy was their marriage that Harriette (one of their fifteen children) resolved by the age of ten to live as unrestrainedly as her easy conscience would allow. The clockmaker's leisure was so devoted to mathematical problems that his children were forbidden to speak to him and conversed together in whispers. He was perhaps so engrossed that he did not notice the departure of his beautiful daughters on the primrose paths to ever-cosy bedchambers. Amy was the first to leave, and where she led, the other sisters followed. Julia Johnstone, who tried to emulate the success of Harriette's *Memoirs* by publishing her *Confessions in Contradiction of the Fables of Harriette Wilson*, suggested that before becoming the Earl of Craven's mistress, Harriette had been seduced by someone less boast-worthy. But the succession of Harriette's noble protectors and would-be protectors was genuine enough (even if for the purposes of blackmail or comedy she omitted others less aristocratic or ridiculous). Harriette did not drive lovers in tandem. She was off with the rich Earl of Craven (with his cocoa trees) before she was on with penurious Honourable Frederick Lamb. It was only when Lamb proved too stingy that she transferred her attentions to the Marquess of Lorne, to whom she claims she would have been faithful, if he had been faithful to her. According to her lights she was an honest woman. Her account of the Regency demi-monde in which courtesans of the highest class entertained the aristocracy "kept the gay world in hot water" in Sir Walter Scott's day. For us the *Memoirs* are sheer enjoyment; the rivalry between Harriette and her lisping sister Amy; the alliance of Harriette, Fanny, her favourite sister, and Julia Johnstone as "The Three Graces"; and her shrewd young sister Sophie's nobbling of Lord Berwick in marriage.

Across her pages flit the Dukes of Wellington and Leinster, Lord Hertford

(Thackeray's Marquess of Steyne), Beau Brummell, Lord Granville Leveson Gower, the 6th Duke of Devonshire, Sir William Abdy come to confess his distress at the elopement of his wife, the witty Lord Alvanley, a corps of foreign diplomats, whip-loads of English politicians, the wicked Lord Byron with a gift of £50. "The wit is poor," wrote Scott, "but the style of the interlocutors exactly imitated."

We owe this impudent masterpiece to Harriette's sense of justice. Lord Worcester, while still a minor, fell madly in love with Harriette (then in her thirties). The affair lasted for three years but when he wanted to marry her, his father the Duke of Beaufort arranged an annuity of £500 a year provided she gave up Worcester and went to live abroad. Harriette kept her side of the bargain, but when the Duke tried to settle for an outright payment of £1,200, she took the advice of Henry Brougham and published her *Memoirs*, in four small volumes. They created such a sensation that each time a fresh volume came out, such a crowd collected outside the publisher's shop that a barrier had to be erected to control the queue. Harriette hoped for twenty editions but thirty were sold in the year; and a French version in six volumes appeared, "corrigée par l'auteur" with coloured plates which led to a denunciation as a most "disgusting and gross prostitution of the Press".

Those who had enjoyed Harriette's favours did not enjoy her revelations. Frederick Lamb, by then a distinguished diplomat, threatened, but did not take, legal action. Meetings were held at various clubs, White's, Brookes's and the United Services, as to what should be done. A Piccadilly stone mason called Blore, whose boorish advances Harriette had pilloried, was encouraged to prosecute and was given £300, and Hugh Evans Fisher was awarded rather more. As Harriette and her publisher had netted some £10,000, such damages were trifling. Though both suits had been successful, none of Harriette's noble victims was prepared to incur the publicity of a lawsuit. It was decided, knowing that Harriette was a creature of her word, to make up a purse and buy her silence.

She had said that she had few prejudices apart from an inability "to endure any mean between men of the highest fashion and honest tradesmen". But with the dowry of her profits and her hush-money, she married a *bourgeois* M Rochefort with whom she lived in France until his demise. Then Mme Rochefort returned to England, where she dwelt a pious widow until her death in 1846, unrecognisable as the notorious young lady of pleasure, whom Sir Walter Scott described as "far from beautiful, but a smart, saucy girl, with good eyes and dark hair, and the manners of a wild schoolboy".

CHAPTER FIFTEEN

Revolutionary Ladies

In the first three-quarters of the 18th century the ladies who fell out with society became merely notorious. The American Revolution of 1776 and the French Revolution of 1789 gave their successors hope of founding new societies in which they would have an honoured place.

There was room in Georgian society for the conventional woman, whether she was moral or immoral. Harriette Wilson played the game as honestly as Mrs Thrale, Maria Edgeworth or Jane Austen. The cards were the same though the game was different: commerce, rather than whist, Faro or old maid. Hers were not the standards of a "pious fanatic", such as Selina Countess of Huntingdon, leaders of fashions such as Georgiana, Duchess of Devonshire, political hostesses such as Lady Holland or Mrs Crewe, but they conformed to the rules of the demimondaines who mixed not with ladies of the highest society, but with their husbands.

Life was all very well for blue-stockings like Lady Mary Wortley Montagu, Mrs Chapone, Mrs Elizabeth Montagu *et sa galère*. They had rich husbands, if not money of their own. They did not have to earn a livelihood. Their *salons* were warm, comfortable and so refined. No icy blasts swept the foothills on which they had their poetic *fêtes champêtres*. They might be Tory or they might be Whig; if the former, the sanity of Farmer George was their concern; if the latter, they prayed for his madness and a Regency with full powers for appointment to the sinecures, so necessary to relieve the only debts a gentleman or lady needed to honour, those of the gaming table.

Excluded from these games were the Dissenters, deprived of political power because of their religion in the same way as Roman Catholics but for different reasons. The Roman Catholics had begun by being suspect as Jacobites and remained suspect as owing an allegiance to the Vatican superior to their allegiance to the Monarchy. The Dissenters had begun by being suspect as refusing to acknowledge the Church of England, as by law established, and ended as Jacobins. Between Jacobites and Jacobins was a great gulf. But neither were accommodated in Hanoverian England.

Chief among the Dissenters were the Unitarians, who accepted God the Father but rejected the Divinity of God the Son. Unitarian ministers like Dr Price and Dr Priestley were not only theologians but eminent men of science and mathematics, and also progressive political reformers.

Nonconformity was a slippery slope. Embarked on it, nobody could be sure where he or she would end. From unitarianism some glissaded into deism and ended up downright atheist. From political reform, others, led by the events of the American War of Independence, slipped into Republicanism and after the storming of the Bastille into secret societies and euphoric revolution.

For young men and women, poor in pocket, rich in ambition, as deprived of opportunity as they were fertile in ideas, socially and sexually as repressed as they were hungry for satisfaction, the American and French revolutions fused an explosion of idealism.

The philosophers had been administering their purgatives for years. The Scottish Freemasons and the French Encyclopaedists had been scribbling away their prescriptions while Britain and its colonies grew more and more sick. And, what was more important, clever men and women who ought to have made their mark in, and on, society were thrust into humiliating jobs. Tom Paine, for example, the Thetford inventive bridge designer wasted time as a staymaker and excise man, until his genius burst forth in writing for the American revolutionaries the *Common Sense Papers* which inspired Washington's victories. With American Independence came the first opportunity for men (and women) to remake a society according to a new plan without regard for the legacy of the past.

The Declaration of Independence was the greatest challenge in the history of mankind (unless one accepts as historical the problems which faced Adam and Eve expelled from the Garden of Eden). Here was an area, not yet fully settled, but vaster than Europe, which the framers of the American Constitution could make a political lesson from the New World to the Old. In England, Mrs Catharine Macaulay had foreseen this possibility and that it must include freedom for women.

A disciple of Mrs Macaulay was Abigail Adams, the wife of John Adams, one of the drafters of the American Declaration of Independence. In March 31, 1776, she wrote him a letter that has become famous.

. . . in the new Code of Laws which I suppose it will be necessary for you to make I desire you would be more generous and favourable to them (the women) than your ancestors. Do not put such unlimited power in the hands of the Husbands. Remember all Men would be tyrants if they could. If particular care and attention is not paid to the Ladies we are determined to foment a Rebelion, and will not hold ourselves bound by any Laws in which we have no voice, or Representation.

That your Sex are Naturally Tyrannical is a Truth so thoroughly established as to admit of no dispute, but such of you as wish to be happy willingly give up the harsh title of Master for the more tender and endearing one of Friend. Why then, not put it out of the power of the vicious and the Lawless to use us with cruelty and indignity with impunity? Men of Sense in all Ages abhor these customs which treat us only as the vassals of your Sex. Regard us then as Beings placed by providence under your protection and in imitation of the Supreme Being make use of that power only for our happiness.

Mrs Adams was better at reasoning than at spelling. It was logical that if the Colonists were justified in fighting the British on the principle that there should be no taxation without representation, the same principles should be observed in the framing of the American constitution. But her husband replied:

As to your extraordinary Code of Laws, I cannot but laugh. We have been told that our struggle has loosened the bands of Government everywhere. That Children and Apprentices were disobedient—that schools and Colledges were grown turbulent—that Indians slighted their Guardians and Negroes grew insolent to their Masters. But your letter was the first Intimation that another Tribe more numerous and powerfull than all the rest were grown discontented.—This is rather too coarse a Compliment but you are so saucy, I won't blot it out.

Depend upon it. We know better than to repeal our Masculine systems. Altho they are in full Force, you know they are little more than Theory. We dare not exert our Power in its full Latitude. We are obliged to go fair, and softly, and in Practice you know We are the subjects. We have only the Name of Masters, and rather than give up this, which would compleatly subject Us to the Despotism of the Peticoat, I hope General Washington, and all our brave Heroes would fight . . .

Though Mrs Adams was not convinced by her husband's arguments, she was beguiled by his flattery. Perhaps because her own relationship with her husband was tender, she accepted that the role of women was to

Charm by accepting, by submitting sway
Yet have our Humour most when we obey.

This was the accepted philosophy of little women who made good wives and great ladies who made good hostesses. Considerable power might be exercised by women, provided it was by guile or charm, not as of right. The male would not accept the female as his equal. She was either his superior as in delicacy, or his inferior, as in strength of mind or body.

Adams was more worried by his wife's arguments than he admitted to her. He opened his mind to his friend James Sullivan. Theoretically the only moral foundation of government was the consent of the people. But how far should principle be carried? To adolescents as well as adults? To women as well as men? To the poor as well as the rich? To the illiterate as well as the educated? To negro slaves and indigenous Indians as well as white colonists? Sullivan returned a negative answer to all these questions. Government must reside in the hands of adult white males of property. The revolutionary Tom Paine might disagree, but John Adams won the day. The War of Independence had not effected a revolution, but established a successful revolt, transferring government from the propertied classes in Britain to the propertied classes in the American states. It was in Europe that its revolutionary repercussions were most felt.

Condorcet, a French atheist in revolt against his Jesuit training, advocated the immediate advancement of women to equal rights in *Lettres d'un Bourgeois de Newhaven* (1787). Following the storming of the Bastille and the flight of the King, it seemed likely that the equality of the sexes would be recognised. In Metropolitan France there were none of the racial complications of negro slaves and tribal Indians. But Talleyrand's report on *Public Instruction* ignored Condorcet's ideas of liberty, equality and sorority. He proposed instead that French girls should be educated with their brothers in public schools only up to the age of eight and thereafter they should stay at home, learning the domestic crafts and sciences to qualify them for wifely and maternal duties.

This provoked Mary Wollstonecraft to dash off in six weeks *A Vindication of the Rights of Woman* (1792), three hundred pages of passionate pleading, which was to make her for a time the most famous woman writer in Europe. Though not well-argued, it still has the power of intense conviction, based upon personal experience.

At the time of writing, she was a young woman of 33. I used the word "young" designedly. Emotionally she was immature. Naturally bossy, she had been forced at the age of twenty to take over the management of her family, because of her widowed father's drunken irresponsibility. She bossed her sisters, her girl friends like Fanny Blood, her pupils, whether as school-teacher or governess. Not very good at managing the affairs of others, she was incompetent at managing her own. There was so much wrong with society that she could blame on to it what was wrong with herself; a lack of charm, total absence of humour, fear of sex, pride in her intellectual superiority and contempt of her social superiors and above these loneliness, lovelessness and a tendency to depression. She was drawn towards the reformists and in Joseph Johnson, the radical bookseller, she found a man who appreciated her talent. He had published her first book, *Thoughts on the Education of Daughters*, before she went to spend a disastrous year as governess to the daughter of Lady Kingsborough (daughter-in-law of that Lord Kingsborough who had befriended little Mrs Pilkington at the end of her life). When Mary returned to London, furious at Lady Kingsborough's anger at her trying to alienate the affections of her charge, Johnson gave Mary more work; articles for his monthly *Analytical Review*, translations from the German, Dutch and French, the reading of manuscripts. He also published her own work, a novel, stories for children, and polemics. When Burke produced his *Reflections on the French Revolution*, she rushed in with a *Vindication of the Rights of Man*, which gave her the formula for her celebrated *Rights of Woman*.

Through Johnson she met the prominent radicals of her day, Drs Price and Priestley, Tom Paine, William Blake, William Godwin and the Swiss writer-artist Henry Fuseli. She found herself among people with ideas of intellectual, political and sexual freedom broader than any she had allowed herself, or had encountered among the Unitarians. Johnson was a bachelor, who had lived for some years with Fuseli. There is no evidence that they had homosexual intercourse; but certainly Fuseli was what they called then "hermaphrodite". He had been in love with men as well as women; and part of his trade was in pornographic drawings. His conversation ranged wide and also broad, with a licence before ladies that Georgian gentlemen allowed themselves only among themselves or with women of pleasure.

Mary had taken a puritanical attitude towards sex in her *Vindication of the Rights of Woman*. But she fell in love with Henry Fuseli, the bohemian bachelor. Unfortunately it was just at the moment when he had decided to become Fuseli the Academician, by marrying Sophia Rawlins, a pretty young artist's model with no great intellect but a love of respectability. He regarded Mary as "a philosophical sloven, with lank hair, black stockings and a beaver hat". But he found her either stimulating as a companion or useful as a foil to Sophia Rawlins. If Allan Cunningham's *Lives of the Painters* is to be believed, Mary fell in love with Fuseli at first sight.

She lacked the guile of less emancipated women. She did not know how to make advances by appearing to retreat. The portrait painted in 1791 shows her in daunting pose. William Roscoe, the Liverpool radical who commissioned it, thought it made her look an "Amazon". But it is more like Counsel for the Prosecution; and one can understand Fuseli's hesitation, if it was his favours she was prosecuting. Yet the friendship lingered on after Fuseli's marriage, until Mary had the effrontery to suggest that she should move in on the Fuselis to give Henry the spiritual love which would complement the bodily satisfaction afforded him by his wife. Mary could not bear to live separately. Mrs Fuseli put her foot down and that was the end of that.

The *ménage à trois* was not unknown at that time. Indeed the Devonshire household in which Georgiana the wife, and Lady Elizabeth Foster the mistress of the 5th Duke of Devonshire lived together, and were brought to almost simultaneous childbirths, was the most exciting scandal of the time. But it was conducted, considering its flagrancy, with the utmost decorum. Though decorous, Mary Wollstonecraft's rejection was so flagrant that she decided to leave London for revolutionary Paris.

There is something more squalid about the failures of idealists than those of conventional rakes or sinners. Johnson's partner, Thomas Christie, for example, had gone to France, fallen in love with a married Frenchwoman, Catherine Claudine, and got her with child. They had returned to London, where their baby was born, and named Julie, after the sentimental heroine of Rousseau's *La Nouvelle Héloise*. But when divorce laws were passed in France enabling Catherine to be rid of Citoyen Claudine, Thomas Christie abandoned his mistress and married a carpet heiress from Finsbury Square. It was no more shabby than Lord Pembroke's elopement with Miss Hunter and subsequent return to his wife, after he had made Miss Hunter pregnant and told her to enter a nunnery. But the sancti-mony of high-minded free love makes it seem so.

By Christie's shabby behaviour Mary Wollstonecraft had been forewarned before she went to France. But Paris in 1793 had something of the hectic spirit of Spain during the early days of the Civil War in the 1930s: at least for foreign expatriates. There were lots of English and American sympathisers trying to experience at first hand a revolution which since it was French they could only observe at second hand. On William Blake's advice, Tom Paine had fled to escape prosecution for the Second Part of his *Rights of Man*. What euphoria he must have felt to be elected Deputy for Calais on his arrival! What disillusion at having his advice disregarded! What despair at being imprisoned during the Terror! What thankfulness to the God whose non-existence he was proclaiming in *The Age of Reason*, when the death mark which should have sent him to the guillotine was chalked on the wrong side of his cell door!

Mary lived in Paris to see many of her French friends like Madame Roland sent to the guillotine, Condorcet rejected, degraded, imprisoned and escaping the blade by poison. She lived in a house from which her host and hostess had fled. The French which she had been proud of reading she was little able to talk. Servants listened to her orders but did not obey them. It was cold. She fell ill. The King was daily driven from his prison to his trial past her window. She wrote to Johnson, on whose notes of hand she lived:

> Though my mind is calm, I cannot dismiss the lively images that have filled my imagination all the day.—Nay, do not smile, but pity me; for, once or twice, lifting my eyes from the paper, I have seen eyes glare through a glass-door, opposite my chair, and bloody hands shook at me. Not the distant sound of a footstep can I hear.—My apartments are remote from those of the ser-vants. . . . I wish I had even the cat with me!—I want to see something alive; death in so many frightful shapes has taken hold of my fancy.—I am going to bed—and, for the first time in my life, I cannot put out the candle.

Revolutions de-moralise at the beginning; and they end by de-humanizing. The Tyranny, with its ever-present menace of death, shocked Mary into a sexual awareness of which the author of the *Vindication of the Rights of Woman* would have been ashamed. When a Frenchwoman boasted of having no sexual desire, Mary answered, "So much the worse for you, madame, it is a default of nature." She was not alone in this demoralisation. William Wordsworth, having got Annette Vallon with child, left her with friends, promising he would come back and marry her. When their daughter was born, he went to London to earn some money for the three of them and stayed to write *The Prelude* and *The Excursion* in repentance. Helen Maria Williams, whose poems had inspired Wordsworth's youth, took John Hurtford Stone from his wife and children in Paris. Stone combined business with revolutionary fervour. His associate was an American, Gilbert Imlay, an American army captain, who had written a couple of books.

When Mary first met Imlay at the Stones, she disliked him. She did not realise that when he had left America in 1786, it was to avoid a burden of debts. But she did not trust him. Soon however his attentions, his flattery and good looks won her.

In April 1793, when war broke out between Britain and France, all foreigners were forbidden to leave the country. But as an American who was, though he did not tell her this, planning to join in a French expedition to wrest the Louisiana colonies from Spain, Imlay was less suspect than the English ladies who had come to support the Girondins in France. He was what those who dislike four letter words call an adventurer. Mary in Paris appeared younger than she had done in London, because less severe in her dress and moral judgments. To Imlay the idea of a mistress who was famous and self-supporting was stimulating. His confession that he had lived with other women made him only the more attractive to Mary. Given her passionate love, Imlay would want no other. In his memoirs of her, William Godwin transposed from the recollection of his own experience in 1796 a view of what she must have been during her honeymoon with Imlay three years before.

> Her whole character seemed to change with a change of fortune. Her sorrows, the depression of her spirits, were forgotten, and she assumed all the simplicity and vivacity of a youthful mind. She was like a serpent upon the rock, that casts its slough, and appears again with the brilliancy, the sleekness, and the elastic activity of its happiest age. She was playful, full of confidence, kindness and sympathy. Her eyes assumed new lustre, and her cheeks new colour and smoothness. Her voice became cheerful; her temper overflowing with universal kindness; and that smile of bewitching tenderness from day to day illuminated her countenance, which all who knew her will so well recollect.

The fulfilment of love made her less concerned with the failure of the revolution. During the Terror her friends were imprisoned, but she remained free because Imlay registered her as his wife at the American embassy. Any hopes of equality of rights for women disappeared, but these mattered less than her joy at conceiving a child by the man to whom she had given allegiance like any old-fashioned spouse.

Imlay's pleasure in Mary as a mistress waned as her joy at being pregnant waxed. Footloose, he had no intention of being chained by a family. He discovered urgent business in Le Havre, while she remained in Paris, writing *A Historical and Moral View of the French Revolution* to prove to herself and others that pregnancy was no bar to work. Visits to her friends in prison, the sight of blood beneath the guillotine, the execution of those she considered the true leaders of the revolution shook her faith not in the theory of violent political change, but in the practice in this instance. Europe, she thought, would be in a state of convulsion for the next fifty years. Meanwhile, there was Imlay to worry about. Since business kept him at Le Havre (renamed Havre-Marat) Mary joined him there only to find that business now took him back to Paris. They were together however for the birth of the baby on what across the Channel was May 14, but according to the French revolutionary calendar the 25th of Floréal. Her name was registered as Françoise, but in English was Fanny, after Mary's beloved friend, Fanny Blood.

Despite the Terror, Mary would have liked to stay in France. The Gallic way of life appealed to her (and no awkward questions were asked about marriage lines). But Imlay found business reasons to go to London; and amatory reasons for remaining there. During the bitter winter of 1794/5, Mary waited for him in Paris, depending for money on what she could extract from Imlay's friends.

In her middle thirties, Mary had acquired the attraction of a sexually awakened woman. She had admirers and could have formed another connection, if she had resigned herself to the realisation that what had been to her a grand passion was to Imlay a past fancy. In the summer of 1795, accompanied by a lively French maid, Marguerite, she went to London, hoping to disentangle Imlay from his new love. When Imlay refused to set up house with her, she attempted suicide with laudanum.

Shamed into doing something about her, Imlay proposed that she should go to Scandinavia on a business trip for him. This would get her, the baby and the maid out of the way and might even bring him some money. Surprisingly, Mary agreed. Action was perhaps a better analgesic to soothe the pain of rejection than laudanum. While she was abroad, she continued a correspondence with the father of her child the effect of which could only have been to alienate him still further by the denunciation of his inferiority and the parade of her noble passion.

By the time she returned, Imlay had found himself yet another woman, an actress, with whom he proposed openly to live. What made this so humiliating was that Imlay's desertion of her after he had ceased to want her was in accordance with the principles of freedom, which they both accepted. By coincidence at about the same time, William Godwin, revising the second edition of *Political Justice*, added to his section on Marriage a consideration of Infidelity, which he considered justifiable unless there was concealment.

Just as Dr Johnson refuted Bishop Berkeley by kicking a stone, Mary Wollstonecraft refuted the arguments of Godwin and Imlay by jumping off Putney Bridge. She found this method of suicide more difficult and agonizing in fact than Goethe had in fiction. It did not even induce Imlay to establish a *ménage à trois* with herself and the actress. Instead he found an excuse to go to Paris.

Mary picked up the threads of literary life. She collected her letters on Scandinavia for a travel-book, prepared a new edition of her *Original Stories* and even attempted a comic drama based on her experiences. When Imlay returned from Paris, Mary met him a couple of times without distress. The affair was over.

Within a month, she called, alone and uninvited, on William Godwin. She had known him for some years without any flirtation. He was now aged 40, the distinguished author of *Political Justice*, a bachelor, unattached to any woman but on the look out for a bed-mate. Indeed at that time he was in pursuit both of Amelia Alderson, a young lady who had published anonymously a novel *The Dangers of Coquetry* and also of Mrs Elizabeth Inchbald, the 43 year-old actress, novelist and playwright. Mrs Inchbald, having experienced the miseries of the marriage bed, preferred the role of *allumeuse* to mistress: but she liked Godwin as an escort.

Mary needed a man and she had picked on Godwin. Godwin needed a woman, but he did not pick on Mary until he had made a proposal (decent or indecent) to Amelia and been rejected. Amelia's womanly confession to Mary that Godwin was ready to "devour her" (Amelia) precipitated Mary's taking him as her lover.

Begun in an atmosphere of high-minded non-contractual free love, their affair descended unsmoothly to reality. When Mary found herself pregnant, she was alarmed when Godwin did not immediately propose marriage. She was frightened at the prospect of being the unmarried mother of two children by different fathers. She was four months gone before the philosopher agreed to abandon his principles and make an honest woman of her. When Mrs Inchbald (or "Mrs Perfection" as Mary called her) heard of the marriage, she insulted them both on the spot. Jibes and sneers came from friends, who considered they had fallen from their high principles into an abyss of conformity. Mary protested to Amelia, "I still mean to be independent, even to the cultivating sentiments and principles in my children's minds (should I have more) which he disavows." She did not feel it necessary to mention that a child was well on the way. Godwin advertised his independence by hiring separate rooms in which he worked and slept. He had a flirtation with a Miss Pinkerton and when the time for Mary's lying in came, he spent the day working in his rooms, receiving messages from Mary, the last of which read, "Mrs Blenkinsop tells me that I am in the most natural state, and can promise me a safe delivery. But that I must have a little patience."

Fanny had been born easily and Mary expected a rapid second labour. It was unexpectedly long. It began at 5 a.m. and the baby (another girl, to be named Mary) was not born until 11.20 p.m. At 3 a.m. next morning Godwin was told that the placenta had not come away and was asked to fetch Dr Poignand, chief obstetrician at the Westminster Lying-In Hospital.

Today the removal of a placenta is a simple operation and the risk of septicaemia minimal. Not so for Mary Godwin. All attempts failed. For eleven days, the woman who had twice attempted suicide fought to keep alive, the husband who had flirted with the idea of marriage overwhelmed by the passion he now felt for the wife he had insufficiently cherished.

He had tried to eradicate religious superstition from her mind: but she had answered, probably when wounded by the attentions of Miss Pinkerton, "How can you blame me for taking refuge in the idea of God, when I despair of finding sincerity on earth?" Now as she died, she gasped, "Oh Godwin, I am in heaven!"

"You mean my dear," the troubled atheist replied, "your symptoms are a little easier."

Godwin buried her where they had married less than six months before, in the little church of St Pancras, with the Fleet River running beside the yard. He had never lived under her roof during her lifetime, but after ten days removed his things to her house in the Polygon. Fanny and the baby had been farmed out among friends; but they were responsibilities which Godwin would have to bear. Marguerite, the French maid who had been to Fanny as much as her mother and more than her father, was dismissed. A friend of Godwin's sister, Louisa Jones, moved in to the Polygon to keep house and tend the children. What Coleridge called a "cadaverous silence . . . quite catacombish" descended on the household.

As a bachelor, Godwin had subsisted; as a widower with two children he was pressed for money. He sat down to write his *Memoirs* of Mary Wollstonecraft, making the sort of desperate amends to a less than perfect marriage that seventy years later Thomas Carlyle attempted on the death of Jane Welsh. It was no sort of biography. Some friends and relatives he did not approach; others whom he approached refused to cooperate. The *Memoirs* are passionate, hectic and frank to indiscretion. The ideas for which Mary had fought, the rights she had written to vindicate were reduced by the example of her life to a scandalous anarchy. He wrote from love and remorse, but he could not have destroyed her lifework more thoroughly if he had written out of hatred. His friends were appalled: his enemies were exultant. Roscoe wrote:

> Hard was thy fate in all the scenes of life,
> As daughter, sister, parent, friend and wife
> But harder still in death thy fate we own,
> Mourn'd by thy Godwin—with a heart of stone.

CHAPTER SIXTEEN

Revolutionary Daughters

The hypotheses of one generation may prove fallacious, yet be accepted as truths by the generation succeeding. Fanny Imlay and Mary Wollstonecraft Godwin were to grow up as faithful believers in the *Rights of Woman* and *Political Justice*. But William Godwin, as he looked round for a second wife who would take over the housekeeping functions of Miss Jones and give his daughters maternal, and himself conjugal, love, found few candidates for the post.

He first tried a young literary lady, Miss Harriet Lee, who with her sister kept a school in Bath. She would have been able to provide his daughters with free education when they reached school age. But she rejected the middle aged philosopher of free love. Then he proposed to Mrs Maria Reveley, Mary Wollstonecraft's friend and disciple, lately widowed. But she preferred the security of marriage to a business man, John Gisborne, less famous but more affluent. It was not until a widow woman, Mrs Clairmont, moved next door and hailed him from the balcony with the incredulous words, "Is it possible that I behold the immortal Godwin?" that he realised he had found his mate.

Mrs Clairmont was the relict of a Swiss. She wore green spectacles and had two children, a son Charles of Fanny's age and a daughter Mary Jane a few months younger than Mary Wollstonecraft Godwin. They were married in 1803 and in 1805 produced a son, who was called William after his father.

Godwin had been capable of high philosophy as a bachelor; or even when, living under a separate roof, his first wife had earned her own living. As the breadwinner for a family of seven, he was forced to lower his standards. But even though his principles flew out of the window, the wolf did not go away from his door. When a correspondent asked how his children fared under Mary Wollstonecraft's system of education, he replied with evasive pomposity.

Your enquiries relate principally to the two daughters of Mary Wollstonecraft. They are neither of them brought up with an exclusive attention to the system of their mother. . . . The present Mrs Godwin has great strength and activity of mind, but is not exclusively a follower of their mother; and indeed, having formed a family establishment without having a previous provision for the support of a family neither Mrs Godwin nor I have leisure enough for reducing novel theories of education to practice, while we both of us honestly endeavour, as far as our circumstances permit, to improve the minds and characters of the younger branches of our family.

Godwin was past his literary prime. He never wrote another philosophical work to equal *Political Justice*, or a novel of the calibre of *Caleb Williams*. His wife tried to start a publishing bookselling business dealing in children's books. Hazlitt wrote for her; Charles and Mary Lamb gave her their *Tales From Shakespeare*. Godwin wrote a number of histories and fables under a pseudonym. But the business was undercapitalised. Though it struggled on for years, it was only with the assistance of loans, which Godwin came to regard as tributes to which he was justified for his benefactions to humanity.

Fanny Imlay (or Godwin as she was now called) was temperamentally withdrawn. She could not compete with her younger sister, who as the child of Godwin as well as the Wollstonecraft was regarded with special attention by visitors. Mary was intelligent, imaginative and beautiful. Godwin had a more intense relationship with her than with any of the other children of his household or with his second wife. It is possible that he felt a deeper and less troubled love towards this daughter than towards her mother. Mary Godwin was devoted to him, accepting his greatness in a way her mother had never done. The more he became a parody of himself, the more Godwin relied on her respect, her conviction that he was genuine.

Richard Holmes in *Shelley, the Pursuit*, that splendid book, writes "Mary was not spoilt as a child, however; Godwin was far too conscientious a father, treating her stringently, and deliberately sending her away for lengthy periods to stay with his friends, the Baxters, in Scotland." There may have been a further reason. "That damn'd infernal bitch, Mrs Godwin", as Charles Lamb called her, hated the memory of Mary Wollstonecraft, and even more the presence of her daughter. Perhaps Godwin sent Mary to the Baxters partly to spare her the hatred of her step-mother, partly to preserve his own image intact.

When Percy Bysshe Shelley wrote to hail Godwin as his master, the needy old boy recognised manna from heaven. Here was a wealthy baronet's son, needing advice, acknowledging loyalty. Here was the younger generation, rallying to his support, offering a possibility of shoring up his tottering little publishing house. The young man had been sent down from Oxford for atheism, and married the beautiful and persecuted daughter of a retired *hotelier*. He was a poet, a perfectibilist, a Godwinian. Godwin wrote, he advised, he saw a pot of gold at the end of a rainbow. He and the Shelleys must meet. But when Godwin took the journey to the end of the rainbow at Lynmouth, there were no Shelleys there. They had vanished.

Mrs Godwin was furious. Godwin would have been furious, if he hadn't still seen a prospect of advantage. Lynmouth in Devon was a long, expensive journey.

But his patience was rewarded. Percy Bysshe and Harriet Shelley came to visit the Godwins at their bookseller's shop and residence in Skinner Street, Holborn.

Godwin treated Shelley as a son and the enchanting Harriet as a daughter-in-law. He gave him cautious counsel about Wales, about his family financial affairs, and his future studies. He showed Shelley the splendid books they were publishing and dropped a hint about the need for further capital.

Shelley was a dangerous idealist. He had married Harriet not out of love but pity. In Ireland he had attempted to start a revolution with *An Address to the Irish People* of thirty pages which was printed so badly that "the lower classes" for whom it was designed would not have been able to read it if they had known how to read. It attracted more attention from the Home Office than from the Irish people. He had tried to set up a radical commune in Wales from which to circulate his *Declaration of Rights*, but could not persuade his relatives to finance him. He had thrown himself into a scheme for reclaiming land in North Wales and headed the list of subscribers with the promise of £100 which he did not possess. He had persuaded Miss Hitchener, a Sussex schoolmistress, to give up her job, and then tiring of her intellectual and physical attractions promised to pay her £100 a year for her pains. Only one payment was made, equivalent to a sum which he had borrowed and not repaid. The subscriptions which he swore would be forthcoming for the Reclamation Scheme, never materialised. He neglected to pay his tradesmen's bills, but sent £20 to head the subscription list for John and Leigh Hunt, who had been imprisoned for two years and fined £500 each.

His revolutionary zeal was boundless and sank like water into sand. He was a man of words, not deeds. His ideas were cultivated strains of the wild flowers of Godwinian thought. Godwin was enthusiastic at being chosen as Shelley's mentor. It reassured him that his own philosophy was not as outmoded as in middle age he sometimes feared. And from a disciple with such expectations of inherited wealth, the Master hoped to derive some assistance in furthering his educational projects (or, in plainer words, to get some money).

When the Shelleys first met the Godwins, in 1812, Harriet wrote, "Need I tell you that we love them all. . . . His (Godwin's) manners are so soft and pleasing that I defy even an enemy to be displeased." For most of the five and a half weeks the Shelleys spent in London, seeing Godwin daily, Mary Godwin was in Scotland. But Fanny, "very plain, but very sensible", soon made friends with Shelley. He took more notice of her than most guests at Skinner Street; drew her out, teased her and displayed his poetical and revolutionary selves to her. Though his voice was high, his fancies were still higher; and Fanny fell more than a little in love with him. What Mary the fourteen year-old felt towards Shelley or he towards her at this time, we do not know. It was not until mid-June 1814, when Mary was three months short of being seventeen, that friendship began and within a few days blazed to passion.

Mary had become a beautiful young woman, whose hair, like Harriet's, seemed to form the halo about her delicate face, which Shelley found so spiritually attractive.

Shelley's marriage with Harriet had been disintegrating over the past twelve months. In the previous year, she had given birth to a daughter, Eliza Ianthe. Paternity was a responsibility Shelley could not bear. But even as he planned to separate from his wife, he bound himself closer to her. On March 22, 1814, he went through a second marriage with her at St George's, Hanover Square, in case their Scottish marriage was invalid; and in the same month, she conceived a second child by him, who was to be born a month prematurely in November.

At that time he fancied himself in love with Cornelia Boinville, the eighteen year-old daughter of a French revolutionary; and *before* he met Mary Godwin in June, he had lived in imagination what he was to experience.

I recollect that one day I undertook to walk from Bracknell to my father's (forty miles). A train of visionary events arranged themselves in my imagination until ideas almost acquired the intensity of sensations. Already I had met the female who was destined to be mine, already had she replied to my exulting recognition, already were the difficulties surmounted that opposed an entire union. I had even proceeded so far as to compose a letter to Harriet on the subject of my passion for another. Thus was my walk beguiled, at the conclusion of which I was hardly sensible of fatigue.

His wooing of Mary must have given him the impression of being *déjà vécu*, the performance of a drama already written. While Godwin imagined that he was helping to settle Shelley's complicated financial affairs in a manner which would be profitable to them both, Shelley was seducing the affections of Mary Godwin and her half-sister Jane, ghoulishly choosing as trysting place Mary Wollstonecraft's grave in St Pancras's Churchyard. Not that they needed much seduction. Atheism, free love, the rights of women, liberty, equality, political justice were the rusks on which they had cut their baby teeth.

Shelley presented Mary with a copy of *Queen Mab*, with a facetious inscription on the fly-leaf. Beneath it, Mary wrote, "I am thine, exclusively thine. I have pledged myself to thee and sacred is the gift." Beside her mother's grave, she offered him her body and soul. It was Sunday, June 26, and they walked back to Skinner Street arm in arm, accompanied by Jane, bewildered and envious.

Next day Shelley imparted the joyous news to the professor of free love. To his astonishment, Godwin was flabbergasted. The tricky negotiations to secure Shelley a loan against his inheritance had not been finalised and now Shelley had the madness to disclose, with the frankness which Godwin had advocated in *Political Justice*, his plan to live with Mary and asked for his consent. "I expostulated with him with all the energy of which I was master," Godwin told a friend, "and with so much effect that for the moment he promised to give up his licentious love, and return to virtue."

On July 6, Shelley's loan (£2,593.10s from Nash, the money-lender) was negotiated, half of which was to be made over to Godwin. From July 8, Shelley was no longer welcome at Skinner Street, except for business meetings with Godwin. But according to Mrs Godwin:

> One day when Godwin was out, Shelley suddenly entered the shop and went upstairs. I perceived him from the counting house and hastened after him, and overtook him at the schoolroom door. I entreated him not to enter. He looked extremely wild. He pushed me aside with extreme violence, and entering walked straight to Mary. "They wish to separate us, my beloved; but Death shall unite us," and offered her a bottle of laudanum. "By this you can escape from tyranny; and this," taking a small pistol from his pocket, "shall reunite me to you." Poor Mary turned as pale as a ghost, and my poor silly (Jane), who is so timid even at trifles, at the sight of the pistol filled the room with her shrieks. . . . With tears streaming down her cheeks, (Mary) entreated him to calm himself and go home. . . . "I won't take this laudanum; but if you will only be reasonable and calm, I will promise to be ever faithful to you." This seemed to calm him, and he left the house leaving the phial of laudanum on the table.

Godwin spent two days writing a ten page letter of advice and warning to Shelley. Unfortunately there was no moral blackmail that he or anyone else could level against the disarmingly frank Shelley. He himself told Harriet of his love for Mary. For Harriet, he said, he had never had more than a brotherly feeling. "It is no reproach to me that you have never filled my heart with an all sufficing passion . . . may you find a lover as passionate and faithful, as I shall ever be a friend affectionate and sincere." This was cold comfort to a wife who had told him that she was pregnant with his second child.

Shelley did not care. His friends Thomas Jefferson Hogg and Thomas Love Peacock would be sure to console the girl. Meanwhile he was staging a re-enactment of the drama which he had staged with Harriet three years before. Then he had eloped to Edinburgh to marry a girl. For this second performance, since he could not marry Mary, he took her to France (not yet recovered from the Battle of Waterloo, six weeks before); and for good measure, he took with them Jane Clairmont. As companion for Mary? An alternative mistress? Another damsel in distress? A soul to be enlightened? Or for sheer deviltry?

They left London in a chaise at dawn. At Dartford they hired four horses to outstrip their pursuers. They reached Dover in twelve hours and hired a small open channel boat, in order to keep ahead. The breeze was fitful and as the moon rose, there was a heavy swell. The wind veered and the sailors debated whether to make for Calais or Boulogne. The summer lightning played across the sky. Mary, who in the chaise had been ill with the heat, sat exhausted between Shelley's knees. In a flight so precipitately romantic, we do not know whether any or all of them were seasick; only that as at dawn they drove upon the sands of Calais, Shelley woke Mary tenderly and said, "Look, Mary, the sun rises over France."

That evening a fat lady landed in Calais. It was Mrs Godwin come to claim her errant daughter. Shelley wouldn't let her see Mary (of whom Mrs Godwin's sentiments were probably "good riddance to bad rubbish"), but Jane spent the night with her mother and next morning went to Mary and Shelley and told them she was returning home.

What sort of prospect would Skinner Street hold for her? Drudgery in the house and bookshop, the only means of escape some post as governess? Ahead lay freedom, travel, adventures of the body and spirit. "Take an hour to decide," said Shelley.

Jane went to her mother and told her that she intended to stay with Mary and Shelley. Mrs Godwin returned by the next packet, perhaps consoling herself that it was Mary Wollstonecraft's daughter and not hers who would bear the disgrace of losing her virtue.

It is not the province of a book devoted to Georgian ladies to penetrate the labyrinth of Shelley's motives. Mary Godwin's are luckily simpler. She was the child of Mary Wollstonecraft (in her bold revolutionary hat) and of William Godwin (the author of *Political Justice*, not the sanctimonious old sponge of Skinner Street). From early childhood she had realised that great things would be expected of her when she grew up. She was no ordinary girl, but the representative of two revolutionary philosophers. She had to prove that they were right; that the Christian religion was a myth and Christian morality a misguided convention. For her, as for Shelley, the elopement was as much a public gesture as a private act. They were on the stage, performing not merely to their contemporaries but to posterity. Even Jane felt this, though it was not until 1816 that she felt her role demanded a change of name from Mary Jane to something more romantic.

All three of them kept journals; Mary and Shelley jointly, and Jane, as usual, on her own. All three of them attempted novels, Shelley *The Assassins*, Mary *Hate* and Jane *The Ideot*. ("This has been for years a favourite plan of mine," the sixteen year-old "wallflower" wrote. "To develop the Workings and Improvement of the mind which by Common people was deemed the mind of an Ideot, because it conformed not to their vulgar and prejudiced views.") But nothing came of their writing, except a *History of a Six Weeks Tour* (1817) extracted from the journal of Mary and Shelley. Their idiotic escapade lasted no longer, because they ran out of money. After they had been abroad a fortnight, Shelley wrote Harriet asking her to join them. But Harriet forced them to return by blocking his supplies of money.

By mid-September, they were established at the first of many London lodgings. Mary was pregnant. Jane was sleep-walking, the prey to nightmares. Harriet was expecting any week. "Perhaps I have done you injury," Shelley wrote her, "but surely most innocently and unintentionally, in having commenced any connexion with you." In a P.S. he added, "I do not apprehend the slightest danger from your approaching labour. . . . Your last labour was painful, but auspicious. I understand that cases of difficulty after that are very rare." And in a P.P.S., "I am in want of stockings, hanks and Mrs W's posthumous works."

From Mrs W's posthumous works, Harriet could have learnt that Mrs W. had not apprehended the slightest danger from the labour after which she had died. Harriet was luckier. On November 30, she was brought safely to bed of an heir, Charles Bysshe.

Shelley was continuously flitting to avoid the duns. The two and a half thousand pounds he had raised in June had vanished. But in January 1815, the same month in which Mary gave birth to a daughter who lived only two weeks, Shelley's grandfather died and serious negotiations started with his father for a settlement of their finances. Not that it made for a settlement of their ways of life.

In pursuit of perfectibility and flight from debt, they were never long in one place. In just over a year Mary gave birth to a second child (William, who survived for two and a half years). In October Fanny Imlay killed herself by poison in a Swansea hotel; and in December Harriet Shelley's body, in an advanced stage of pregnancy, was fished out of the Serpentine. Fifteen days later, Mary, child of the woman who had failed to drown herself off Putney Bridge, married Percy Shelley; and her father, professor of free love, welcomed them back to Skinner Street. "According to the vulgar ideas of the world," William wrote his brother, "she is well married, and I have great hopes the young man (the eldest son of Sir Timothy Shelley of Field Place in the County of Sussex, Baronet) will make her a good husband."

Though by December 1816, William Godwin felt proud, Shelley guiltless and Mary secure, Jane Clairmont was in a condition which did not embarrass her, but which needed to be hidden from her mother and step father.

In 1814, when she decided at Calais to go on with Mary and Shelley rather than return to Skinner Street with her mother, she had expected more than she received. She hoped perhaps that she would share Shelley as a lover. Instead, Shelley made horror games with her, when Mary was in bed, sleeping the sleep of the loved and pregnant. Brought up on Gothic romances, Jane was fascinated and terrified by Shelley's plays on her imagination. She may have produced poltergeistic phenomena. At any rate she thought she did: and like any sceptical atheist, she had a susceptibility for the supernatural.

Her position on their return to England had been precarious. She had no money, except once when she was lucky enough to win a lottery. She was faced with three possibilities, all distasteful: to live as a wallflower with Mary and Shelley; as a drudge in Skinner Street; or as a governess, in the same way that the great Mary Wollstonecraft had been forced to do with the Kingsboroughs.

In the spring of 1818, she had resorted to a desperate expedient. There was Mary, the mistress of the poetic genius Shelley, heir to a baronetcy. She would fly higher. Byron was a lord, a poet whose genius was acknowledged and whose poems brought him guineas by the thousand. Shelley was a professed free lover. Byron was a practised one. The world knew from *Don Juan* his plentitude of exotic mistresses. Lady Caroline Lamb had made her passion the scandal of London. For a short time Lady Oxford had flaunted him as her lover. His wife

Annabella Milbanke had borne him a child and now was trying to divorce him as a madman. He was wide open to love.

For her assault on Byron, Mary Jane thought her Swiss surname would pass muster, but she could not decide whether she would be Constantia (which might scare a lord afraid of constancy), Clare, Clara, Clary or Claire, variations of fame and splendour.

It did not matter. What Byron saw was an eighteen year-old girl, not very beautiful, but vivacious, unsophisticatedly wrong-headed, pretending to want to write for, or act in, the theatre, but really begging him to take her maidenhead. It is possible that he would not have encouraged her further, if he hadn't discovered the connexion with Godwin. And the fact that she was not Godwin's daughter, but merely the daughter of the damn'd infernal bitch whom Godwin had married, made her proposal to spend a night with him out of London, at the same time attractive and trivial.

In April she insisted on showing Byron off to Mary at his rented house in Piccadilly Terrace. This in her mind was the beginning of a wonderful relationship, Byron a recruit to a Shelleyan community. For Byron, it was only a minor boredom, added to the major boredom of debts, nullity suits and Milbanke nuisances, which he would have to go to Europe to avoid. Like William Hickey, James Boswell and innumerable 18th century philanderers, he felt no guilt in taking or discarding mistresses.

When Byron planned to go to Geneva to avoid his creditors, "Claire" persuaded Mary and Shelley to take her there in advance of her lover. Wishing "to escape that contempt we so unjustly endure", Shelley had been thinking of going to Cumberland or Scotland, but the prospect of meeting Byron, to whom he had sent a copy of *Queen Mab*, turned the scale in favour of Switzerland.

As for Byron, "What could I do?" he wrote his half-sister Augusta Leigh. "A foolish girl in spite of all I could say or do, would come after me, or rather, went before me. . . . I could not play the Stoic with a woman who had scrambled eight hundred miles to unphilosophise me." He enjoyed talking to Shelley, as one poet (who had sold 14,000 copies of a poem in one day) to another (who was soon to try to suppress *Queen Mab* as juvenile). But the devotion of Claire became tedious. He tried to put her off with cautionary tales. He had had a Turkish girl who was unfaithful to him sewn into a sack and tossed in the Bosphorus. The original of his Thirza was a girl he had seduced and given two children. When he refused to marry her, she committed suicide and he could not erect a stone in her memory because she was buried at a cross road with a stake through her. Claire noted, "He said he fretted very much about her death, but nothing, not even that, would have made him marry her because she was of mean birth." Whether it was true or not, the warning was plain. Claire need not think he would marry her if she became pregnant, even if she used Mary Wollstonecraft's blackmail of threatened suicide.

By July Claire knew she was pregnant. Shelley discussed with Byron what should be done about the baby. He and Mary would take Claire home and look after her lying-in so that the Godwins knew nothing. Byron first suggested the baby should be sent to his half-sister's to be cared for: but at Claire's insistence he agreed that for the first seven years it should live with one or other of the parents. Anything for a life free from romantic Godwinians. "I forgot to tell you," he wrote Augusta, "that the demoiselle who returned to England from Geneva went there to produce a new baby B. who is about to make his appearance."

This was in August 1816, before the suicides of Fanny Imlay and Harriet Shelley and the marriage of Mary to Shelley. At Bath on January 13, 1817, Claire gave birth to a daughter, whom she christened Allegra after the gaiety which she felt, and hoped Byron would share, at her birth.

The idea of a natural daughter did give Byron some pleasure, provided that he did not have to see the child's mother. "Although I never was attached nor pretended attachment to the mother, still in case of the eternal war and alienation which I foresee about my legitimate daughter, Ada, it may be as well to have something to repose a hope upon," he wrote Augusta. "I must love something in my old age and probably circumstances will render this poor little creature a great and perhaps my only comfort . . ."

As foresight, it was tragically inept. Allegra died of typhus at the age of five, in an Italian convent, unvisited by her mother or father. Before that time Mary Shelley's daughter Clara and her son William were also dead, in consequence of Shelley's impetuosity and Mary's obedience. Three months after Allegra died, Shelley himself was drowned, but not before he had given Claire a baby which miscarried and his children's nurse a daughter who survived for eighteen months. Byron himself died on April 19, 1824, two years to the day after the natural daughter he anticipated would cherish his old age.

Of Mary's children, there only remained Percy Florence, so named after his father and the city in which he was born. He was a very ordinary boy, untainted by genius, talent or romanticism. He went to Harrow, Byron's old school, where to his mother's relief he never conceived an original thought. When he was seven, he became heir to the baronetcy through the death of Harriet's son, Charles Bysshe; and in 1844, on the death of his grandfather, he succeeded to the title and his father's legacies were paid.

These included £12,000 to Claire Clairmont. She could have married Thomas Love Peacock perhaps. At least Maria Reveley thought so. "How much suffering she might have been spared if she had married Peacock!" she exclaimed. We have no evidence that Peacock ever proposed to her. He may well have been content with setting her down as Stella in his *Nightmare Abbey*. And Mrs Reveley may merely have been reflecting how much suffering *she* had avoided by rejecting William Godwin and marrying John Gisborne. We do know that Claire might have married Maria's son, Henry Reveley. But at the time of Henry's proposal Byron and Allegra were still alive. Instead, she became a governess; what Shelley had warned her she would have to be, if she returned from Calais with her mother instead of venturing on with Mary and him across war-torn Europe.

With her legacy from Shelley Claire lived on to the age of 81. A young

American writer called Henry James met her at a tea-party in Florence. It was not until after she died on March 19, 1879 that he realised that the gentle old lady had once been the hoyden who flung herself so audaciously into the arms of Lord Byron.

What a scandal those revolutionary daughters had caused in Georgian times! Yet their principal faults had not been perversity but innocence. As Claire herself remarked, "Our upbringing unfitted us entirely for intercourse with vicious characters. . . . Nothing could be more refined and amiable than the doctrines instilled into us, only they were utterly erroneous."

Bibliographical Note

The Grand Century of the Lady is intended more as an historical excursion than a scholarly dissertation. To compile a bibliography of the sources from which I drew this book as full as the index to its contents would hamper readers rather than aid them. Wandering throughout that vast bookstore The London Library, in St James's Square, I have, like a raven, pilfered here a trinket, there a gaud. To their staff and treasury of 18th and 19th century books, my main acknowledgments are due.

But I would like to thank certain other writers either for information or for indications of where to go for further research. Elizabeth Burton's *The Georgians at Home* is a most delightful and intelligent study of everyday life which taught me much and indicated what I should supplement if possible rather than repeat. Peter Fryer's *The Birth Controllers* (1965) is the source for much of the chapter on breeding: and Norman Hartnell's *Royal Courts of Fashion*, 1971 and Elizabeth Ewing's *Fashion in Underwear* for a little in the chapter on Fashion. Most of my sources, when modern, have been indicated in the text. But I must confess my debt to Hope Costley-White, for her charming *Mary Cole, Countess of Berkeley* (1961) and to Claire Tomalin for her thoughtful *Life and Death of Mary Wollstonecraft*. In my text, I have paid tribute to Richard Holmes' *The Pursuit of Shelley*, but here I should acknowledge my debts to my good friends Rosalie Glynn Grylls for her *Mary Shelley* and *Clair Clairmont* and Malcolm Elwin for *Lord Byron's Wife* (1962) and *The Noels and the Milbankes*, 1967. I do not think that I quoted a single sentence from any of these volumes, but my debt is great in understanding. The same is true of many other recent books: the *Byron Letters and Journals* edited by Leslie A. Marchand, Professor Aspinall's Correspondence of *George Prince of Wales and George IV*.

The list of sources is almost endless.

But if instead of a Bibliography, I had to recommend someone wanting to study the England of the 18th century, I would recommend *Parson Woodforde's Diary*, William Hickey's *Memoirs* and Cobbett's *Rural Rides*. For the splendours and miseries of the Georgian Lady, let me recommend the Autobiography of Mrs Delany (if necessary retold by Simon Dewes, her descendant in *Mrs Delany*, Rich & Cowan, undated), the life of Mrs Thrale (later Mrs Piozzi), the diaries of Miss Frances Burney (later Madame d' Arblay), *The Memoirs of Harriette Wilson* and, for good value, *The Adventures of Fanny Hill*, by John Cleland. Cleland wrote *Fanny Hill, or the Memoirs of a Woman of Pleasure* in two parts, which were published in 1748 and 1749. He was paid twenty guineas for the copyright by the bookseller-publisher Griffiths, who is said to have made a profit of £10,000 from its sales. A frank, delightful, erotic novel, it aroused such religious resentment that Cleland was summoned before the privy council, to whom he pleaded poverty. He was not punished, but a bookseller named

Drybutter who had tried to gild the lily by salacious additions was made to stand in the pillory. Lord Granville, on behalf no doubt of many of his peers who kept Fanny Hill in their libraries, awarded Cleland a pension of £100 a year "in order that he might make a worthier use of his talents", in the words of the *Dictionary of National Biography*. He never wrote anything half as good, but it was a civilised way of appeasing the unco' guid and recompensing the impoverished Cleland for a little masterpiece.

Index

(References to illustrations are enclosed in parentheses.)

Abdy, Sir William 153

Ackerman, R. 47

Acting, rhetorical 64, natural 64

Adams, Abigail 155-6, (71)

Adams, John 155-7

Adams, Samuel & Sarah. *The Complete Servant* 20-23, 25, 32, 41

Addison, Joseph 24

Alderson, Amelia 162

Algarotti, Francesco 127

Amelia, Princess daughter of George III. White gloves and fan at age of 3 43

American Declaration of Independence 155. War of Independence 7, 12, 154, 157

Andrews, Mr & Mrs 92, (53)

Angelo, Henry, *Reminiscences* 51. Vauxhall Affray 54. visits Vauxhall with Rowlandson 54-55. "Angelo, Old", *See* Tremamondo

Ann, Queen 9, 10, 11, 36, 38, 78, 118

Archer, Lady. Gambling house kept by 84

Argyle, Duke of. Verdict on Beggar's Opera 61. Archibald, Duke of 130.

Armistead, Mrs 136-7

Arne, Susanna. *See* Cibber.

Arne, Dr Thomas Augustine. Music to Romeo & Juliet 67. Intervenes in "Susanna's" marriage 70-71

Auriol, family 93

Austen, Cassandra 94

Austen, Jane 35, 94, 113-5, 154. *Emma* 35, 94, 113, 114. *Northanger Abbey* 113. *Persuasion* 113. *Pride and Prejudice* 94. *Sense and Sensibility* 106, 114. *The Watsons* 114, (49)

Austin (?). 9 months after (1)

"Backscratchers" for verminous scalps 41

Barry, Spranger, Irish actor 63, 66-67

Bassett, Mr & Mrs Francis 119, 121

Bate, The Rev. Henry (Dudley). In Vauxhall 54. Reports on Sarah Siddons 71

Bath 108, (60)

Beaufort Duke of 153

Beaumarchais Mariage de Figaro 43

Beauty Patches 42

Beckford, William 80

Beggar's Opera, The, on fans 43, 61-62, 63. Revival 69

Bellamy, George Anne, Irish actress 63. As Juliet 67. Auditions in Teddington barn 68, 69

Behn, Mrs Aphra 144

Bentham, Jeremy 17-18

Berkeley, Frederick Augustus Fitzhardinge, 5th Earl of 137-140

Berkeley, Admiral Sir George Cranfield 140

Bertin, Mlle Rose 39, 45

Bess of Hardwick 21

Bessborough, Henrietta Frances Countess of 77, 78, 86, 137

Blackburne, Dr Archbishop of York. His mistress and natural son 136

Black magic 11, 35

Blackwell, Alexander, printer-apothecary 99-100

Blackwell, Elizabeth, his artist-obstetrician wife 99-100

Blake, William 12, 157, 159

Blood, Fanny 157, 161

Blue stockings 112

Boaden, on Master Betty's debut 73-74

Bolton, Duke of 62

Bolton, Duchess of, Godmother to "Con Phillips" 144

Bolton, Miss as Polly Peachum 62

Boswell, James 16, 81, 105, 107, 171. *Life of Johnson* 116, 117

Bowles, Catherine, surgeon 101

Bramble, Squire 52. On "gardy loo" 99

Brandon, Colonel 106, 114

Brangton, the Misses 53

Brighton, Pavilion 44, 46

Bronte sisters 113

Brookes, Mr, anatomist of Blenheim St. Panic in his Zoo 59

Brougham, Henry 153

Brownlow, Lady on Queen Adelaide's ginger complexion 75-76

Bruce, Lord. Recommends Sarah Siddons to Garrick 71

Brummell, Beau 44, 46, 153

Brunswick, Caroline, wife of George IV 14

Buckinghamshire, Albinia Countess of 84-85

Bunbury, Sir Charles 88, 118
Burney, Dr 16
Burney, Charlotte 42
Burney, Edward Francesco 94
Burney, Fanny 16, 17, 50, 51, 55, 94, 107–8, 117
Burns, Robert. On a louse 41
Byron, Lord 35, 94, 153, 170–2. *Don Juan* 170
Byron, Lady (Annabella Milbanke) 171

Campbell, Dr John. Thirteen bottles of port at a sitting 34
Canals 12
Carlisle House 55–57
Carlton House 44–46
Carlyle, Thomas and Jane 163
Casanova 16, 55–56, 122
Cato Street Conspiracy 18
Cave, Edward "Sylvanus Urbanus", 106
Centlivre, Mrs epilogue to *The Gamester* 78–79, 144
Charke, Mrs Charlotte 63, 149, (73)
Charlotte, Queen, Wife of George III 94, 123
Charlotte, Princess, d. of Prince Regent 14. Given fan at age of 2, 42–43. Her birthday party 43. Marriage 45–46. Prays for fleas 99
Charlotte, of Mecklenburgh-Strelitz, Queen 14. Revealing wedding garments of 39–40. Snuff taking 43–44. Court dress 46, 47, 94
Chatsworth, equipped with ten water closets 98
Chelsea Hospital 50
Chesterfield, Lord. Has all letters directed to Ranelagh 51. Writes songs for Beggar's Opera 62. On marriage 123. With "Con Phillips" 144–5, 148.
Cholmondeley, Captain 68
Cholmondeley, Earl 68
Cholmondeley, Polly 68
Clairmont, Mrs 164. Marries Godwin 164, 165, 168–9
Clairmont, Mary Jane (Claire) 11, 164, 168, 169, 170, 171, 172–3. *The Ideot* 169. Bears Byron's daughter Allegra 172
Cleanliness, not practiced always even by royalty 42
Clive, Kitty. Fatness 30. Irish birth 63. As Portia 64–65. Marriage and career of 69–70. Dr Johnson on 69–70. Compared with Garrick 70, 71, 74. As Cleopatra 94
Clogher, Dean of. Life saved by holly tree 37
Cobbett, William 12, 20
Coffee House. The Bedford Covent Garden 60, 65
Coke, Lady Mary 128–31, 142–3

Coke, Thomas, Earl of Leicester 128
Coke, Lord. His heir 128–31
Cole, family. Ann, *See* Farren. Mary, *See* Berkeley. Susan, *alias* "Mrs Turnover" 137–9
Coleridge, S, T 163
Colman, George the Younger. On toupée 41
Colonies. North American 17. West Indies 17. East India 17. India 18. Fear separation to 25
Concannon, Mrs, gambling hostess 84
Condorcet, Marquis de. *Lettres d'un Bourgeois de Newhaven* (1787) 157, 159
Congreve, William. On Beggar's Opera 61
Contraceptives 15, 16. Cundum sellers 16
Copyright, *Modest Plea* for, Mrs Macaulay 17
Cornelys, Sophie, *alias* Miss Williams 56
Cornelys, Mrs, Theresa 55–57
Cosmetics. Preparation of for freckles and various pimples 22–23. Poisonous properties of 41–42. Bill to prosecute use of cosmetics as witchcraft 45
Coutts, Thomas banker 17, 86
Coventry, Lady. Killed by white lead 42
Crapper, Thomas 99
Craven, Earl of 152
Crewe, Mrs (later Lady) 79–80, 154
Cruickshank, George 9, (11–14), 16
Cumberland, Duke & Duchess of 32. Liable to be trodden on in Ranelagh 51
Custance, Mr and his mistress Miss Sherman 136

Daly, Irish Theatre Manager 68, 74
Dashwood, Elinor 114
Dashwood, Marianne. Views on marriage 106, 114
Dashwood, Sir Francis 145
Defoe, Daniel 15–16
Delane, Dennis, Irish actor 63. As Merchant of Venice 64
Delany, Mrs Mary 14, 38, 118–23, 140
Delany, Rev. Patrick 122, 145
D'eon, Mlle le Chevalier 11
Dering, Sir Edward 116
De Seingault, Chevalier, *alias* Casanova 56
Devonshire, Georgiana 5th Duchess of 17, 41, 77, 79, 102, 154, 158, (48)
Devonshire, William 5th Duke of 58, 79, 94, 158
Devonshire, William 6th Duke of 153
Dighton, Richard. Country ball (39)
Dodsley, publisher 147
Douglas, Catherine, Duchess of Queensbury. Patronises Gay 61–62
Douglas, Charles, 3rd Duke of Queensbury 61–62, 142

Douglas, William, 3rd Earl of March, 4th Duke of Queensbury 81–82, 142–3

Edgeworth, Maria 113, 124, 154
Edgeworth, Richard Lovell 113
Egan, Pierce 55
Encyclopaedists 11, 155
Entail 17, 116
Evelina 17, 50, 51. In Vauxhall 53. At Marybone 53–54, 68, 107–8, 109

Fangotherapy 103
Fans 42–43
Farren, Anne, née Cole 137, 139
Female spectator. On ram butting a lady in Picadilly 37–38
Fenton, Lavinia, actress 62. Duchess of Bolton 62
Fielding, Henry, *Amelia* 54, 55, 65, 67. *An Apology for the Life of Mrs Shamela Andrews* 135. *Joseph Andrews* 135. *The Battle of the Poets* 150. *Tom Thumb* 150
Fisher, Kitty, actress killed by cosmetics 42, as Cleopatra 94 (43)
Fitzclarences. Children of Dorothy Jordon, morganatic wife of the Duke of Clarence (King William IV) 15, 75
Fitzhardinge, Thomas Moreton 140–41
Fitzhardinge, William, Baron Seagrave 1st Earl Fitzhardinge 139–41
Fitzherbert, Mrs 139, (74)
Flea catchers employed by George III and the Prince Regent 99
Fleetwood, Theatre Manager 64, 151
Fontange, Mlle Originator of hair style 40
Foote, Samuel 64, 67
Foster, Lady Elizabeth 94, 158
Fox, Charles James 80, 118, 136–7
Fox, Henry 1st Lord Holland, 80–81, 118
Fox, Henry 2nd Lord Holland, 80
Fox, Henry 3rd Lord Holland, 136–7
Fox, Lady Elizabeth wife of 3rd Lord Holland, 143, 154
Franklin, Benjamin 101–2, 103, 105
Free love, 19, 158, 159, 164
Fuseli, Henry 157, 158
Fuseli, Mrs 158

Gainsborough, Thomas Pantheon 58, 91–93, (48, 53, 54a, 54b, 57)
Gambling, Games 77, 78. Royal Province of Groom Porter 77. Gambling act of 1739, 83. Of 1745, 83. Gambling houses kept by the Ladies Mordington and Cassilis 83–84. By Albinib Lady Buckinghamshire et. al. 84

Garrick, David. At Pantheon 58. His career 65–67. Life with Peg Woffington 67. Marries the dancer Violette, 68. Acts Orestes at Teddington 68. Last season 71–72. Made actors respectable 72. Peeps through keyhole at the Johnsons 105–6, 112
Garrick, George 105–6
Gay, John 60, 61–62
Gentleman's Magazine, The 13, 78, 106
George, Ist 9, 10, 11, 14, 38, 77, 78, 122, 123
George II, 11, 14, 61, 78, 91, 136, 146
George III, 11, 14, 39–40, 75, 99, 100, 118, 123, 136, 154
George IV, 9, 11, 14, 16, 32, 44, 46, 47, 48, 58, 77, 99, 100, 136, 138, 139
Gillray, James 9. On gambling 84–85, (47)
Glorious revolution, 1688, 9, 10, 36
Godwin, Mary Wollstonecraft. See Shelley, Mary
Godwin, William 157, 160. Career 161–3, 171, 172. *Memoirs* of Mary Wollstonecraft 163. *Political Justice* 162, 165. *Caleb Williams* 165
Goldsmith, Oliver On Immoderate Tails 40. *She Stoops to Conquer* 60. Irish playwrights 63, 68, 123. *The Citizen of the World* 110–12, 113.
Gordon, Duchess of. Insults Duke of York's mistress 58
Gower, Lady 94
Gower, Lady Evelyn 127
Graham, James 101–3
Granville, Bernard 118, 119, 121
Granville, Mary. *See* Delany Mrs
Granville, Lord Leverson Gower 86, 153
Gronow, Capt. von On Queen Charlotte's nose 43. On snuff-taking at the Pavilion 44
Guy, Richard 96

Hamilton, Emma Lady 24, 93, (63)
Hamilton, Horatia 24
Hamilton, Sir William 24
Hanway, Jonas 46
Harley, Jane Elizabeth, Countess of Oxford 16, 170
Harrington, Jane Countess of 56, 91, 92, (55)
Haymarket theatre 56. Migrates after fire to Pantheon 58
Hazlett, William On Mrs Siddons 72
Head-dresses. Mrs Delany on 38. *Tête de Mouton* 38. George Colman on 41. Decorations for 40–41. Lice in 41. Combs etc., 47. (22, 24, 25, 36)
Health, Goddess of, Emma Lady Hamilton reputed to have been 102, like a cauliflower 103

Health, The Temple of 102–3
Herrick, Robert 36
Hervey, Augustus 42
Hervey, John Lord ("Sporus") 127
Hickey, William 171
High life, Below stairs 51, 60
Highmore, John (2, 66, 67)
Hogarth, William 9, 90, 103. *Mariage à la Mode*, (4, 5, 62, 64, 65) *The Harlot's Progress* (44)
Hogg, Thomas Jefferson 168
Hoppner, John 94
Horse racing, Ascot Heath 86. Epsom Downs 86. Newmarket Heath 80, 82, 86, 142. York 86–87. Races, The Derby, the Oaks 88, 118
Hospitals, 95–96
Howard, John. Penal Reformer 97
Howe, Mary Countess of (54b)
Hulkett, Sir John & Family
Humphreys, Ozyas 94
Hunt, John & Leigh 166
Hunter, Kitty 144, 158
Hunter, Dr Sir William 100
Huntingdon, Selina, Countess of 154
Hutton, Mrs G. P. Sells secret of digitalis to Dr Withering 101

Ilchester, Lord and Lady 118
Imer, actor father of Therese Cornelys 55
Imlay, Fanny (Françoise) 161, 163, 164, 165, 166, 170
Imlay, Gilbert 159–161
Inchbald, Mrs Elizabeth 144, 162
Italian Opera House 57, 58

Jacobites, 10, 108, 118, 121, 122, 154
James, Henry 173
James I 10
James II 9
Jenner, Dr 96–97
Jervas, Charles 91 (51)
Jockey Club, The 82, 87–88
Johnson, Jenny. *See* Cibber Jenny
Johnson, Joseph 157–8
Johnson, Dr Samuel 10, 24, 30. On Hanway 46. At tea with Garrick 67, 68. On Kitty Clive and Mrs Porter 69–70. Writes his name on the hem of Mrs Siddon's garment, 72. Marriage 105–7, 108. On mean marriage 117–18. On double standards of chastity 132. *Life of Johnson* 116
Johnstone, Lady Cecilia 130
Johnstone, Julia. *Confessions in Contradiction of the Fables of Harriette Wilson* 152

Jordan, Mrs Dorothy 15. Her debut 74. Aliases 74. Seduced by Daly 74. Her children by Daly 74. By Ford and the Duke of Clarence 74–75. Her rise and fall 75
Josephine, Empress 46

Kauffman, Angelica 93, 94, (76)
Kean, Edmund. Earnings of 73
Kemble, Charles 71. John Philip 71, 73. Roger 71. Sarah 71. Sarah d. of Roger and Sarah, *See* Siddons
Kendal, Duchess of 123
Kenyon, Mr (Later Lord) 84–85, 94, (47)
Kenyon, Mrs (Later Lady) 94
King, Gregory *Observations on the State of England* 13
Kingsborough, Lord 149, 157
Kingsborough, Lady 157, 170
Kingston, 1st Duke of, Evelyn Pierrepoint 124–7
Kneller, Sir Godfrey 90

Lady's Calling 110
Lamb, Charles & Mary *Tales from Shakespeare* 165
Lamb, Elizabeth, Lady Melbourne 16
Lamb, Caroline Lady 46, 94, 170, (72)
Lamb, Frederick 16, 152, 153
Lamb, George 16
Lamb, Peniston, Sir William. Lord M. 16
Lamb, Peniston 16
Language, Changes in 14–15
Lansdowne, Lady 38, 119, 122
Lansdowne, Lord 118, 119
Laroche, Miss. Life saved by stays 37
Lascelles, Mrs Edwin (Lady Harewood) 91–92, (56)
Lawrence, Sir Thomas 94
Le Fanu, Alicia, Mrs Joseph 108, 125
Le Fanu, Henry 109, 125
Le Fanu, Joseph 108
Le Fanu, Père 109
Leigh, Augusta 171
Lennox, Lady Sarah 88, 118
Life in London 55, (41)
Ligonier, Penelope, Viscountess 91, (57)
Linley, Elizabeth (Mrs Sheridan) 92, (54a)
Linley, Mary (Mrs Tickell) 92, (54a)
Linley, Thomas 92
London clubs. Almack's 80, 86. Almack's Ladies Club 83. Brooks, 153. Kit-Cat 124. United Services 153. White's 80. Old Clubs and New Clubs, 81, 82, 143, 147, 153

Lowndes, T. Publisher 17

London Daily Post On Garrick's debut 66

London Magazine, The 107

Lunardi, 9. In Pantheon with his balloon, dog and cat 58

Macaulay, Mrs Catherine *Letters on Education* 17. *A Modest Plea for the Property of Copyright* 17. One of nine living Cases 93, (70). Takes quack-doctor Graham's brother as second husband 101, 155

Macklin, Charles 63–67

Madame Rena, prima donna 141–2

Malthus, Rev. *On Population* 13, 19

Mapp, Mr 103

Mapp, Mrs bonesetter 103–4. "Mrs Mapp" mare 104

March, Lord *See* Douglas, William, 4th Earl of Queensbury

Marie, Antoinette, Queen 38, 45, 46

Marlborough, Sarah Churchill, Duchess of 11, 21, M90–91

    artindale, Henry. Croupier and moneylender 84–85

Master Betty the young Roscuis, Irish actor 63, 73–74

Meade, family 145

Meade, Colonel 148

Mears, Mrs Martha gynaecologist 100

Medmenham 11, 35, 145

Melford, Lydia 49, 52, 56

    Memoirs of Harriette Wilson 152–3

    Memoirs of Letitia Pilkington 148–9

    Memoirs of Mary Wollstonecraft 163

Menus 30–31

Merveilleuses Les 45

midwifery, Introduction to the practice of, Dr Thomas Denman 100

Midwives, Mrs Kennon, Mrs Draper et. al. 100

Mill, James 18

Mill, John Stuart 18, 19

Milliners, Mlle Rose Bertin 39, 45. Mrs Tempest 39

Misson. On Patches 42

Montagu, Edward Wortley M. 124–8

Montagu, Lady Mary 11. On uniform perfection of Court Ladies 42. On Lavinia Fenton 62. Small-pox 96. Career 123–128, 131. Richardson more lewd than Rochester 134. An Italian Pamela 135. Cousin of Fielding 135. In Kit Kat (3). In Turkish dress (50)

    Montagu, Mrs Bluestocking 93, 116, 142, 144,

148, 154

More, Hannah 109, 112, 124

Napoleon, Disapproval of décolleté, preference for white 46. Napoleonic Wars 7

Narrative of her life by Charlotte Charke 149

Nelson, Ad. Lord 24

Nicholls, Dr Frank Writes commissioned attack on men-midwives 100

North, Christopher On Mrs Siddons 72

O'Brien, Lady Susan nee Fox Strangeways 14, 15, 19, 24, 88, 118

O'Brien William 118

Old maids petition 61

Opera house (41)

Opie, John (75)

Paine, Tom 155, 157, 159. Common Sense Papers 158. *Rights of Man* 159. *Age of Reason* 159

Pamela in High Life 134. Pamela ill. J. Highmore, (2, 66, 67)

Pamela or Virtue Rewarded Written in 2 months 133. Earlier letter novels by Alciphron, Montesquieu, 134. Success and translation 134–5, 138, 141, 152

Pantheon 53. Views of Walpole and Dr Johnson 57. Created by Wyatt, ambition of Mrs Hard-castle 57. Guests 58. Lunardi at 58. Fire 58–59. Painting by Turner 137

Paris fashions, 38–39, 46, (21)

Parsons, Mrs E. "In the family way" 14

Peachum, based on Jonathan Wild, thief taker 61

Peachum, Polly. Played by Lavinia Fenton 61

Peacock, Thomas Love 168, 172

Pembroke, Earl and Countess of 144, 158

Pendarves, Squire of Roscow Castle 119–22

Pepys, Samuel 50, 78

Petersham, Lady Caroline stews chickens at Vauxhall 51

Phillips, Tersia Constantia 144–5. Writes *apology* 145, 152

Pierrepoint, Evelyn See Kingston Duke of

Pierrepoint, Lady Mary *See* Montague, Lady Mary Wortley 114

Pilkington, Elizabeth 149

Pilkington, John Carteret 149

Pilkington, Laetitia 145–52, 157

Pilkington, Matthew 145. Author of *Dictionary of Painters* 149

Pimples 22–23

Piozzi, Gabriel Mario 117

Piozzi, Mrs *See* Thrale Mrs

Pitt, George 91

Place, Francis 17–18

Pleasure gardens, Cuper's or Cupid's Gardens 49. Marybone Gdns 49. Excellent Food 51. Described by Angelo and F. Burney 51, 53–54. Fireworks 53. Ranelagh House, Rotunda and Gdns 50. 'Runelow for my money' 51, 52. Spring Gdns Old and New 49

Political justice, William Godwin 161, 165, 167

Polly Banned by Lord Chamberlain earns John Gay over £1,000 in subscriptions 62

Pompeati, Italian dancer husband of Theresa Cornelys, 55

Pompeati Mrs *See* Theresa Cornelys

Pompeati Guiseppe, son 56. *alias* Count d'Aranda, alias, Mr or Sir Joseph Cornelys

Pope, Alexander. Suggests theme for Beggar's Opera 61. Note in *The Dunciad*, on Macklin's Shylock 65. On Garrick 66. On marriage 105. Lady Mary Wortley Montagu 127, 146. On Cibber 149

Population 12–13

Porter, Mrs Elizabeth marriage with Dr Johnson, 105

Porter, Mrs Mary actress 67. Dr Johnson on 69–70

Portland, 2nd Duchess of 122, 123

Prince Regent *See* George IV

Praz, Mario 92–93

Precedency 32

Prisons, Marshalsea 27–28, 145, 148. Fleet 27, 145

Pritchard, Hannah 30. As Rosalind 66

Pulteney, Heiress 109

Pupil of Nature; or Candid Advice to the Fair Sex by Martha Mears 100

Quadrille Party (45)

Quakers 44–45, 142

Quin, James 63, 66–67

Race horses Vinganillo, Thornville 87. Gimcrack, Eclipse, Diomend 88, 118

Raffald, Mrs 28, 31

Raftor, Catherine *See* Clive, Kitty

Raftor, Jeremy 70

Ranelagh, Viscount (late Earl of) Ranelagh 50

Recamier, Mme. 46

Reform Bill 1831 9, 10. Reformists Correspondence Societies 85

Reid, Sir William & Lady, eye-Doctor 101

Repository of Arts 47

Reveley, Henry 172

Reveley, Mrs Maria 164

Revolution, French 21, 36, 45, 154

Reynolds, Sir Joshua. At Pantheon 58, 68, 72, 91, 92, 93, 94, 112, 55, 56, 59)

Rich, John, manager of Lincoln's Inn Fields Theatre 61

Richardson, Samuel 132, 133–5, 147, 148. *Pamela* 132–4, 138. *Clarissa Harlowe* 134

Rivals, The 123

Roads 11

Robinson, Mrs Perdita 136

Rochefoucauld, 34, 142

Rochester, Lord. Lewd poems of 134

Rogers, Samuel. On Mrs Siddons in retirement 73

Roland, Madame 159

Roman Catholics 10, 154

Romney, George 93, (63)

Rothwell, Richard (78)

Rouge et Noir, by Charles Persuis (C. Dunne) 79

Rousseau, J. J. 21, 158

Rowlandson, Thomas 9. At Vauxhall 54. Gambling at Devonshire House 79, (37)

Royal Academy 90

Royal College of Physicians 96

Royal Marriage Act of 1772 14

Russell, Dr of Brighthelmstone 98

Samuel, R (70)

Sandwich, John Montagu 4th Earl, 35

Sandwich, Lady 40

Sanitation 13, 97, 99

Saxe-Coburg Neiningen, Amelia Adelaide Louise Theresa Caroline, Princess of 75–76

Saxe Gotha, Princess Augusta of, wife of Frederick Prince of Wales 14

Schessile, C. 71

Scott, Sir Walter 152, 153

Sebastian and Laetitia 126

Selwyn, George 80, 81, 147

Sensual love 10

Servant, The Complete, by Samuel and Sarah Adams 20–23, 25

Servants etc., Advice to in General 21–22. Butler 21. Cook 21. French Chefs 34. Footman and boys 20, 21. Governess 15, 23. Housekeeper 20. Lady's Maid 22–23. Mrs Thrale's "Sophy" Maid of all Work 20. Nurses 15, 21. Teachers 15, 21. Tutors 15

servants, Directions to by Dean Swift 20, 23

Shakespeare 60. *As you Like it* 66. *Hamlet* 64.

Julius Caesar 64. *Macbeth* 72, 73. *Merchant of Venice* 65–66, 71–72. *Othello* 64, 66. *Richard III* 66, 74. *Romeo & Juliet* 67

She Stoops to Conquer 60, 68, 123

Shelley, Charles Bysshe 170

Shelley, Harriet 165–170

Shelley, Mary 11, 162–169 (78) Hate 169. *History of a Six Weeks Tour* (with P.B) 169. Mary's children, Clare & William died young, Percy Florence 172

Shelley, Percy Bysshe 11, 35, 165–72. *Address to the Irish People* 166. *Declaration of Rights* 166. *Queen Mab* 167. *The Assassins* 169

Shelley, Sir Timothy 176

Sheridan, Alicia (*See* Le Fanu)

Sheridan, Betsy 32, 108, 125

Sheridan, Charles 108, Mrs Charles 108

Sheridan, Richard Brinsley 60, 63, 73, 108. *The Rivals* 123. Mrs R. B. 92, 93, 108, (20)

Sheridan, Thomas, Irish actor 63, 108, 109. Mrs Thomas (née Frances Chamberlain) 108

Siddons, Mrs Sarah. Witness of Pantheon holocaust 58. Career 71–73. Compared with Mrs Cibber 72. Her best roles 72. Accused of stinginess 73, 74. Portrait by D. Downham (42). By Reynolds as Tragic Nose (59)

Siddons, William 58, 71–74, 93

Sloane, Sir Hans 96, 100

Sloper, Sir William 70–71

Smellie, Dr William, obstetrician 100

Smith, Mr & Mrs & Aunt Everard (19)

Small pox 96–97

Smollett, Dr Tobias 52, 99. *Adventures of Humphrey Clinker* 49, 52

Smugglers 28, 39

Snuff 7, 43–44

Stael, Mme de 55

Stanley, Ann Lady 118, 121

Steele, Sir Richard, Irish playrwight 63. Looks lost by gambling, 79, 126

Stephens, Catherine actress, Countess of Essex 62

Sterne, Laurence *Tristram Shandy* 7. *Sentimental Journey*, 24. Calls Smollett. Dr Smellfungus 99

Stevens, Jane. Sells her Bladder pill prescription for £5,000, 104

Strafford, Lady 130

Stuart, Lady Louisa 125, 128

Sturt, Mrs 32. Masquerade at Hammersmith 32. Gambling House 84

Suffolk, Henrietta Howard, Countess of 91

Swift, Jonathan *Directions to Servants* 20, 23. On chamberpots 98. On marrying 133. Friend of Gay 61, 122, 133, 141, 145, 146

Tatler, The 126

Tattersall's 88

Thornton, Colonel 87–88. Thornton, Mrs 81, 87–88, (46)

Thrale, Mrs 10. On Servants 21. On delicacy of language 24. Rouge addiction 42. On fans 43. On mean marriage 117, 154

Thrale, Mr 21, 34, 117

Thraliana 117

Thurlow, Lord Chancellor 62

Toilet (5, 7)

Tories 10, 12. Political beauty patching 42

Torond, Francis (19)

Townley, Charles *High Life, Below Stairs* 51, 60

Townshend, Lady On Kitty Clive's face 70

Tremamondo, Dominico Angelo Malevolti "Old Angelo" 58

Trusler, John Proprietor of Marybone Gardens, professional chef 51. Father of Betty 51, and of Rev. Dr John Trusler

Trusler, Rev. Dr John 26–7. *The Honours of the Table* 31–32. On *Table Manners* 32–34

Tunbridge Wells, Misfortune of a false eyebrow at 42. Betsy Sheridan at 108, 109–110

Turner, J. M. Sketches ruins of The Pantheon 59

Twyford, Mr Jacobite. Lover of Mary Granville 119, 120, 121

Tyers, Jonathan & Family 49–50, 52

Tyrconnel, Lady Mistress of Duke of York 58

Umbrellas 46

Unitarianism 11

Up and Down (38)

Vanderbank, John 90

Van Dyck, Sir Anthony 90

Van Somer 90

Vassall, Elizabeth, Lady Holland 143

Vauxhall. *See* Pleasure Gardens

Veneral disease 16, 97

Vermin 97, 99

Vernon, Caroline 84

Victoria, Queen 11, 77, 100

Villiers, Barbara, Duchess of Cleveland 119

Villiers, George, Duke of Buckingham. *The Rehearsal* 66

Villiers, Henry 119–20

Vindication of the Rights of Woman 17, 157

Voltaire 10, 12, 95, 127. On *Pamela* 134

Wales, Frederick Prince of, fecundity of 14. Patron of Vauxhall Gardens 49. George, Prince of, *See* George IV

Walpole, Horace, 4th Earl of Oxford. On Queen Charlotte's wedding dress 39–40. On Lady Fortrose killed by whitelead 42. On Ranelagh and Vauxhall 50–51. On Almack's & Carlisle House 56. Calls Pantheon "a winter Ranelagh" 57. Despises Garrick 66. On Kitty Clive 70. Miss Vernon's way of paying debts 84. On Elizabeth Linley 92. On Dr Graham 102. On Archbishop of York 136. On "Con Phillips" 144

Walpole, Sir Robert, 1st Earl of Oxford. Pilloried in Beggar's Opera gets Lord Chamberlain to ban Polly 62

Walsingham, Dady 123

Washington, George 155

water, Mineral properties of 98. Drinking water impurities of 98

Water closets 98, 99

Waterloo, Battle of 46. Bridge 49

Wellington, Duke of 153

Wesley, C. & J. 10, 45

Wet nurses 97

Whales 38

What d'ye call it by John Gay 61

Whigs 9, 10. Political beauty-patching 42

Whitefield, G. 10, 45

Wigs (7, 9)

Wilkes, John 35, 58

Wilkinson, Tate. On Mrs Siddons 72. Auditions Dorothy Jordan 74

William & Mary 9, 10, 83, 90

William IV (Duke of Clarence) 15, 75–76, (60)

Williams, Sir Charles Hanbury 61

Willis, Dr Francis 100

Wild, Jonathan 61

Wilson, Harriette 152–3, (77)

Winchester, Bishop of. Pinches Brummell's snuff 44

Winsor, Frederick Albert 86–7

Wit, a wit outwitted (69)

Withering, Doctor, His Cosmetic Lotion 22. *London Pharmacopeia* 101

Woffington, Peg, Irish actress 63. As Nerissa 64. As Rosalind 66. Mistress of Garrick 67. At Teddington 68, 69, 74

Woffington, Polly. *See* Cholmondeley, Polly

Woodforde, Rev James 26, 28, 29, 77, 136

Wollstonecraft, Mary, *Vindication of the Rights of Woman* 17, 19, 21, 157. *Thoughts on the Education of Daughters* 157, 158. Career 157–63. *A Historical and Moral View of the French Revolution* 160. *Original Stories* 161, (75)

Wordsworth, William 159

Worsdale, Painter 146

Wortley, Anne 124–5, Wortley, Edward. See Montagu, Edward Wortley

Wyatt, James, Architect, builds Pantheon 57. Sees it burn from Salisbury Plain 59

York, Duke of, defends his mistress at Pantheon 58. Helps Foote 64

York Herald 87

Zoffany, Johann 93